BUILDING THE NEW WORLD

STUDIES IN THE MODERN ARCHITECTURE OF LATIN AMERICA 1930–1960

VALERIE FRASER

VERSO

London · New York

For Tim and Christina

First published by Verso 2000
© Valerie Fraser 2000
All rights reserved

The moral right of the author has been asserted.

Verso
UK: 6 Meard Street, London W1V 3HR
USA: 180 Varick Street, New York, NY 10014–4606

Verso is the imprint of New Left Books

ISBN 1–85984–787–0
ISBN 1–85984–307–7 (pbk)

British Library Cataloguing in Publication Data
A catalogue record for this book is available from the British Library

Library of Congress Cataloging-in-Publication Data
A catalog record for this book is available from the Library of Congress

Designed and typeset by Illuminati, Grosmont
Printed and bound in Great Britain by Scotprint, Haddington

CONTENTS

PREFACE AND
ACKNOWLEDGEMENTS

Every book has a history, and the preface is the author's opportunity to in-dulge in historical reconstruction, and in this case there are at least two versions. One version could be dated back to the summer of 1969 when as a first-year undergraduate at the University of Essex I was meant to be spending a term at the Universidad Nacional Autónoma de México. I and my fellow students were refused entry to Mexico, apparently on the grounds that we came from an institution with a reputation for breeding radical activists, and were there-fore a danger to national security. I knew little about Mexican politics but I did know that the new campus at which we were due to study had a reputation for the startling originality of its art and architecture. My frustration at not getting to see any of this only confirmed my interest in Latin America.

The more prosaic version is that after a period researching the colonial architecture of Peru I felt the need for a change. Teaching at undergraduate and graduate level suggested new areas of research and revealed gaps in the literature. During visits to Latin America, even when the main focus was the colonial period, I began to build in visits to the monuments of modernism including, eventually, the UNAM campus. British academics will correctly surmise that a book with the publication date 2000 has an eye to the forth-coming Research Assessment Exercise by which departments are judged and rewarded on the quantity and quality of their research output. I had naively assumed that I could produce a book on modern Latin American architecture relatively quickly and easily in order to meet the RAE's requirements, but it has proved neither quick nor easy. I can only add that once I realized what a Pandora's box of exciting material I had opened up, had it *not* been for the RAE this book might have taken another ten years to write and would have been many times longer. I hope that the pressures of the tight timetable are not too evident; certainly none of those acknowledged below is responsible for any shortcomings or oversights.

In researching and writing this book I have been helped by a great many people. I was already toying with ideas on the subject when Bernardo Moncada Cárdenas came to spend the academic year 1993–4 at Essex as a Research Fellow in our department. We made plans for a co-authored study and although these were shelved Bernardo played an important part in the book's early stages. In Venezuela the following year he was invaluable, showing me round Mérida and Caracas, sharing with me his tremendous knowledge of Venezuelan architecture of all periods and introducing me to other experts in the field. I am grateful to Max Pedemonte for his memorable tour of the Caracas Metro, to Paulina Villanueva for her warm welcome, to Cecilia Fajardo-Hill for help with bibliography, contacts and photographs, and to Gloria Carnivale of the Venezuelan Embassy in London. In Mexico Xavier Guzmán Urbiola was generous with his expertise and his enthusiasm, and without the help and friendship of Horacio Carvajal and Liliana Domínguez I should not have been able to do and see so much in the time available. Thank you, too, to Juan Manuel Santín of the Mexican Embassy in London. Maria Marta Camisassa's understanding of modern Brazilian architecture has been a significant influence over the years and her insights as we drove around Minas Gerais together were inspirational. Others who have helped with material, information and ideas on Brazil include Rachel Sissons, João Diniz, Roberto Luís de Melo Monte-Mór, Augusto César Baptista Arenal, Conrad Hamerman and the very special Osvlado Aurelio da Silva, who showed me round the MES building in Rio de Janeiro which he himself had helped to build in the late 1930s. In Cuba I much appreciated the help and kindness of Reinaldo Peñalver Moral and Tania Bruguera. Although this book does not include more than a passing reference to Argentina, Fabio Grementieri's erudite architectural tour of Buenos Aires helped to bring a number of general issues into focus.

Many students past and present have contributed to the formulation of the argument via discussions and seminars, and more specifically by bringing back books and photographs from their research trips, answering questions, and helping with contacts and bibliography. Adrian Locke, Marcia Bonnet, Suzy Hartman, Alison McLean-Cameron, Gabriel Pérez-Barreiro, Simon Richards, Paula Terra Cabo, Helen Thomas – thank you all. Maria Clara Bernal, Magdalena Mayo and Isobel Whitelegg did much of the picture research and their help was invaluable. Thanks, too, to Chris Morgan and Barry Woodcock for drawing the plans.

I am very grateful to the Leverhulme Trust, the University of Essex Research Endowment Fund and the University of Essex Research Promotion Fund for their support for my various research trips over the years, and to the British Academy for a generous grant towards the cost of illustrations. Many ideas were tried out in lectures and conference papers and in particular I am grateful for invitations to the BRASA III conference in Cambridge in 1996, to Wellesley College, Massachusetts, March 1998 and to Lima to the International Conference En el Umbral del Milenio, May 1998. This book would not have been possible without the University of Essex Albert Sloman Library's exceptional holdings of Latin American material or the help of the specialist Latin American librarian Chris Anderton and the staff at the Inter-Library Loan desk. I am deeply grateful to the staff at Verso, to Jane Hindle, Gillian Beaumont, Sophie Arditti, and especially Lucy Morton for all their encouragement, hard work, patience and care.

I have enjoyed tremendous support from many dear friends and colleagues including especially Neil Cox, Dawn Ades, Tim Laughton, Michaela Giebelhausen, Jules Lubbock, Thomas Puttfarken, Gabriela Salgado and Libby Armstrong of the Department of Art History and Theory at the University of Essex. A special word of thanks to Alice Friedman for her invaluable encouragement and for patiently answering so many queries about modern architecture in Europe and the USA.

Thanks, as ever, to Tim Butler without whom none of this would have been possible, and a special thank you to Christina, our daughter, who with unwavering good humour has put up with endless long journeys, walked many miles of hot city pavements, waited patiently while we took photos or talked to our many guides and fellow-enthusiasts, on one condition: that once in a while we would stay in a hotel with a swimming pool.

PICTURE CREDITS

The author and publishers would like to thank the following for the use of illustrative material: pp. 16, 115, 153, 154, 155, 202, © Fondation Le Corbusier; p. 30, courtesy Xavier Guzmán Urbiola; pp. 31, 33, 71, Pl. 3, Helen Thomas; pp. 35, 72, courtesy Archivo Fotográfico de la Dirección de Arquitectura del Instituto Nacional de Bellas Artes, Mexico; p. 37, courtesy Instituto Nacional de Bellas Artes, Mexico; p. 43, courtesy Museo Casa Estudio Diego Rivera y Frida Kahlo, Instituto Nacional de Bellas Artes; pp. 48, 57, courtesy Universidad Autónoma Metropolitana; p. 54, from Rafael López Rangel, *La modernidad arquitectónica Mexicana: antecedentes y vanguardias 1900–1940*, Mexico 1989; p. 59, photograph Aerofoto, from the archives of the family of Mario Pani, courtesy Louise Noelle; p. 67, after Louise Noelle and Carlos Tejeda, *Catálog Guia de arquitectura contemporánea: Ciudad de México*, Mexico 1993; p. 111, after Claudio Perna, *Evolución de la geografía urbana de Caracas*, Caracas 1981; p. 147, after Rachel Sisson, *Rio de Janeiro as Capital*, Rio de Janeiro, 1987; pp. 194, 204, after Henrique Mindlin, *Modern Architecture in Brazil*, London 1956; p. 70, photograph Luis Márquez Romay, from the archives of the Instituto de Investigaciones Estéticas, Universidad Nacional Autónoma de México, courtesy Louise Noelle; p. 86, photograph Marianne Goeritz, courtesy Henry Moore Foundation; pp. 92, 98, 101, courtesy CINAP, Galería de Arte Nacional; pp. 95, 99, courtesy Ernesto Armitano; p. 97, courtesy Centre Historique des Archives Nationales; p. 103, after Marta Vallmitjana (co-ord.), *El Plan Rotival: La Caracas que no fue*, Caracas 1991; pp. 109, 119, 127, 128, from Sibyl Moholy-Nagy, *Carlos Raúl Villanueva and the Architecture of Venezuela*, New York 1964; p. 109, El Universal; Pl. 14, photograph Mike Roberts; p. 117, courtesy Juan Pedro Posani; Pl. 22, courtesy Taller de Arte Carlos Cruz-Diez; p. 149, photograph Augusto Malta, courtesy Jennings Hoffenberg Collection; pp. 157, 160, 161, 175, 186, 187, 192, photographs by Marcel Gautherot, © Instituto Moreira Salles; p. 178, photograph Marcel Gautherot, courtesy R. Burle Marx & Cie Ltd; p. 167, from Gerardo Ferraz, *Warchavchik e a introdução da nova arquitetura no Brasil: 1925 a 1940*, São Paulo 1965; Pl. 24, Pl. 25, Maria Marta Camisassa; p. 183, F. S. Lincoln; p. 185, Oscar Niemeyer Foundation; p. 208, Frances Loeb Library, Harvard Design School; pp. 223, 227, 239, 243, 255, courtesy Arquivo Público do Distrito Federal, Brasília; p. 233, photograph Augusto Cesar Baptista Areal; pp. 228, 236, after Willy Stäubli, *Brasília*, New York 1965; p. 248, from John A. Loomis, *Revolution of Forms: Cuba's forgotten Art Schools*, New York 1999; pp. 63, 78, Pl. 6, Pl. 7, Tim Butler. All uncredited photographs are by the author. Every effort has been made to trace the sources of photographs; any errors will be rectified in subsequent editions.

INTRODUCTION

A survey of the major studies of twentieth-century architecture published in English in the last twenty-five or so years might suggest that there is not really enough to warrant a book on modern architecture in Latin America; indeed, it would be easy to get the impression that very little was built in the region at all during the last hundred years.[1] The perversity of this omission from the literature is rendered even more peculiar when we consider that Le Corbusier was the single most influential figure of the period, and that Brasília is probably the closest to a grand-scale realization of his theories and ideas to be built anywhere in the world.[2]

But such myopia is relatively recent. From the 1940s to the 1960s the USA was extremely interested in developments in Latin America. In 1939 the Brazilian pavilion at the New York World's Fair had created quite a stir, and in 1943 the Museum of Modern Art in New York staged the exhibition Brazil Builds, which included an impressive array of contemporary architecture by over twenty different architects.[3] The catalogue drew attention to the way in which building in Brazil was both modern and Brazilian, as well as identifying the technical advances from which US architects could usefully learn. In 1955 the influential critic Henry-Russell Hitchcock mounted another exhibition at the Museum of Modern Art, Modern Architecture in Latin America since

1945, an extensive and enthusiastic survey of modern architecture in the region. Hitchcock points out areas in which Latin America was ahead of the USA: 'In certain fields, notably university cities and public housing, the United States in recent years has had little to offer as extensive in scope or as brilliant in design as the best in Latin American work.'[4] He assumes an evolutionary model of architectural development, with the USA and Latin America making uneven progress along the same path. The catalogue introduction justified the exhibition in these terms: 'Because the quantity of Latin American building exceeds our own, the appearance there of predominantly "modern" cities gives us the opportunity to observe effects which we ourselves only anticipate.'[5] It is worth pointing out that at this date Brasília was not even on the drawing board.

This exhibition was followed by a flurry of enthusiastic English-language publications, several of them by Latin American authors, including well-illustrated monographs on individual artists,[6] studies of production in individual countries, especially Mexico, and some broader surveys.[7] An example of the widespread popularity of the subject is Brazilian architect Henrique Mindlin's *Modern Architecture in Brazil*, which appeared in 1956 in French and German as well as English, and was distributed around the world by six different publishing companies in Rio de Janeiro, New York, London, Amsterdam, Paris and Munich. My own second-hand copy, which originally belonged to a firm of chartered architects in Nairobi, was undoubtedly purchased because Brazil was seen as an important player in the field of contemporary architecture. For these few decades Latin American architecture was valued for its inventiveness and its confidence, and for the way it combined modern and national or regional characteristics.[8] Brasília in particular, planned in 1957 and inaugurated in 1960, inspired several admiring publications.[9]

Brasília, however, also marked the end of the love affair. This was one ambition too far, and the architectural establishment in the USA and Europe turned against it. Under the tutelage of the critic and historian Sigfried Giedion, the 1958 graduate seminar in Harvard studied the plans for Brasília and found them wanting.[10] They felt that Brazil should have called in international planning experts or commissioned Le Corbusier to help. So Brazil, which for twenty-five years had been admired for its achievements in architecture and town planning, was suddenly considered insufficiently experienced to design its own capital city. Non-specialist interest persisted into the early 1970s, after which Brasília, along with the rest of Latin American modern architecture, more or less disappeared from the English-speaking world's view of the achievements of the twentieth century. Architectural history continued to be written in Latin America, of course, and has taken an upturn in recent years, producing some excellent specialist research, but those who write about Latin American architecture are themselves often also architects, and so doubly inside.[11] Given the lack of interest in the subject in the USA and Europe, it is hardly surprising that they tend to address themselves rather than a wider audience, but it reinforces the tendency to overlook Latin American architecture. I believe it would be hard to find an architectural history course in a university outside Latin America where the region features on equal terms alongside, say, German or Italian, French, Finnish or Japanese modern architecture.

This book therefore attempts to redress the balance by considering examples of the sort of architecture which attracted international attention in the 1940s and 1950s. The underlying premiss is that from the 1930s to the 1960s several countries in Latin America were indeed producing highly innovative architecture, and the world was right to sit up and take notice. By way of introduction I outline below some general issues of terminology and sources which are applicable to Latin America as a whole, before explaining the reasons for my particular focus on production in Mexico, Venezuela and Brazil.

The Modern Movement in architecture and urbanism

The term *modern* is notoriously wide-ranging – nowhere more so than in Latin America, where, during the nineteenth century, the newly independent nations, many of them under thoroughly authoritarian regimes, sought to promote an image of themselves as modern. To be modern was to be an autonomous nation, to be forward-looking and optimistic and to believe in progress, but it also meant to be up to date, and in this the standards were still set by Europe. For the elites of Latin America in the nineteenth and early twentieth centuries, being modern meant being familiar with the latest ideas and fashions of Europe, from novels and clothes to theories of town planning. It meant having a house with a bathroom and electricity, and wallpaper from Paris. In terms of architectural style, the term 'modern' could be applied to almost anything that was – or, at least, was considered to be – fashionable in Europe. In other words, in some ways the modern was almost synonymous with the foreign. But at the same time, from a traditional European perspective one of the defining characteristics of Latin America – or, rather, the combined continents of America – was always that it was new and young, in contrast to Europe, which was old; so it was a smooth and natural process for the young nations of Latin America, as they gained confidence in the earlier decades of the twentieth century, to appropriate and extend this, and claim the fashionable designation *modern* for themselves.

The architecture with which this book is concerned, however, belongs to a much narrower definition of the term 'modern'. This architecture belongs to a specific movement variously referred to as the Modern Movement, or *modernism*, which has its roots firmly in the radical theory and practice of modern architecture in Europe in the early twentieth century. From the late 1920s onwards, a generation of idealistic young architects in Latin America borrowed ideas from Adolphe Loos, from Walter Gropius and the Bauhaus, from the Russians and the Italians, and above all from Le Corbusier. Theorists and practitioners in Latin America as in Europe, well aware of the loose nature of the term 'modern', often called it simply the *new*, and understood newness in many different ways.[12] These can be summarized as follows: it was understood as new first and foremost in the sense that it made use of new technology and new materials – glass, steel and reinforced concrete. These innovations, in releasing building from its traditional structural constraints, allowed for completely new architectural forms: instead of load-bearing walls, a structural skeleton could support floors, ceilings and roof; internal space could be more flexibly arranged; and walls and partitions could be all of glass – daylight and fresh air were regarded as essentials of healthy modern living. In theory, at least, this new architecture could meet new demands – for motorway flyovers, for example, or to create breathing space in cities by raising high-rise buildings up on stilts. It could meet – with machine precision as well as speed and efficiency – the new demands of the emerging new society for mass housing, large-scale hospitals and educational facilities. In line with a dominant strand in contemporary European theory, many Latin American architects believed that the new architecture could play a part in fostering a different, more socially inclusive society.

The architecture built according to these technical and functional considerations conformed to an entirely new aesthetic vocabulary, and carried with it a new terminology. Louis Sullivan's dictum that 'form follows function' took on new life as the technical horizons expanded, and theorists argued that the new architecture was so purely rational, so firmly based on the realization of the precise functional requirements using the full range of modern technology available, that the result would be a style-less architecture. New architecture was therefore without ornament or decoration; it was seen as honest, logical and thoroughly rational, as true to the needs, technology and spirit of the new machine age. The term 'International Style' was applied by North American commentators to the particular formal characteristics of this new (European) architecture: the use of an internal structural skeleton and glass façades in a rectilinear 'cubistic mode', to use Frampton's term, where the traditional aesthetic concern for mass was replaced by a concern for volume. As Hitchock and Johnson put it in the catalogue of their defining exhibition The International Style (1932): 'The prime architectural symbol is no longer the dense brick, but the open box.'[13]

In Europe the new architecture was a response to the interlinked processes of urbanization and industrialization. Rapid urbanization had created social and environmental problems that urgently needed to be addressed; industrialization could provide architects with radical means with which to do so, and allowed them to think, plan and build in entirely new ways. The most influential body in the field of urbanism was the CIAM, the Congrès Internationaux d'Architecture Moderne, founded in 1928 by a group of twenty-four European architects.[14] The CIAM argued that architecture – or rather *building* – was unavoidably linked to political and economic factors; that in order to replace the slums that resulted from uncontrolled urban expansion with decent housing, architecture had to transform itself from a craft-based practice into a building industry by rationalization and standardization of component parts; and that there would have to be a move away from individual towards more collective living arrangements. In the 1930s the CIAM became more or less an organ of Le Corbusian theories, and the emphasis shifted from that of how best to provide proper housing for the working class (during the Depression years) to a broader concern with city planning.

The Charter of Athens, a document drawn up during the 1933 CIAM meeting and heavily influenced by Le Corbusier, identified the problems in existing towns and cities as overcrowding, traffic congestion, pollution, inefficiency and the disintegration of social order, the root causes of which were industrialization and uncontrolled private speculation.[15] The Charter of Athens architects put forward a series of radical – and essentially utopian – proposals for rethinking the urban fabric from scratch, with a view to transforming disorder into order. The city was conceived as an efficient machine or industrial complex, organized around what the Charter identified as the four functions: housing, work, recreation and traffic circulation. The city should be strictly zoned to ensure efficient communication between housing, work and recreation; and, at least in the areas of housing and recreation, space should be arranged in a way that would foster a more collective and egalitarian mode of living. It argued that all urban planning should be under the aegis of architects, and assumed a powerful centralized government that would delegate to them the powers necessary to put their plans into practice.

The largely European membership of the CIAM in the early 1930s looked at their own cities and dreamed of having the power to sweep away all the dirty old inefficient streets and buildings and replace them with steel and glass towers set in spacious parks, with traffic speeding past at a safe distance, but nowhere in Europe, of course, were the authorities either willing or able to embark on such a radical programme of urban renewal. In Latin America it was different: the cities were much smaller and there was very little industry, so the need was not so much for renewal as for planned expansion. It seemed possible that with careful planning it would be possible to leapfrog the problems created by the Industrial Revolution in Europe, and plan ahead for urban and industrial growth. It is not surprising, therefore, to find aspects of CIAM thinking informing the various university cities and large urbanization schemes of the 1940s and 1950s, and of course Brasília.

For modernizing governments, modern architecture seemed to bring together all the various essential components of construction: utility and strength with economy and modernity. Disciples would also argue that due care and attention to the purpose, involving the full exploitation of the potential of modern materials, would inevitably result in beauty: in all, a perfectly interconnected logical conclusion. And since urban theorists of the early twentieth century believed with an almost religious zeal in the benefits of fresh air and daylight, these too – at least in the eyes of the modernist architects – were best accommodated using a plain, pure style of architecture.

Therefore the new architecture, especially organized in conformity with the new urbanistic principles, offered Latin American governments the means to appear modern in a variety of senses. Most obviously, it implied a modernizing economy, with industries producing cement, steel and glass, even when those industries were in their infancy, or indeed – as in the case of the world's first high-rise slab block, the Ministry of Education and Health building in Rio de Janeiro, begun in 1936 – when most of the materials had to be imported from abroad. In fact, at no time during the period under discussion were any countries in Latin America sufficiently industrialized to mass-produce more than a few of the prefabricated elements on which the theory of the new architecture was predicated.

Nevertheless the new architecture could create a very visible – and often literally high-profile – image of a young, dynamic nation with an expanding economy and a growing industrial infrastructure. It could also be used to signify a modernizing government that was actively shaping its people's future. In Latin America during the years 1930 to 1960 the interests of idealistic architects and ambitious governments broadly coincided over the possibilities offered by the new architecture, even if their priorities were slightly different: the largely left-leaning practitioners believed that modern architecture could improve the lot of the fast-growing and acutely underprivileged masses, while governments of both left and right patronized these young men in the belief that modern architecture could serve the interrelated purposes of promoting an image of national progress (and, for those governments which cared about such things, this included improvements in social welfare) and, more importantly, stimulate industrial development.[16] Governments embraced the new architecture as part of a modern image, as a way of promoting themselves through showpiece projects like government ministries and university cities, or because it offered ways of housing large numbers of people at minimal cost. In different ways and to different degrees, the new architecture and town planning of Latin America were part of a larger utopian project to transform society and build a new world.

Translating European theory into Latin American practice

Latin American architects and planners embraced much of the rhetoric of European modernism, and in particular of Le Corbusier. Le Corbusier visited Latin America several times and his writings of the 1920s and 1930s were avidly consumed by the younger generation of architects. He put the case for the new architecture with clarity and passion and echoes of his ideas are found everywhere: ideas about an architecture appropriate for the machine age, the irrelevance of ornament, the house as a machine for living in, the 'Five Points towards a New Architecture' which new technology made possible. The terminology of Latin American architecture is spattered with Le Corbusianisms: the term *unité d'habitation*, which Le Corbusier devised to refer to residential blocks that included other functions such as shops and social spaces, becomes translated into Spanish and Portuguese as *unidad habitacional*; his term for a sunscreen – *brise-soleil* – is retained in the French in Spanish-speaking countries, while in Brazil it tends to turn into *quebra-sol*; and his *pilotis* is universally used for piers, stilts or piles that raise a building above ground level.[17]

This receptivity to Le Corbusian neologisms should not surprise us. The elites of countries like Brazil, Argentina, Mexico and Venezuela, which had fast-growing economies in the 1920s, 1930s and 1940s, were in fact very up to date, very *modern*. They were as at home in Europe, especially Paris, as they were in their own capital cities. As in the nineteenth century, they continued to be educated in Europe, communicated in French almost as easily as in their own language, welcomed European intellectuals into their homes, and subscribed to European books and journals.[18] Paradoxically, these close links were reinforced by the political upheavals in Europe – the Spanish Civil War, the rise of Fascism and the Second World War – which encouraged intellectuals to emigrate to Latin America. Among them were several architects who were to become extremely influential in their adopted homes: Candela, Cetto, Goeritz and Meyer went to Mexico; Mujica to Venezuela; Bonet and Dourgé to Argentina; Warchavchik to Brazil. But Latin America was not a passive or indiscriminate recipient of European ideas. This is most clearly expressed in the metaphor of cannibalism adopted by a group of Brazilian intellectuals in the 1920s to define their relationship with European culture as that of ritualized violence, of deliberate, selective ingestion, by which the foreign product was transformed into something entirely Brazilian.[19] Not everyone saw it in quite such aggressive terms, but among the intelligentsia there was always an element of reflexivity about the consumption of European culture.

It is also worth remembering that Latin America had considerable impact on Europe during this period.[20] Artists, architects and their patrons criss-crossed the Atlantic in both directions. Painters like Diego Rivera, Wifredo Lam and Tarsila do Amaral had studios in Paris, and perhaps had more influence on artists like Picasso, for example, than Picasso would ever have cared to admit. Le Corbusier is the prime example of this complex relationship. He was hugely excited by his various visits to South America, especially his first in 1929, when he travelled in Argentina, Uruguay and Brazil, lecturing on his theories of architecture and town planning. He had just published *The City of Tomorrow and its Planning*, in which he proposed – in terms that anticipated the Charter of Athens – that the solution to Paris's problems was to sweep away the old city centre and start again, so he was overwhelmed with excitement at the possibilities for radical experimentation offered by the cities of South America. They were still small, but growing fast.

Like many modernists, Le Corbusier was inspired by flying, by the clarity of vision and sense of power it engendered.[21] Flying over Buenos Aires, Montevideo and São Paulo, he imagined new cities suited to the new, modern world of America, with superblocks and superhighways completely replacing the existing city structure.[22] From the air these new cities would read as simple legible patterns, announcing the clean, tidy lives of the inhabitants within. In the case of Rio, the last place Le Corbusier visited on his 1929 tour, he could no longer ignore the larger-than-life landscape. Instead of imposing a rigid geometry, here his superhighway 'unrolls in an elegant, ample, majestic curve', and sweeps around the coast.[23] The superhighway was to be 100 metres high, and built on top of ten storeys of offices and housing, which in turn were to be raised up on 30-foot-high piers. This is the point at which the generous curve first enters Le Corbusier's vocabulary – as in 1932, for example, when the central feature of his plan for Algiers is a similar long snake of a motorway incorporated into an enormous, extended residential block.[24]

Le Corbusier's shift to more curvilinear forms, inspired as it was by his experience of Brazil, may in turn have played a part in validating the curve in

Brazilian eyes – or, rather, it may have reinforced an existing tendency, encouraging the Brazilians to lay claim to what was already rightfully theirs. Indeed, Latin American intellectuals tended to be sceptical of foreigners, and were aware that Le Corbusier's enthusiasm for Latin America was often deeply patronizing. The Brazilian writer Mário Andrade, commenting on his arrival in São Paulo in 1929, lamented that Latin Americans still felt it necessary to invite famous Europeans to come and tell them how to think.[25] It is clear, however, that Le Corbusier provided a particularly attractive challenge to the younger generation of architects, and they used his ideas as a springboard for their own developments.[26]

The USA and Latin American modern architecture

The USA is the other important reference point in this story. One aspect of Le Corbusier's thinking that would have been congenial to Latin American architects and intellectuals was his scepticism about US culture, which he saw as modern but overly materialistic and lacking in poetry. He argued that Buenos Aires could learn from New York's mistakes to grow into a city that could rival or surpass it.[27] Le Corbusier's attitude is similar to that first articulated in Latin America in 1900, when the Uruguayan poet José Enrique Rodó contrasted Latin America's rich cultural and spiritual heritage, derived from its Mediterranean roots, with the cold, utilitarian Anglo-Saxons to the north.[28]

There were those in the USA who recognized this too, and viewed Latin America's close ties with Europe, its vivacious, adventurous Latin culture and its rich colonial heritage, with envy. In 1924, for example, the English émigré Alfred Bossom published a book of photographs of colonial Mexican architecture, taken on a recent visit. He found it all very exciting, a reflection of the adventurous, daring spirit of the Spanish conquerors and thus an appropriate style for the similarly adventurous spirit of contemporary 'Americans', a term he uses inclusively or exclusively according to the context:

> Mexico! Not to visit Mexico is not to know the Western Hemisphere. Not to have
> viewed the monuments of its romantic past is not to sense the inner meaning of
> American traditions, nor to fully grasp the development of the American people.[29]

In the captions to the photographs he points out features of colonial Mexican
architecture that could be adapted to contemporary buildings.

In fact, this had already been happening for several decades. Mexico was
inevitably the main focus of US interest in Latin America, and from the end
of the nineteenth century US architects and theorists, anxious about their own
cultural and especially architectural identity, repeatedly turned to the south for
inspiration.[30] The product of the enthusiasm for the Spanish colonial past was
the California Mission style, which drew on Mexican sources as well as California's own Spanish heritage, and in fact went on to become a source of
inspiration for neocolonial revivals in Latin America.[31] US hostility to European modernism paved the way for the rapturous reception Mexican Muralism
received in the 1920s, while it encouraged architects to turn their attention to
pre-Columbian cultures. The 1920s saw some remarkable Mayan revival buildings in the USA, most famously those by Frank Lloyd Wright.[32] The Mexican
Francisco Mujica contributed to this tendency in 1929 with a book which
argued that the skyscraper was an essentially American form, with its roots in
the pyramids of ancient Mexico.[33]

In 1944 the US town-planning expert Francis Violich was among those
who continued to appreciate the sense of history and romance to be found in
Latin America:

> In comparing the planning of the cities of Latin America with that of the cities of
> the United States, it is at once apparent that her technicians have profited by closer
> contact with Europe. The result has been the development of two divergent types
> of cities in the Western hemisphere: those of the United States, impressive but un-
> gracious; and those of the Latin American countries, historic and old-world like, but
> thoroughly delightful and human.[34]

This was soon to change, and ten years later the contrast for Hitchcock was
not with the old but with the new: '[In Latin America] the flavour of city after

city strikes the casual visitor... as being more modern than anything but a Houston or a Miami Beach at home.'[35] In 1964 the architectural critic Sibyl Moholy-Nagy also compared Latin America very favourably with the USA as a place where great things can happen, while recognizing, not without envy, that it was the oligarchic governments which made such artistic autonomy possible:

> It is a curious cultural side-light that the much deplored semi-feudal state capitalism of South America guarantees to architects of gigantic public works the supremacy of their decisions, while the democratic, free-enterprise states of Europe and North America established long ago the strangling interference of the lowest 'common' design denominator.[36]

This interest in the architecture and town planning of Latin America is paralleled by growing political and economic attention to the region. From the mid nineteenth century the USA had been anxious to promote the cause of Pan-American unity, and in 1933 the 'Good Neighbour' policy consolidated a variety of initiatives designed to protect and promote US interests in Latin America. One of the more subtle ways of doing this was under the cloak of culture – promoting exhibitions of Latin American architecture, and funding architects and town planners to go and lecture and advise, during which time they could also learn, and no doubt identify opportunities for US trade and industry. In the 1940s the intention was also to build a consensus in the region in favour of the Allied powers, and culture was a way of pursuing this aim. The Brazil Builds exhibition in New York in 1943 had an explicitly diplomatic role: 'The Museum of Modern Art, New York, and the American Institute of Architects in the spring of 1942 were both anxious to have closer relations with Brazil, a country which was to be our future ally.'[37] There were various other initiatives to encourage such links, as in 1945, when the Department of State sent the architect Richard Neutra on a lecture tour to Brazil.

The very real critical interest in modern Latin American architecture which exhibitions like Brazil Builds succeeded in generating is intriguing. As we have seen, US architects of the early twentieth century sought out formal features that could be classified as 'American' at a time when European modernism was regarded with deep suspicion.[38] Hitchcock and Johnson mounted a challenge to this search for an American architectural identity when they introduced the new architecture to New York in 1932, veiling its European origins and playing down its social implications by using the term 'International Style'. The logic of this 'new' modern architecture was that it supposedly rendered all cultural, historical or national references unavailable or unjustifiable, and was thus 'style-less'.[39] The new architecture did not immediately have much impact in the USA, however, and critics like Hitchcock watched with fascination as a group of Latin American architects appropriated European modernism, complete with social implications, internalized the rules of this 'style-less style' and then proceeded, with great dexterity, to translate it into an American product. In other words, Latin American architects demonstrated that they understood the rules but did not need to be confined by them; that it was possible to be both modern and regionally or nationally specific at the same time.

They enjoyed opportunities beyond the dreams of European or US architects, most notably huge commissions for university cities, for urban development schemes, and, in the case of Brazil, for a new capital. For such projects funding was not a major issue, and the architects were given considerable autonomy in terms of social considerations as well as in aesthetic and constructional matters. They also enjoyed a plentiful supply of cheap, relatively skilled labour. The rising tide of inward migration to the cities provided a huge workforce whose traditional skills in constructing houses of wood and adobe were easily adapted to what was to become the mainstay of modern Latin American architecture: reinforced concrete. The realization of the many imaginative concrete forms devised by architects and engineers in so many different countries was dependent on armies of skilled and semi-skilled labourers who assembled the scaffolding and wooden shuttering around the iron reinforcements, and mixed and poured the wet concrete into place.[40]

With government backing, Latin American architects experimented with ways of adapting the European theories to contemporary Latin American reality, and each country came up with its own solutions, combining the modern and the national in different ways. They achieved this using a variety of means: by the incorporation of works of art or indigenous flora; by the use of local materials or techniques; by formal references to colonial architecture, or to indigenous culture, past or present; or merely by the use of traditional colours or textures. They could exploit topography or geography, such as the proximity of landscape features or of older buildings, to establish a contextual dialogue. In tropical regions the climate encouraged new developments with space – living and working areas could be extended into the open air, while gardens could penetrate into interiors – and necessitated experiments to counter the force of the sun by means of screens, blinds and louvres, which in turn contributed to a building's visual impact. Sometimes it is not so much a matter of the fabric of a building but the purpose for which it was designed, or the people who use it, that contribute a distinctive national or regional note. All this gives Latin American modernism its own identity.

Building new worlds

I want to stress, however, that the Latin American modern architecture with which this book is concerned is not an uncritical reworking of European modernism with the addition of some decorative local colour, but a deliberate and more profound adaptation of or challenge to European models. In this it constitutes an 'alternative modernism', to appropriate a term coined to describe Latin American art.[41] During the period under consideration, Latin American intellectuals were very aware of their cultural and historical dependence on Europe, and of the economic and political power of their northern neighbour. These factors formed a backdrop against which they set about building their own version of the new world; we, too, must bear them in mind when we consider their achievements.

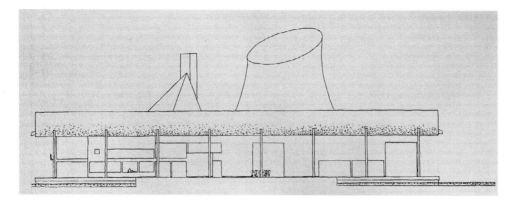

Le Corbusier, drawing of Chandigarh Assembly Hall, Punjab, India, 1951.

A single example, not otherwise discussed in this book, can serve as a paradigmatic example of Latin America's own brand of architectural modernism: the headquarters of the United Nations Economic Commission for Latin America (Comisión Económica para América Latina, CEPAL) in Santiago de Chile. By definition this is a building of continental rather than national or regional significance, characterized by its range of reference, its social and historical inclusivity (Plate 1). Begun in 1960, it is a mature example of the type of Latin American modern architecture with which the rest of this book is concerned. It was designed by Emilio Duhart, a Chilean architect with impeccable modernist credentials: he had trained with Gropius at Harvard, and then worked in Paris with Le Corbusier. He intended the building to be a 'monumental, visible expression of spiritual and social endeavours'.[42] The shell-like spiral central conference hall refers most directly to Le Corbusier's Assembly Hall in Chandigarh in the Punjab and so, appropriately, links Latin American economic development with that of India. It also pays homage to newly inaugurated Brasília, Latin America's own spectacular achievement in the field of modern architecture and city planning, where Niemeyer had used a similar Le Corbusian spiral for the little chapel attached to the presidential palace.

The CEPAL conference hall also suggests older architectural precedents: the round tower of the Caracol of Chichén Itza in Mexico, for example, and the curved wall of the Inca Observatory in Machu Picchu. And in Santiago the jagged peaks of the Andes provide the architecture with a spectacular backdrop, just as they do in Machu Picchu. These Latin American references are in tune with the organization's purpose as a unifying force within the region. CEPAL had been set up in 1948 to promote economic integration within Latin America when it became clear that US-driven Pan-Americanism, formalized into the Organization of American States in that same year, was not going to provide the level of economic aid to which Latin American countries felt their membership entitled them.[43] During the 1950s, CEPAL promoted a theory of development throughout Latin America which emphasized 'state-directed industrialization as the means by which underdeveloped countries could achieve rapid economic growth and a more favourable position in world trade'.[44] An International Style building would have been inappropriate for such an institution, and Duhart has made its regional responsibilities explicit in the architecture.

In contrast to such large-scale political, historical and cultural associations, however, the concrete blocks around the main entrance bear the impress of individual human hands, as a reminder of the Commission's social responsibilities. The purpose of economic integration was, after all, to improve the lot of the ordinary people of Latin America. These hands pressed into wet cement, personal and poignant, also point to the paradox of modernist architecture in Latin America: that so much of it was built not using industrial techniques and mass-produced units, but by the use, precisely, of manual labour and manual dexterity, human muscle and sweat.

Emilio Duhart, CEPAL building, Santiago, Chile, detail of façade, c. 1966.

Latin America produced a wealth of architecture during the twentieth century, but my concern in this book is with the cases where there was what we might call an alliance between modernizing governments and modernist architects. During the era of optimism and relative economic growth – between 1930 and 1960 – three countries, Mexico, Venezuela and Brazil, produced not just a few isolated examples of modern architecture: they planned and built on a grand scale, and in accordance with the new theories, for a new world. The governments of these three countries, despite their very different political standpoints, embraced the new architecture as an efficient means of promoting an image of a progressive nation-state. They invested in city planning and public services, in schools, universities, hospitals and social housing, and in the respective ministerial buildings to administer these new responsibilities. The theoretical link between the new architectural aesthetic and what was called an 'architecture of social concern'[45] meant that where a government patronized prominent works in the new style, as in the case of the Ministry of Education and Health in Rio de Janeiro, the style of the building announced that government's good intentions to a national and international audience more effectively than any ministerial mission statement.

Within these three countries the central case studies were not hard to choose. In 1967, Jean Franco, in her unsurpassed *Modern Culture of Latin America*, had already identified three major examples of modern architecture: the University Cities of Mexico and Caracas, and Brazil's new capital, Brasília, all from the 1950s.[46] These state-funded urban schemes remain the examples which most readily spring to mind in any discussion of modern Latin American architecture, and so formed my starting point. They did not, however, occur in a vacuum, and my intention has been to provide these relatively well-known examples with a context by exploring aspects of the theory and practice of architecture during the preceding two decades.

The first chapter deals with Mexico, where a central issue was the relationship between architecture and muralism. In the mid 1960s a critic said of Juan O'Gorman that he was 'a good painter and a rebellious, good architect. This is exceptional in Mexico, where good painters no longer abound, and rebellious architects simply are not supposed to exist.'[47] The story of modernist architecture in Mexico is intertwined with the better-known story of the Mexican muralists, and Juan O'Gorman's personal journey through both means of expression provides a route through this chapter. Even when he was a young man, O'Gorman's arguments in favour of a strictly functional, minimalist form of modern architecture sat awkwardly with his belief in the importance of beauty and art – a belief strongly promoted by José Vasconcelos, the influential Minister of Education during the early 1920s and patron of the muralists. Radical architects like O'Gorman had to carve out a route for themselves in the wake of the success of the muralists, and the route they chose sometimes seems deliberately antagonistic to art. The two periodically converge, most famously in the University Library, where O'Gorman was involved with both the architecture and vast mosaic murals.[48]

In the chapter on Venezuela the Ciudad Universitaria (University City) in Caracas is of central importance. Here, in contrast to the almost exactly contemporaneous CU in Mexico City, the architect Carlos Raúl Villanueva chose to involve painters and sculptors from the start, designing the different buildings with a view to incorporating art wherever possible. The result is a complex where there is an almost seamless transition between art and architecture, where a wall is also a decorative screen, or where a panel of stained glass is a wall. Villanueva commissioned works of art from both Venezuelans and foreigners, so that the CU also represents the integration of European abstraction into Venezuela, and of the arts into the heart of the educational system. This in turn is part of a wider concern for other forms of integration in and through architecture in Venezuela, where there is no dramatic break between the old and the new. Villanueva's – and Venezuela's – earliest urban scheme was the reconstruction of the dilapidated district of El Silencio, where neocolonial façades integrate new-style housing blocks into the old urban centre. The subsequent development of the Centro Simón Bolívar effectively serves to link together the colonial city, including the pseudo-old El Silencio district, and the new, so integrating the past into the present and the future. More recently, in what I suggest is a continuation of the Venezuelan integrational tendency, the Caracas Metro system has actively sought to establish links between different sectors and social groups of the city by means of art, architecture and urban planning.

The last and longest chapter looks at Brazil, a more complex case than either Mexico or Venezuela. A history of modern architecture that leads to Brasília has to begin in the capital which Brasília was built to replace, Rio de Janeiro, but must also take into account certain other developments, notably in São Paulo and in Belo Horizonte. The principal actors are Lúcio Costa and Oscar Niemeyer, who respectively drew up the urban plan and designed the architecture of Brasília, but both were strongly influenced by a third central player, Le Corbusier, especially during his second visit to Brazil in 1936. During his first visit in 1929, however, Le Corbusier had met in São Paulo the young architect Gregori Warchavchik, who was largely responsible for disseminating ideas about the new architecture in Brazil. Another important figure was the landscape gardener Roberto Burle Marx, whose collaboration with Niemeyer encouraged the latter in his use of the curvaceous forms that were to become the hallmark of Brazilian modern architecture. The key projects are the Ministry of Education and Health building in Rio de Janeiro, begun in 1936 and the proving ground for many of the most important architects of the future, and the city of Brasília, whose construction, it was believed, 'would generate a new mentality in the country, one of accelerated optimism, achievement, and confidence in Brazil's own abilities to make "the big push" toward self-sustaining growth'.[49] This was but a more ambitious version of the ideas behind much of the modern architecture of Latin America discussed in the following pages.

ONE

MEXICO

If anywhere in Latin America should have produced a new architecture, it was Mexico in the years immediately following the Revolution of 1910–17. There was an urgent need for a physical infrastructure to support the new regime and enable it to implement its health and education programmes and to house the increasingly urbanized workforce, because the new constitution of 1917 had included resolutions concerning the universal right to a state education, health care and affordable housing. The Revolutionary government also needed new ministerial buildings to administer these programmes – buildings which, by their very presence in the city, would also demonstrate the seriousness of the government's intentions.

In the field of the visual arts, however, it is the muralists rather than the architects who spring to mind in connection with the early achievements of the Mexican Revolution, and the relationship between the muralist movement and architecture during the 1920s is central to an understanding of the heterogeneous nature of subsequent modernist architecture in Mexico. In the early post-Revolutionary years there was no caucus of articulate, powerful radicals among the architectural community, whereas the muralists – especially the big three, Diego Rivera, David Alfaro Siqueiros and José Clemente Orozco – immediately seized the opportunity to transform traditional practice.[1] They were noisy, talented, energetic and highly politicized; with strong government backing, their work began to appear in prominent public places from the early 1920s, and they quickly achieved tremendous popular support both in Mexico and abroad.

The muralists' early success set the agenda for architecture in two important ways. First, a rather narrow and distorted idea of 'plastic integration' was in effect forced upon architects by the muralists, who wanted new buildings to include appropriate walls for them to paint; second, because the aesthetic of Mexico's first modernist architecture was essentially minimalist and abstract, and involved the rejection of all decorative detail on ideological grounds, the successful incorporation of the figurative narratives and allegories of the muralists was inevitably going to be difficult. There were additional, related problems in that, for example, a taste for extensive walls of glass limited the possibilities for external mural decoration. And there is the question of nationalism. Muralism quickly established itself as a form of expression that was both Mexican and modern, but for architecture this proved to be much harder – partly, of course, because the terms of the debate had already been established by the muralists. Some architects succeeded in grasping this particular nettle, but in general the state did not: it wanted an architecture that was unequivocally modern in the sense of the so-called 'International Style' of modern, but with nationalist accents provided by the muralists. These are the tensions that form the backbone of this chapter. The architectural solutions are highly diverse: imaginative, flamboyant, surprising, and at times awkward, but the very awkwardness is part of the excitement, evidence of the struggle to find new solutions to contradictory demands.

Vasconcelos, muralism and neocolonial architecture

The key figure behind the success of the muralists was the philosopher and political activist José Vasconcelos, Minister of Education between 1921 and 1924. Vasconcelos, a passionate believer in the progress of humanity from a material state via a rational state to a spiritual state, saw education as the key to Mexico's progress towards the desired third state.[2] Vehemently anti-positivist, he saw education not as narrowly vocational but as transformative and life-enhancing in an almost mystical way, and he understood the potential support for an educational programme that a public mural art could bring. He perceived art as a way of awakening the illiterate masses to what he saw as true aesthetic beauty rather than as a vehicle for any specific political message. This in turn was part of his broader vision of Mexico's position on the international stage, as the crucible in which what he called the universal cosmic race, the *raza cósmica*, would be created.[3] This, he argued, would be achieved when all the races of the world were evenly intermingled, and he believed that Mexico was providentially poised between Europe and Asia, and therefore well placed to draw the best from all these sources: from the indigenous cultures of America, from the heritages of colonial Latin America, of Greece and of the Orient.[4] Vasconcelos's view was that the rich culture thereby created, 'the Latin awakening which today throbs in history', would challenge that of the materialistic and spiritually desiccated Anglo-Saxon nations, especially that of the USA.[5] In order to achieve the *raza cósmica* the Mexican people needed to know and value these diverse cultures, above all their own, and that meant education: this was where the muralists had a vital supporting role to play.

The Ministry of Education building

Vasconcelos's first initiative in this direction came in 1921, when he commissioned a series of murals of Mexican landscape and women in traditional dress for the walls of the Ministry of Education, then still under construction.[6] This building typifies the way in which architecture in the early post-Revolutionary years was constrained and compromised in ways in which the muralists were not. While the government of President Obregón was drawing up the necessary legal and constitutional documentation to create the new Ministry, Vasconcelos set about building it a permanent home. Money

Federico Méndez Rivas, Ministry of Education, courtyard, Mexico City, 1920–21
(photograph c. 1983).

was very tight, the site he chose in the centre of Mexico City was part building lot, part older structures, and the architects he approached wanted to undertake detailed and time-consuming research before starting work. Vasconcelos was impatient. He urgently needed a suitable centre from which to administer his ambitious educational plans, but he also wanted it to be – as he said in his inaugural address – a symbol, a building with noble proportions, 'as firm and clear as the conscience of the mature Revolution'. He chose an engineer, not an architect, to design it, Federico Méndez Rivas, an otherwise unknown figure but one whom Vasconcelos considered to be a 'man of action'. In under a year, with the help of 600 workers and craftsmen, Méndez Rivas had built a grand three-storey palace organized around two spacious courtyards, with 'high arches and wide galleries' of the sort Vasconcelos had requested. He took his cue from the existing architecture of the old colonial Law School to produce an academic building that harked back to the neoclassicism of the late-eighteenth-century reformer Manuel Tolsá, whose work Vasconcelos greatly admired. In other words, although the building's function was a central plank in the Revolutionary government's aims and its construction was a triumph of revolutionary enthusiasm, it did not mark a radical change of architectural direction. And this is evidently what Vasconcelos wanted. He did not want something in what he referred to disparagingly as the 'modern' style favoured by the dictator Porfirio Díaz, with mean proportions and 'iron tubes' instead of columns; he wanted something of stone, with the nobility and grandeur he associated with the Spanish colonial past.

As an influential intellectual in the years immediately following the Revolution Vasconcelos is perhaps exceptional in the degree to which he regarded the colonial period as a cultural golden age, but he is not alone in his affection for colonial architecture. In 1922 the anthropologist Manuel Gamio praised it as a genuinely Mexican expression, produced by a workforce that was predominantly Indian, and adapted to 'the climate, the earth and the sky of Mexico',[7] and the possibility of recuperating this 'Mexican' style to meet the needs of a modern society had been recognized even before the Revolution. Jesus Tito Acevedo and Federico Mariscal, two architect-members of the Ateneo de la Juventud, a group of young writers and artists that started meeting in 1907 with the aim of building a new Mexican culture, had argued for a new national architecture based on a reworking of the colonial legacy to meet the needs of modern society.[8] The neocolonial style, therefore, came to be the mode favoured by the Mexican government in the early post-Revolutionary years. This may seem paradoxical, because a century earlier success in the struggle for Independence in Mexico, as elsewhere in Latin America, brought with it a rejection of the architectural style of the high colonial period. In fact a distaste for baroque and rococo flamboyance was part of a broader shift in values that was to lead to the social and political upheavals of the early nine-teenth century. After the foundation, under royal patronage, of Mexico's Academy of Fine Arts in 1785, first the baroque altarpieces were stripped out of the churches and then, after Independence, many of the churches and other colonial buildings were themselves demolished. This was part of a reaction against centuries of Spanish cultural and political domination, but also, in the case of the destruction of some of the university buildings in the centre of Mexico City, it was a demonstration that the newly independent government would tackle pockets of conservative resistance to its liberal programme. As elsewhere in Latin America, the later nineteenth century became a period of tremendous architectural eclecticism, with dictatorial governments such as that of Mexico's Porfirio Díaz looking to France as a suitable model of progress, and patronizing a Beaux-Arts type of simplified classicism as part of a broader raft of modernizing measures.

But at the end of the nineteenth century, while architectural modernizers were still tearing down examples of the colonial baroque, artists such as José María Velasco were beginning to incorporate them into their paintings as picturesque details that helped to establish the distinctive 'Mexican' qualities of their land- and cityscapes. Privately, too, many members of the elite maintained their colonial mansions in good order, and in some cases were quietly engaged in reconstructions. Foreigners who fell in love with Mexico, and who were therefore not so involved in questions of the ideology of style, favoured the colonial over the more anonymous alternatives and this, in turn, helped to validate it in the eyes of Mexicans. The boundary between colonial and neo-colonial easily became blurred in such circumstances. By the time of the Revolution, therefore, the memory of Spanish colonial rule was overlaid with feelings of national pride and self-confidence so that, paradoxically, the neo-colonial style became – of all the many architectural styles available in the second decade of the twentieth century – uniquely acceptable to the Revolutionary government. It represented a rejection of the style favoured by the previous regime, and it was regarded as genuinely Mexican.

This is the architectural and ideological background to the Ministry of Education building, but as a building it has been eclipsed by the fame of Rivera's murals. Vasconcelos himself had no notion of the revolution he was initiating when he approached Rivera to co-ordinate the mural programme. Mediterranean culture lay at the heart of his plans for the new Mexico, and Italian Renaissance frescoes were the model he had in mind, but he left the artists to their own devices. Led by Rivera, Orozco and Siqueiros, they transformed his vague ideas of spiritual improvement through the contemplation of idealized beauty into a vital, powerful and throughly modern artistic language, and while each responded to the challenge in his own very distinctive way, the mural movement is unified by its exploration of new forms of art with explicitly political content, and by its public nature. In other words, in form, content and context it marks a break with the type of academic easel painting which preceded it.

There is no equivalent rupture in architectural style: the period 1910 to 1930 is one of evolutionary rather than revolutionary change. There are at least three reasons for this. First – and perhaps most obviously – architecture, especially high-profile state-funded architecture, is an expensive and time-consuming business, and from identifying a location through the various planning and construction stages it necessarily involves many different people and interest groups. Second, unlike painting, architecture was, as a branch of engineering, an established and respectable profession and so inevitably more conservative in its instincts, although had there been a politically radical pressure group within the profession equivalent to that of Rivera, Orozco and Siqueiros, the situation might have been different. Third – and perhaps most importantly – Vasconcelos had little interest in or understanding of architecture as a potentially transformative power, and certainly did not see it as playing a role equivalent to that of art, music or poetry in his campaign for aesthetic and spiritual education.

The National Stadium and Benito Juárez School

Two other projects can serve to illustrate Vasconcelos's architectural priorities, both built during his term of office in Colonia Roma, a new suburb in the south of Mexico City: a national stadium designed by José Villagrán García (1901–92) and, facing it, a school by Carlos Obregón Santacilia (1896–1961).[9] Both these architects were important figures in subsequent architectural developments and their careers typify this evolutionary strand of early-twentieth-century architecture in Mexico. The stadium was built in 1924, and Vasconcelos took an unusually active interest in it. He was determined that it should be more than 'a mere race track': he wanted it to be an open-air theatre, acoustically designed to enable the human voice to be heard without amplification but at the same time large enough to seat 60,000 people. At the inauguration, which he arranged to be brought forward so that he could take part before his formal resignation as Minister of Education, the amphitheatre was filled with a massed chorus of 12,000 schoolchildren, followed by a thousand couples dancing a *járabe*. It is telling that he saw its concrete construction as a necessary evil, not as a symbol of modernity:

> I detest those iron buildings, in the style of American skyscrapers, that will have to be demolished in fifty years. I admire peoples who build for eternity whether with stone, like the Romans, with brick, like the Babylonians, or with simple, massive and durable adobe like the Incas of Peru. But the strength to support stands for sixty thousand people can only come from concrete, which is frightfully expensive.[10]

Villagrán García's design, however, was in tune with Vasconcelos's tastes. The structure was simple, massive and traditional, with colonial-style arcades and a very grand double stairway, reminiscent of the garden façades of Italian Renaissance palaces.

The second important project overseen by Vasconcelos was the Benito Juárez School built between 1923 and 1925 by Carlos Obregón Santacilia, again in the new suburb of Colonia Roma.[11] The construction of schools was,

José Villagrán García, National Stadium, 1924 (photograph *c.* 1930).

of course, a central part of Vasconcelos's educational programme, and the Benito Juárez was one of the most important of those constructed under his tenure of office: a two-storey neocolonial building comprising a girls' wing and a boys' wing, each ranged around a spacious courtyard and linked by the library block. On the main street façade the rhythm of the windows suggests the articulation of a grand cultural institution, but without the overlay of columns and entablatures: in the Benito Juárez School the walls are smooth and empty, the main detailing being the finials which emphasize the staggered roof line in the manner of a traditional rural hacienda. The design conflates

Carlos Obregón Santacilia, Benito Juárez School, Mexico City, façade, 1923–25.

ideas of education and *mexicanidad*, and so represents Vasconcelos's educational and social aspirations: it involves the reappropriation of the colonial past in pursuit of a future populated with better-educated, more aesthetically sensitive people, while also relating to but also progressing from other educational and cultural buildings in the city. In both this school and the contemporaneous stadium the sense of simplicity and strength, and the lack of architectural articulation, are similar to those found in the rural mission churches of the sixteenth century rather than to the more textured surfaces and ostentatious designs of later colonial buildings. It must be said, however, that the neocolonial style achieved its brief popularity almost by default, and that Vasconcelos's own ideological position in relation to the colonial past was highly dubious:

> One day in Oaxaca, while I was looking at the old houses with their noble coats of arms and the patios with their beautiful stone arcades, I noticed how small the white

population was, and how many Indians from the surrounding highlands were invading the streets, wrapped in their blankets, silent and impassive. And I understood the whole tragic process of the history of Mexico; it lies in this displacement, in the exhaustion of the conquering and civilizing Spanish blood.[12]

Change was not long in coming.

Ministerial Deco

After their brief experiments with the neocolonial style, both Carlos Obregón Santacilia and José Villagrán García moved on, but in different directions. Obregón Santacilia, as the protégé of Vasconcelos, was well placed to become more or less the official architect of the Revolution; during the 1920s he received government commissions for several high-profile buildings.[13] Among the most important was the Ministry of Health and Social Security building (1926–27), which marked a turning point in urbanistic as well as architectural terms. It is in striking contrast to the Ministry of Education building, which belonged to an earlier era both in its neoclassical style and cloistered plan, and in its location in the heart of the old colonial city, two blocks from the Cathedral. The site chosen for the new Ministry building, of almost equal importance to the Ministry of Education in terms of the government's aims, was at the other end of the Paseo de la Reforma from the old city centre, so effecting a geographical break from the past. It uses a triangular plot with the main façade on the corner, opening out behind into two arms with a formal garden between, as opposed to the traditional square block with interior patio; and is in a boldly Art Deco idiom, the style which replaced the short-lived neocolonial for important government commissions.[14]

This is a sober building, as befits its function, but in line with Deco architecture elsewhere the overall impression is of grandeur and elegance, with ostentatiously high-quality materials and craftsmanship in the Beaux-Arts tradition, and with great attention to the ironwork and light fittings. Obregón Santacilia flourished in the Deco mode: it allowed him to be modern in the

Carlos Obregón Santacilia, Ministry of Health and Social Security, Mexico City, detail of main façade, 1926–27.

sense that it provided an alternative to the classical language, with large areas of smooth plain wall, articulated only by shallow stepped recessions in the wall surface around the doors and windows, and also Mexican in that Deco, as an inclusive and mildly iconoclastic style, encouraged a nationalist accent. The sculptural details are particularly interesting in that in style and content they are suggestive of early colonial stone carving, of European designs and motifs imbued with an Aztec aesthetic via the hand of the indigenous craftsman. As with the Ministry of Education, this office was responsible for fulfilling the Revolutionary promises, and Obregón provided the government with a showpiece of modern design, but with a Mexican accent. As a building which helped to reorientate the city, it could also be read as a symbol of the reorientation of Mexican politics.

Clinical functionalism

The architect in charge of the new Ministry's programme of hospital construction, however, was José Villagrán García, who had a rather different agenda. Having won his spurs with the National Stadium in 1924, he was appointed architect to the Department of Public Health in 1925, in which year he built the Institute of Hygiene at Popotla. This complex of buildings has been almost completely destroyed, but at the time it marked a major shift towards a functional style of architecture: horizontal and rectilinear, with flat roofs and plain façades, and a minimum of decorative detail. The sanatorium was a simple, symmetrical design, almost like a traditional Renaissance cross-plan hospital, and the reinforced concrete structure was undisguised. Obregón Santacilia described the work – in a journal produced by the cement industry – as having 'the simplicity and perfection of a machine', where everything from the organization of space to the smallest detail was designed to fulfil a specific purpose.[15] In his later sanatorium at Tlalpan in Huipilco, begun in 1929, Villagrán further refined his method of working. He began with a rigorously detailed investigation of the practical requirements, the spaces and their various functions before designing anything. He therefore eliminated everything that was not absolutely essential and fitted to its purpose.[16] Using this method, Villagrán designed a succession of hospitals to meet the needs of the growing population, his language becoming ever more sparse. The results were good, functional hospitals, clinics and sanatoria, always pleasantly light and airy, constructed speedily and economically. The emphasis was always on the comfort and convenience of the patients and staff rather than considerations of appearance, but these buildings also served to promote a very modern image of the new Ministry as an active agent of progress and social reform – an image that

José Villagrán García, Institute of Hygiene, Popotla, 1924 (photograph c. 1930).

accorded well with the emphasis on cleanliness and hygiene which was so much a part of the language of modernism.

Obregón Santacilia and Villagrán García were both professors in the School of Architecture while Juan O'Gorman (1905–82) was a student there, and during the mid to late 1920s he worked for both as a draughtsman: for Obregón on the Benito Juárez School, and for Villagrán on the Institute of Hygiene at Popotla.[17] In his autobiography O'Gorman pays tribute to Obregón, for whom he had enjoyed working, but he has little to say in favour of Villagrán: he feels that he underpaid him, and he plays down Villagrán's influence on his own architectural development.[18] In fact, after his brief flirtation with neocolonial ideas, Villagrán's chosen route was a pragmatic functionalism which, in practice, was not far removed from that taken up by the vociferously radical slightly younger generation of architects in Mexico, among whom O'Gorman was a leading figure. O'Gorman's antipathy towards Villagrán was probably therefore at least partly a result of his own egocentricity: he later wanted to claim for himself the honour of having been the first Le Corbusian functionalist in Mexico. Villagrán, on the other hand, chose to emphasize his independence from non-Mexican influence, claiming that he began building in a functionalist mode before he had even heard of Le Corbusier.[19] Both men claimed to have been influenced by a third, little-known figure, the architect Guillermo Zárraga, who introduced new ideas from Europe via his column in the Sunday edition of the *Excelsior* newspaper, and also gave classes in architectural theory.[20] O'Gorman quotes Zárraga as saying: 'Today we have to make an architecture which meets the needs and the means of production of our country', and acknowledges that Villagrán developed these ideas too.[21] For Villagrán, reinforced concrete and simple, functional, cubic architecture were a means to an end. For O'Gorman, they were the basis of an ideology.

Architecture and revolution

It was the muralists rather than the architects who first identified the exciting possibilities offered by the new architectural techniques and materials. The radical manifesto 'A Stridentist Prescription' (1921) borrows directly from Marinetti's Futurist Manifesto, and celebrates 'the wonderful skyscrapers that everyone detests' as the architecture of the future.[22] It is significant that the appended 'Directory of the Avant-Garde' seems to list almost every imaginable contemporary avant-garde artist and writer, but not a single architect. In Spain in the same year Siqueiros published his 'Three Appeals for a Modern Direction to the New Generation of American Painters and Sculptors', in which the first appeal, for artists to embrace the future, includes the following passage:

Stridentist movement woodcut by Ramón
Alva de la Canal, *Edificio/Building*, 1926.

Let us live our marvellous dynamic age! Let us love the modern machine which provokes
unexpected plastic emotions, the contemporary aspects of our daily lives, the life of
our cities under construction, the sober practical *engineering* of our modern buildings,
devoid of architectural complications (immense towers of iron and cement stuck in
the ground), comfortable furniture and utensils (plastic materials of the first order)…[23]

Siqueiros is borrowing from the language of contemporary architectural theory
in Europe: an enthusiasm for engineering and a contempt for 'architectural

complications' were later to become central tenets of the modernist debate among the more radical young architects in Mexico. Siqueiros's second appeal is for an art stripped of the inessential details:

> the *fundamental essence*, the basis of the work of art, is the *magnificent geometrical structure of form* – the concept, inner workings, and architectural materialization of form and perspective – which, by imposing 'limits', creates the depth and atmosphere of *'volumes in space'*.

He refers to the primary shapes, 'cubes, cones, spheres, cylinders, pyramids – which should provide the skeleton of all artistic architecture', and urges a return not to what he calls 'those lamentable archaeological reconstructions (*"Indianism"*, *"Primitivism"*, *"Americanism"*) based on the work of the ancient inhabitants of our valleys', but to 'the constructive vitality of their work', its 'synthetic energy'; and his final appeal is for the rejection of the idea of a national art: '*We must become universal!* Our own *racial* and *regional* physiognomy will always show through in our work.'[24] Siqueiros's vision of a universal art that will at the same time manifest its regional origins is an issue which also arises with particular force in relation to architecture.

Juan O'Gorman and Le Corbusian theory

This is the context in which in 1924, as a third-year student in the School of Architecture, Juan O'Gorman got hold of a copy of Le Corbusier's *Vers une Architecture/Towards a New Architecture*, which had been published in Paris the previous year. Earlier in his university career O'Gorman had made his mark by complaining to Vasconcelos, then Rector, that there was not enough teaching, and that what teaching there was, was of very poor quality.[25] As a radical-minded young man, a member of the Communist Party, he found it frustrating to have to read Renaissance theorists like Vignola and to study the conventional march of classical architectural styles from Greece and Rome, via the Renaissance, to French and then Mexican neoclassicism. By his third year,

however, things had improved, and in his autobiography he speaks enthusiastically about two tutors in particular: the architect Guillermo Zárraga and the
engineer José Antonio Cuevas. In contrast to Vasconcelos's conservative taste
for traditional materials, O'Gorman quotes Zárraga's demands:

> What have reinforced concrete and the iron frame to do with the classical orders?
> Nothing! What has our civilization, our culture to do with life in ancient Rome, or
> in France during the period of the Revolution, or in Mexico during the time of
> Independence? Nothing![26]

Zárraga argued for new, functional forms that met the needs of the times,
using the new materials, techniques and systems of construction; while from
the engineer José Antonio Cuevas O'Gorman learned the need to understand
the technical aspects of the profession.[27]

This was fertile ground for Le Corbusier's persuasive rhetoric, and the
young O'Gorman read *Vers une Architecture* several times. Indeed, to a highly
politicized young architect in post-Revolutionary Mexico it must have seemed
that this text was a manifesto written specifically for the needs of the new
Mexican state. Le Corbusier attacks all superfluous decoration, whether it be
artificial 'elegancies' borrowed from the past, or the follies of 'Peasant Art' –
so ruling out, from a Mexican perspective, neocolonial, neo-Aztec or folksy
styles.[28] He makes sarcastic reference to 'those young nations which have lately
appeared on the map [where] *Progress* rages', where people exchange their
traditional home for an overdecorated 'up-to-date house *à la européenne* with its
imitation stone stucco and its mantelpieces'.[29] Le Corbusier is adamant that
'Architecture has nothing to do with the various "styles".'[30] Instead, he pro-
claims the supremacy of technology and celebrates the purity of purpose of
the engineers who design ships, aeroplanes or grain stores, and his alternative
to all the 'styles' of architecture is summed up in his famous remark that a
house is a machine for living in, a piece of engineering designed from the
point of view of efficiency and comfort rather than style.[31]

Le Corbusier's tone is passionate, uncompromising and optimistic; he offers solutions to social problems and demands that Architecture rise to the challenge of the new era. The Mexican case was, of course, crucially different from Le Corbusier's scenario. He argued that there had been a revolution in the methods of construction, and a revolution in the concept of what architecture could be; what was now urgently needed, he argued, was an architectural practice that would put these two together to meet the needs of the fast-growing population of urban workers in order to prevent a political revolution. Le Corbusier's aphoristic declamation 'Architecture or Revolution' would have had a special resonance in Mexico in the 1920s: the Mexicans had already had their political Revolution, but the technical transformation Le Corbusier described was only in its infancy, and the 'revolution in the concept of what Architecture is' which he identified (albeit somewhat optimistically, and with himself, of course, as a central player) perhaps entered the consciousness of Mexican architects only as a result of his book.[32] But the Revolution had to pay dividends to those who had fought for it: Mexico needed to make the best use of modern construction techniques in order to build comfortable, clean, hygienic houses for the workers as quickly and as cheaply as possible, and it needed to provide people with education. Decent housing and a decent education: these were what Le Corbusier argued for, and in Mexico, too, these were what the people needed if they were not to be disillusioned. Le Corbusier's combination of optimism and arrogance must have been very attractive to the younger generation of Mexican architects: change for the better was possible, brave young pioneers with the interests of the masses at heart could indeed transform the world, and, however confused the detail or shaky the foundations, there were those in Mexico in the 1920s who were full of confidence in the future, and in the benefits of progress and modernization.

Vers une Architecture offered a challenge to radical young architects like O'Gorman. Whether or not such developments were taking place elsewhere, how far Le Corbusier himself had put his ideas and ideals into practice was beside the point. All Mexico needed was the idea, then it could press ahead and put the theory to work in ways that would be appropriate to the Mexican context. Of course it is easy, with hindsight, to see that O'Gorman's reading of Le Corbusier was very selective, and from his later vehement rejection of Le Corbusier's functionalism is seems unlikely that after his youthful enthusiasm he ever bothered to read the book again. At the time, however, it is not surprising that O'Gorman and his contemporaries, especially Juan Legarreta and Alvaro Agurto, were to select from Le Corbusier the basic elements that suited their political aspirations and their perception of Mexico's needs. For two reasons – because Mexico had so little tradition of architectural theorizing, and because the expectation of artists and intellectuals was that they be active participants in the Revolutionary transformation of society (exemplified by the muralists) – these architects embraced a very minimalist functionalism as the architectural ideal because it was apparently simple, rational and, above all, modern, and offered an immediate solution to Mexico's problems. In following Le Corbusier's rejection of 'style', they also avoided the 'lamentable archaeological reconstructions' despised by Siqueiros.

O'Gorman's first functionalist houses

Inspired by the teachings of Zárraga, by Mexico's manifest need for radical architectural solutions, by his socialist ideals, and by his ambitious and rebellious nature, O'Gorman found in Le Corbusier a set of ideas which articulated and validated his own aspirations. With admirable business acumen for a socialist, he invested the money he earned from working for Obregón in two tennis courts in the increasingly fashionable San Angel district in the south of the city, and in 1929 he built 'the first functional house in Mexico'.[33] The choice of site was particularly good for O'Gorman's self-promotional purposes in that the area had been developed in the nineteenth century with numerous grand mansions, but also the plot itself faced the popular San Angel Inn, a colonial hacienda that had been converted into a restaurant: the old colonial Mexico, beloved of Vasconcelos and the early post-Revolutionary government, together with the eclecticism of nineteenth-century new money, provided a useful foil to the incontestably avant-garde. O'Gorman's house was of re-inforced concrete, and he claimed – with pride – that people visiting the restaurant used to avert their eyes from the horror of it:

> The form was entirely derived from the utilitarian function. The services, both of electricity and sanitation, were exposed. The blocks of concrete [were] not plastered. Only the mud block and partition walls were skimmed. The tanks were visible on the roof. There were no balustrades on the roof and the whole construction was made with the minimum possible work and expense.[34]

He is at pains to stress the point that functional architecture could provide maximum efficiency for minimum work and expense.[35] The house comprised three bedrooms, two bathrooms, living room, kitchen, servant's room with bathroom, garage and covered terrace on the ground floor, and, on the top floor, a studio reached by a flying helicoidal staircase. O'Gorman credits his two mentors with the ideas behind it. He applied José Antonio Cuevas's dictum that architecture should first and foremost be correct in terms of its structural engineering, and then Zárraga's emphasis on the need to be as faithful as possible to the basic human requirements of a dwelling, to apply modern construction techniques, and to take into account the local conditions. So, for example, because in the Valley of Mexico the nights are always cold, there are east-facing windows to catch the first warmth of the sun.

O'Gorman showed off this first functionalist house to his acquaintance Diego Rivera, who was suitably impressed, saying that he found it aesthetically pleasing. In his autobiography O'Gorman says – perhaps somewhat disingenuously – that this surprised him because he had designed the house to be useful and functional, not beautiful. Indeed, he claimed that this house prompted Rivera to invent the theory that architecture arrived at by the strict application of the most scientific functionalist principles was also a work of art. He credited Rivera with realizing that an architecture involving 'maximum efficiency and minimum cost' which was also visually attractive would be of

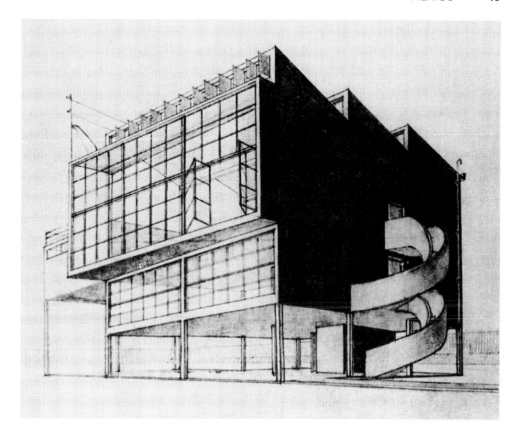

Juan O'Gorman, drawing of Diego Rivera's part of the Rivera–Kahlo studio house,
San Angel, Mexico City, north elevation, 1931–32.

enormous value in the rapid reconstruction of the country.[36] The result was
that Rivera bought the second plot from O'Gorman and commissioned him
to build two interlinked houses in a similar mode for himself and his wife
Frida Kahlo, knowing that to do so would be an effective way of promoting
O'Gorman's architectural ideas in powerful government circles.[37]

In 1931–32 O'Gorman therefore designed and built a complex that was socially as well as architecturally radical: the separate studio-houses reflected Rivera and Kahlo's semi-detached marriage; the cost per square metre was so low that it was almost 'workers' housing';[38] and the zigzag roof line above Rivera's studio was industrial in its origins, so conforming to Rivera's view of himself as a cultural worker. Even more than O'Gorman's first house these were very different from anything built in Mexico before and are explicitly Le Corbusian: they are built using modern techniques and materials, they are partly raised on *pilotis*, they have huge windows – walls of glass in some cases – so that the reinforced concrete skeleton is explicit, the internal divisions are kept to a minimum and they have rooftop patios. They demonstrate that O'Gorman's claim to have read *Vers une Architecture* several times is probably correct, as the design of Rivera's house in particular owes much to Ozenfant's studio-house, built by Le Corbusier and Pierre Jeanneret and illustrated in *Vers*: the zigzag roof, the large metal windows, the external helicoidal stair-way.[39] All the services are exposed: the water tanks on the roof, the rubbish bins, the electric cabling.

It is not, of course, merely a work of engineering, as O'Gorman liked to insist. It is interesting that buildings such as this support Siqueiros's argument that a 'Mexican' art could not be invented using artificial historicisms, but that the *mexicanidad* would in fact emerge of its own accord. The architectural structure is more or less non-site-specific beyond the orientation, and the design is closer to a Le Corbusian studio-house in France than to anything in Mexico, but many of the materials and construction techniques are in fact adaptations of Mexican traditional craftsmanship to the new requirements. These houses might give the impression of being made out of prefabricated units, as advocated by the theorists, but of course they were not. The iron-mongery for the windows and balustrades would have been custom-made locally, the partition walls were of local brick, local tiles were used for the rooftop patios and walkways, the floors were of wood stained with *congo*, a traditional yellow pigment, locally made clay panels were used beneath the roof, and the walls were coloured using the traditional *pasta* technique of incorporating the colour into the plaster skin instead of applying a separate layer of paint. Even the reinforced concrete was not in itself a new technique – it had been used in buildings in Mexico since the nineteenth century, albeit disguised behind stone or plaster – and shuttered concrete with reinforcing rods in the interior is but a small step from the very ancient technique of constructing walls of *tapia*, where soft mud reinforced with stones is supported between wooden shuttering until it has hardened.

The use of colour in the Rivera–Kahlo house is especially interesting in that it could be interpreted as both Mexican and modern (Plate 2). Rivera's house is painted red and white, Kahlo's is a rich saturated blue and white; the window frames are dark red, and the floors of yellowish stained wood. The use of strong colours is typical of domestic housing in Mexico, of course, but Le Corbusier had also used burnt sienna and ultramarine blue in his Esprit Nouveau pavilion in the Paris World's Fair of 1925, and in his Pessac housing project near Bordeaux in 1926. It would be interesting to know if O'Gorman was aware of this, whether it is coincidence, whether the use of such colours stems from a common Mediterranean root, or whether in fact these strong colours were not O'Gorman's idea at all but, rather, a reflection of the tastes of Rivera and Kahlo themselves. Kahlo's later home, the Blue House, is of course blue, with red door and window frames, and green-painted wood and metal work, and her childhood memory of it – as depicted in *Family Tree* (1936) – shows blue to have been its traditional colour, so Kahlo seems likely to be at least the source of inspiration, and perhaps the instigator, of the blue walls on her own part of O'Gorman's design. The fact that it had also been validated by Le Corbusier might have been an added bonus, but there is another distinctively Mexican touch which cannot possibly be attributed to Le Corbusier: the enclosing fence of cacti, in the manner of rural field boundaries. These were part of the original design, as they can be seen in the photographs of the house taken by Frida's father Guillermo Kahlo on its completion in 1932.[40] Again, whether the impetus came from O'Gorman himself or from his patrons is open to question, but the affirmation of popular Mexican traditions in this way is an important element in the rhetoric of Mexican modernism.

O'Gorman's functionalist schools

The need for an architectural renaissance to match that already achieved in art had been identified in an article published in 1926 in the first issue of the magazine *Forma*, in which the author pointed to Rivera as the best person to co-ordinate it.[41] Once he had seen O'Gorman at work, this is indeed what Rivera proceeded to do. In 1932 he invited O'Gorman to meet the newly appointed Minister of Education, Narciso Bassols, at the Rivera–Kahlo house in San Angel so that O'Gorman could explain his theories and describe the advantages of the 'new architecture'. The two got on well. Bassols was impressed above all by the promise of real results which O'Gorman's type of architecture offered, based as it was on the mantra of maximum efficiency for minimum effort, and he embraced the idea of an architecture without art. 'I didn't do architecture,' O'Gorman said, 'I engineered buildings, using the same mental process by which one makes a dam, a bridge, a road, engineering works.'[42] O'Gorman's identification of himself as an engineer was part of the radical rejection of the architect as an outmoded, academic, elitist professional, preoccupied above all with art and ornament, in favour of the engineer, who was perceived as playing a central role in the processes of industrialization and modernization. Again there is a close coincidence with the views expressed by Le Corbusier in *Vers une Architecture*:

> Our engineers are healthy and virile, active and useful, balanced and happy in their work. Our architects are disillusioned and unemployed, boastful and peevish. This is because there will soon be nothing more for them to do. *We no longer have the money to erect historical souvenirs.*[43]

Bassols's priority was to make some real progress on the promise in Clause 3 of the 1917 Constitution: to provide a good state education for everyone.

Vasconcelos had built some schools but, as we have seen, they were in a neocolonial style and, as O'Gorman remarked, they were designed liked monasteries, they were very expensive and did not begin to meet the demand.[44] Bassols must have recognized that traditional architectural practice was never going to be able to provide decent schools in working-class areas. He would have been happy to embrace one of the CIAM's declarations of 1928: 'Academicism causes States to spend considerable sums on the erection of monumental buildings, contrary to the efficient utilization of resources, making a display of outmoded luxury at the expense of the most urgent tasks of town planning and housing.'[45] What matters is not whether or not O'Gorman or Bassols could have read this particular manifesto, but that this was a part of a contemporary current of thought to which both would have subscribed. They were aware of such debates, and of how apposite they were to the contemporary Mexican situation. O'Gorman's proposals were for schools at a fraction of the price of those built under Vasconcelos or proposed to Bassols by other architects. He offered not Architecture but simple, useful buildings, planned in the same way as engineering works were planned: 'eliminating all architectural style and executing constructions technically' – all, of course, with 'maximum efficiency and minimum effort'.[46]

Bassols was convinced, and appointed O'Gorman Head of the Architectural Office of the Ministry of Public Education in 1932.[47] With help from his old master Guillermo Zárraga, then Director of Public Works of Mexico City, O'Gorman proceeded to design and build twenty-four schools in the Federal District between 1932 and 1935.[48] He used a three-metre module as the basis for all the major elements: classrooms were for fifty children and were three metres high with an area of 6 × 9 metres, which would allow for one square metre per child and four square metres for the teacher's podium; corridors were to be 1.5 metres. A quarter of the total wall surface of classrooms was to be of glass, one-third of which had to be openable, and windows should stretch the full length of a south- or south-east-facing wall, 1.5 metres above ground level – in other words, the upper half of the wall. Playgrounds were,

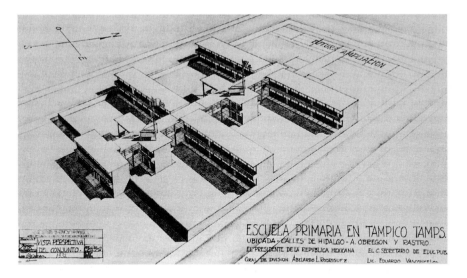

Juan O'Gorman, drawing of primary school in the port of Tampico, Mexico, 1932.

where possible, to be calculated on the ratio of five square metres per child, and there was to be one lavatory for every twenty-five children. Schools were to be painted in strong colours on the outside – red, blue, orange, pink, green or brown – and lighter colours inside to make the rooms bright (Plate 3). These buildings were to be designed to be very low maintenance, and to be extended with minimal disruption when the need arose. There were two basic categories of school: one for urban and one for rural needs. The former type had a reinforced concrete frame, floors and flat roofs, and metal doors and windows; the latter had brick walls and pitched, tiled roofs supported on wooden beams, and wooden doors and windows. In other words, they were adapted to the locality. It was expected that the local population would help with donations of land, materials, money and labour.

Some schools have been demolished and most have been altered, but we can still imagine the impact they must have had at the time, especially in areas where there had previously been no state school at all, or only rudimentary provision in a private home. Modern commentators have criticized these buildings for providing those who were already poor with an impoverished environment, the barest minimum.[49] It is true that O'Gorman took pride in not wasting a penny of the public's money, but in most cases he was providing a school where none had been before. And what was the point of worrying about people's spiritual needs, he asked, when 'what is urgently needed is hygiene. Hygiene of the body and of the mind. Large windows providing lots of light, and lots of WCs.'[50] For children such as those O'Gorman describes as living in shacks among the rubbish dumps, whose education had taken place in tiny, unhygienic, ill-suited locations without playgrounds, these new, brightly painted buildings would surely have seemed exciting, perhaps even luxurious.[51] At the time of their construction, some of the schools were the largest buildings in the area. An early photograph of the school in Colonia Tlahuac shows it as a spacious, open-plan complex with farmland and a few small houses behind. A detail which marks it out as Mexican is again a cactus fence enclosing the playground.[52] In urban schools the street façades had high windows to limit distractions from the street: in many cases these were simply portholes made out of drainage pipes – a marvellously cheap, effective and witty way of providing ventilation while also *demonstrating* the utilitarian, engineering aesthetic.[53] Another O'Gorman touch was to add the words *Escuela Primaria* on the outside of the building, in bold coloured lettering, as if this were a reading lesson in itself.

O'Gorman countered the critics who said that his schools looked Swedish or German, rather than Mexican, arguing that this was simply because the type of building was unfamiliar: their distinctive appearance was the result not of foreign influence but of the rigorous application of fundamental technical principles.[54] Had he been prepared to modify his position slightly, he could have argued that in fact his schools could be considered Mexican because they

Juan O'Gorman, Pedro María Anaya primary school, San Simón Ticumac,
Mexico City, 1932; detail, concrete piping used as ventilation portholes.

were well suited to Mexico's needs and economic situation, and in any case his
polemical rhetoric disguises a less rigid reality. As in the Rivera–Kahlo house,
the use of colour was tremendously important, and O'Gorman himself went
further: he arranged for murals to be painted in many of these new schools.[55]
His conditions were that artists should charge only enough to live on and to
cover the costs of their materials; otherwise he gave them complete freedom
to paint however and whatever they wanted, without fear of state intervention.[56] Several artists took part in this murals-for-schools project, and although
the results have been described as 'rather pedestrian'[57] and few now survive,
the aim was to provide a cheerful, stimulating environment. A contemporary
advocate of O'Gorman's schools argued that the inclusion of works of art was

the essential spiritual component which could serve to awaken the children's artistic desires, and to fulfil their instinctive Mexican delight in images and colours.[58] Vasconcelos's ideas had taken root, even if O'Gorman was reluctant to acknowledge the fact.

O'Gorman and the architectural debate, 1930–33

The schools programme established O'Gorman at the forefront of architectural debates in the early 1930s in Mexico. Bassols asked him to head a new School of Construction Techniques (Escuela de los Técnicos de la Construcción) under the auspices of the National Polytechnic Institute, an organization which had grown out of Vasconcelos's Technical Education programme and was therefore unconnected with the School of Architecture at the University.[59] O'Gorman – together with his former teacher, the engineer José Antonio Cuevas – drew up plans for an education that combined engineering with architecture, and they attracted some of the most politically committed young architects of the generation, including Juan Legarreta and Enrique Yáñez (1908–90) to teach in it. Not surprisingly, this upset the School of Architecture, which, O'Gorman was later to claim, excommunicated him for several years. The debate tended to be overly crudely put. On the one hand there were those who argued for a technically appropriate or scientific starting point to the design process, who wanted to build shells within which individuals could then pursue their various daily activities unimpeded, as it were, by any incommodious or intrusive environmental factors, and there were those who saw it as their duty as intellectuals and professionals to think of architecture in more instrumental terms, as contributing to people's spiritual as well as physical well-being. O'Gorman argued forcibly, if somewhat tautologously, for the primacy of engineering:

> We used our knowledge of the techniques of reinforced concrete, stability, materials, and so on in the construction of schools… and for the first time in Mexico we used

techniques of composition as an engineering process. This was where I discovered for myself the idea that architectural composition was necessary because in technical terms it is not possible to make a building which will function more or less well without applying composition as a technique, and one would have to ensure that the composition was useful in order to make buildings that functioned in the best possible way from the point of view of 'maximum efficiency for minimum effort'. And this was where I also discovered what composition was: the spaces for circulation which served to unite and separate, the useful places for work and those for rest, separated by walls so that [each] should be efficient.[60]

It is as if none of these issues had arisen at all in his previous architectural training, and his training in composition had been concerned exclusively with abstract form, not with the essential practical considerations of how a building would be used. The government, for obvious economic reasons, favoured the new functionalist architecture as the simplest, cheapest route to providing schools, hospitals and housing, although it had the added advantages of being visually modern and up to date in relation to contemporary architectural developments in Europe, and having good socialist credentials.

The deep divisions within the profession came to a head in 1933, at a special conference of the Society of Mexican Architects. Many spoke on both sides of the debate, and O'Gorman was forthright as ever:

The architecture which some call functional or rational, and others call German, Swedish, international or modern, creating confusion with so many names, we shall call technical architecture, in order the better to define it, with the clear understanding that its end is to be useful to man in a direct and precise way. The difference between a technical architect and an academic or artistic architect will be perfectly clear. The technician is useful to the majority and the academic useful to the minority…. An architecture which serves humanity, or an architecture which serves money.[61]

The conference stimulated debate, but came to no agreement; the divisions within the profession were deep, and essentially restrictive to practitioners on both sides.

Social housing

Houses for the workers

Perhaps an even more urgent requirement than hospitals and schools was housing: good, cheap, solid, healthy housing for the increasingly urbanized population. The most interesting early experiments here were those by O'Gorman's near-contemporary Juan Legarreta (1908–34), who in 1928, as an architectural student, had attacked the cast of the Victory of Samothrace in the Academy of San Carlos, shouting 'Death to Art',[62] and who, in his address to the Society of Mexican Architects in 1933, made his anti-establishment position quite clear: 'A people that lives in huts and round shacks cannot *talk* of architecture. We will build the people's houses. Aesthetes and windbags – let's hope they all die – they can come to their own conclusions afterwards.'[63]

Legarreta argued that in order to progress, people had to have better living conditions, and he saw it as his Revolutionary duty to try to provide these. In 1930 he designed an extremely simple, extremely cheap two-storey dwelling for two families, one to each floor, consisting of a kitchen, bathroom and living room, off which were curtained alcoves with fixed concrete bunks for beds.[64] The government, predictably, was very interested in cheap solutions to Mexico's housing problem, and in 1932 the Ministry of Communications and Public Works organized a competition under the direction of Carlos Obregón Santacilia for a 'casa obrera mínima', a minimalist worker's house. Legarreta won with a slightly expanded version of his 1930 design which took into account the way the working-class Mexican family functioned. The house was set back from the street to allow for a small patio, partly shielded by a low wall to create an intermediate space between the public and the private. The door led into the kitchen/dining room, the pivotal point in the house, 'for the mother-worker is centre and symbol of the family'.[65] This in turn opened on to two other crucial spaces: into the relatively large living room, where the family could work, study, celebrate and relax, and out on to another small

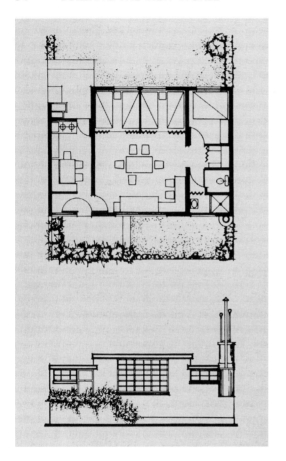

Juan Legarreta, design for a *casa obrera minima*, minimalist worker's house, plan and elevation, 1932.

patio to the back. This last was in effect the mother's own private sphere, with a sink for washing clothes and space to hang them out to dry.

It is interesting, however, that Legarreta, like O'Gorman, does not seem to have acknowledged the intrinsically popular elements in his work, perhaps because to have done so would have reduced the purity of the argument about the necessity for a technical architecture. Legarreta's minimalist worker's house of 1930 featured in 1931 in the magazine *Tolteca*, organ of the eponymous cement company (a subsidiary of Portland Cement), and was accompanied by very enthusiastic copy:

> Into this house Legarreta has not only incorporated the logical, rational principles of the genius Le Corbusier, but has made it speak in the language of our Mexican heart. And its cheerful strong colours mitigate the brilliance of the sun in the valley of Anáhuac.

The article continues with a description of the commodious interior, then the author envisages the integration of such a house with its inhabitants: 'On a little terrace the flower pots and bird cages: Mexico.'[66] Bright, strong colour is obviously an essential element in these early functionalist buildings – in O'Gorman's Rivera–Kahlo house, in his school buildings, and in Legarreta's designs for workers' housing. As we look at architects' drawings, or at early black-and-white photographs, it is easy to forget this. In these early functionalist buildings the colour of the walls was the architects' most obvious aesthetic contribution – beyond, that is, the clean lines and the 'sincerity' of the materials. The plants, the pots and the singing birds were, of course, the way the author of the *Tolteca* article – and presumably Legarreta himself – envisaged the house being used and naturalized. In some ways, perhaps, this sort of architecture could be seen as a genuinely co-operative effort between the architect/engineer at one end and the inhabitants at the other, with, where possible, the active participation of the family members – or, in the case of schools, the community – in the construction process as well. As noted above, the concrete construction was not so very different from traditional techniques of building using shuttered clay. This Mexican type of functionalism diverges sharply from Le Corbusier's various proposals for workers' housing, all of which divorce the design and construction from the future users, placing them firmly in the (better) hands of big industry and specialized factories which he envisaged mass-producing the various parts designed by what he calls 'true architects'.[67] For Le Corbusier, building belonged in the hands of capitalists and individual architects.

In practice, the architecture of both O'Gorman and Legarreta was automatically and unselfconsciously Mexican *and* modern: a radical functionalism, carefully thought through beginning with the needs of the future inhabitants, efficient and cheap. The important point about their work at this time is that it effectively provided an entirely new architectural route, one which marked a clean break from the styles and tastes of the past, which was deeply committed to fulfilling people's most basic needs, and which, in that it made explicit and enthusiastic use of modern technology, was also a visible demonstration of the country's progress and modernity: an education in modernity for the Mexicans themselves, but one with which they could identify. The architectural terminology used at this period was not clear. As we have seen, in 1932 O'Gorman tried to introduce the term 'technical architecture', which is, I think, unhelpful, because neither he nor Legarreta nor Villagrán in fact starts from the technique but from the needs of those who will use their buildings, and from a belief that essential activities and interrelations can be advanced by means of the disposition of the various parts of a building. In other words, the design is a result of close attention to what they felt were the essential human needs, bearing in mind the possibilities of modern technology, and of course always with an eye to the cheapest, quickest and most durable solutions.

Multifamiliares

The problems facing Mexico could not be solved by individuals, and, despite the passionate political commitment of architects like O'Gorman and Legarreta, it was larger, more generalized solutions that were needed, where the personal input was necessarily more limited. To design individual houses – even if, as in Legarreta's workers' housing, they were intended to be replicated across several blocks – was a luxury: production could not meet the demand, and the demand could not be met in the space available. The solution was to go upwards, as O'Gorman had in fact already recognized. His own entry for the

Juan O'Gorman, design for a housing block with communal facilities, 1932.

competition won by Legarreta in 1932 was not for individual houses but for a remarkable *multifamiliar*, multi-family building of workers' housing that makes use of Le Corbusier's 'Five Points towards a New Architecture'. The block comprises six storeys of flats raised on *pilotis*, so from ground level the views are uninterrupted, the spaces continuous; it uses his free plan and free façade, his ribbon windows, and his roof terraces. It breaks from Le Corbusier, however, in that although the block is a long low rectangle in elevation, in plan it describes a graceful undulating curve.[68] This, together with the asymmetry of the balconies, makes it very different from the sort of thing Le Corbusier had suggested in *Towards a New Architecture*, where multistorey housing was four-square and symmetrical.[69] In the drawing O'Gorman also adds some little local details – the Mexican flag and the distinctive vertical cacti of the Rivera–Kahlo plot – and we can be sure he would have wanted the finished building to have been brightly painted.[70]

O'Gorman's ideas for multistorey housing were not taken up. Nor were a variety of subsequent plans, including those of Hannes Meyer, the Swiss architect who had been Director of the Bauhaus between 1928 and 1930, and emigrated to Mexico in 1938 after several years working in Russia.[71] Meyer was full of ambitious plans and projects, arguing for architecture as a powerful force capable, if properly planned, of helping to develop a less individualist, more socialist community. In 1938, in a lecture in the Academy of San Carlos, he declared:

> Architecture is a process of plastic expression of social life. Architecture is not the emotive individual action of the architect-artist. Building is a collective activity.... Architecture is, therefore, a social manifestation indissolubly united to the social structure of its respective society. Separated from its respective society it becomes a fraud, lacking in content, a snobbish toy.[72]

Had Meyer arrived a few years earlier he might perhaps have been able to pick up where O'Gorman and Legarreta had left off, but he was received with suspicion on all sides. For the conservatives his ideas were, of course, too radical; whereas O'Gorman – a fervent supporter of Trotsky, who had arrived in Mexico in 1937 – accused Meyer of being an agent of Soviet imperialism. This was unfortunate, because certainly after the nationalization of the oil industry in 1938 there was money for some major public housing projects, and had there been an articulate, determined group with some clear plans, they might have stood a chance of success. The Union of Socialist Architects did elaborate a project for a workers' city, for example, but it came to nought, and in 1940, after Lázaro Cárdenas was replaced as president by the more cautious Ávila Camacho, such schemes were quietly shelved.[73]

Mario Pani, Centro Urbano Alemán, Mexico City, 1947–49.

It was not until the late 1940s, under the regime of President Miguel Alemán (1946–52), that the arguments about the need for high-density, low-cost housing bore fruit. Mario Pani, educated in Europe, returned to Mexico in 1934, after the first flowering of modernist architecture there. He was interested in questions of urban planning, he had first-hand knowledge of Le Corbusier's ideas about housing and cities from his time as a student at the École des Beaux-Arts in Paris, and he was well connected in government circles. In 1947 he was asked to put in a proposal for two hundred family units for a site in the developing Colonia del Valle to the south of the city centre.[74] Pani's response was to present a study for more than five times the number of dwellings on the same plot and for the same price. The government accepted

Mario Pani, Centro Urbano Alemán,
Mexico City, 1947–49, detail.

and the Centro Urbano Presidente Alemán was constructed between 1947 and
1949. There are six three-storey blocks, and six of thirteen storeys raised on
pilotis, giving the area an airy feel; the complex includes gardens, a swimming
pool, a crèche, primary schools, a central laundry and commercial outlets.
Two-storey duplexes reduced the number of service corridors needed as well
as reducing the number of lift stops, and, as with O'Gorman's early houses
and schools, the high blocks face east to catch the warming morning sun on
the large balconies and windows.[75] The surrounding area, although divided
into lots, was still largely undeveloped, with a mix of private houses, light

industry, and fields still under cultivation.[76] At the time of its inception, to those travelling up Avenida Coyoacán into Mexico City from the south, it must have appeared startlingly new and ambitious.

This was the first urban complex of its type in Latin America. It is an adaptation of Le Corbusian and CIAM ideas which saw the future of the city as a series of slab blocks set in ample parkland and isolated from through traffic, but it is not a copy. Henry-Russell Hitchcock was impressed, but added: 'unfortunately the quality of the execution is not always up to the quality of the design'.[77] His reservations perhaps have more to do with the regional accent than with the quality of the workmanship – more to do with what Villagrán calls the 'barbarous' surface textures which so shocked foreign visitors confronted with certain examples of modern Mexican architecture.[78] Pani's blocks are not the smooth glazed prisms envisaged by Le Corbusier, but richly textured and full of contrasts. The alternating balconies create strong patterns of light and shade, and the wall surfaces are clad in overlapping red hanging tiles and very coarse concrete, both locally produced materials, and cheap, durable and easily maintained, as well as visually interesting. At least on the level of detail these buildings have the irregularities of craftsmanship; they are manifestly *not* machine-tooled and mass-produced in the way required by functionalist architectural theory. The urbanization is now over fifty years old and wearing well, so what Hitchcock regarded as the inadequate quality of the execution has not affected its durability.

Pani was also loyal to the spirit of Vasconcelos. His frugal construction costs at the Centro Urbano Presidente Alemán meant that there was money left over to commission a number of interior decorative panels and a large mural for a specially constructed exterior wall. The artist of the latter was Orozco, but he died in 1949 before completing it. In his later Centro Urbano Presidente Juárez (1950–52) Pani collaborated with the artist Carlos Mérida to introduce coloured mosaic panels on to the façades and around the core of the open staircases. The designs can be read as abstract, but also suggest dancing figures. In his speech at the inauguration of the Ministry of Education building in 1922, Vasconcelos had said that he felt 'a dance rhythm in the air', and his sense of optimism lived on in some of these modern architectural and artistic projects of the 1940s and 1950s.[79]

The Ciudad Universitaria (University City)

The site

The Ciudad Universitaria (CU) of the Universidad Nacional Autónoma de México (UNAM) has been called 'the mythical *topos* for the creation of the new Mexican... the environment where a modern society would be born'.[80] It was also the environment that would demonstrate that, in effect, it already had been born: a showpiece of the Mexican government's achievements in modernizing the country since the Revolution. Before 1950 the state had invested in meeting basic educational needs by providing schools, and since Calles's presidency (1929–34) it had chosen to do so in a distinctively modern but essentially functional idiom. It had also built hospitals and public housing in a similar style. The CU was different. The driving force behind it was Miguel Alemán, under whose presidency the Mexican economy continued to expand, and he was determined to leave a lasting monument to his achievements by the end of his term of office.

The idea of building a university campus in the form of a city had already taken root elsewhere in Latin America – in Rio de Janeiro and Bogotá in the 1930s, for example. In Caracas plans for the construction of a university city began in 1944, and Mexico followed suit. The choice of site was important. It was an area to the south of the city, an uncultivated and sparsely inhabited lava field whose distinctive character had been established by the eruption of Mount Xitle in *c.* 100 BC, but where the remains of a civilization that had been wiped out by the eruption could still be seen. This rocky landscape – called El Pedregal, the place of stones – had been attracting attention for some time:

Juan O'Gorman and Diego Rivera,
Anahuacalli, Mexico City, 1940s.

at the site of Cuicuilco archaeologists had identified an ancient cultural heritage dating back to 500 BC, and therefore quite separate from that of the parvenu Aztecs. Cuicuilco was therefore an evocative symbol of new world antiquity similar to old world Pompeii. In the 1930s the artist Dr Atl 'camped out in a rudimentary shelter among the rocks for some weeks' to produce a series of chalk studies of the bleak terrain,[81] and Frida Kahlo was repeatedly drawn to the Pedregal landscape, using it as the background to several self-portraits.

There were two major architectural insertions into El Pedregal before work began on the CU – one an isolated, quirkily personal project of Diego Rivera's; the other a luxury housing development by Luis Barragán. Rivera bought a plot of land where during the 1930s he worked with Juan O'Gorman on a museum to house his collection of pre-Columbian pottery and sculpture. The result is extraordinary – a sort of modernized Aztec construction to which he gave the Nahuatl name Anahuacalli, or house of Anahuac, the ancient name for the Valley of Mexico. From the outside it is a massively solid truncated pyramid of the local dark-grey volcanic rock with narrow slit windows, like a prison or tomb. The inside is surprisingly light, but comprises an unsettling labyrinth of corridors and stairs with ancient, largely anthropomorphic or zoomorphic artefacts staring from every niche, nook and cranny. O'Gorman was later to claim that his role was largely that of supervisor and constructional engineer, and that he did not believe in such artificial attempts at effecting a renaissance of pre-Hispanic architecture adapted to the needs of the present.[82]

The Anahuacalli was a one-off, but by the 1940s the expansion of the city made this relatively flat – albeit very rocky – area of interest to speculators, among whom was the architect and landscape gardener Luis Barragán. In 1945, in partnership with José Bustamente, Barragán bought 750 acres of El Pedregal, which he later described as follows:

> To the south of Mexico City lies a vast extension of volcanic rock, and, overwhelmed by the beauty of this landscape, I decided to create a series of gardens to humanize, without destroying, its magic. While walking along the lava crevices, under the shadow of imposing ramparts of live rock, I suddenly discovered, to my astonishment, small, secret, green valleys – the shepherds call them 'jewels' – surrounded and enclosed by the most fantastic, capricious rock formations wrought on soft, melted rock by the onslaught of powerful prehistoric winds.[83]

Barragán's 'humanizing' meant the construction of modern, International Style villas set in extensive private gardens created by means of small manipulations and additions to the existing landscape: in other words, a very local setting for the more international language of modern architecture – a way of naturalizing modernism, but without the social or political implications of the state-funded projects.

The CU was very different. The idea had been raised as early as 1928, but for reasons of finance and lack of political will the first move came only in 1943, when the university authorities, recognizing the inadequacy of the conglomeration of schools, institutes and colleges housed in a miscellany of old buildings in the city centre, decided to buy land in the Pedregal district.[84] Despite its superficially inhospitable appearance, El Pedregal was not un-occupied land but rather, as Barragán's text implies, common land or *terrenos ejidales* on which the locals had grazing rights. In order to move in, the university (and, presumably, Barragán and Bustamente) had to buy out the *ejidos*. During the late 1940s discussions and financial negotiations proceeded, plans were drawn up in 1950, and by the end of President Alemán's term of office in 1952 enough had been built to warrant a symbolic foundation ceremony; only two years later the faculties moved out from old university buildings in the city centre to the new campus.

The plan

To build the new campus an umbrella University City Company was founded, and the architects in charge of the overall layout and rationale were Enrique del Moral and Mario Pani, under the co-ordinating direction of Carlos Lazo, but the CU was a highly collaborative project: it is indicative of the open-mindedness of the profession at the time that the basis for the plan was a proposal by a group of students, and the whole programme involved over 150 architects.[85] The plan was influenced by the Le Corbusian ideas of the CIAM's 1933 Charter of Athens, whose utopian declaration that the programme for a new city 'must gather into fruitful harmony the natural resources of the site, the topography of the whole area, the economic facts, the sociological needs and the spiritual values' must have seemed peculiarly apposite to the task.[86] The Charter codified the four functions of the city (housing, work, recreation and traffic circulation), stressed the importance of maintaining a human scale in city planning, and identified as particularly problematic the incompatibility of private enterprise and profit on the one hand, and social responsibility and unfettered city planning on the other. Since the CU site was entirely owned and controlled by the state, the architects had a unique opportunity to put contemporary ideas concerning town planning into practice with a relatively straightforward brief, and without the complications of private interests.

Of course, a university city is not like other sorts of city: it has a single purpose, however broadly one defines education; it has a fixed social structure (successive generations of students; a more permanent but – in Mexico – largely part-time body of academic staff, and permanent full-time administrative staff); and it was planned for a fixed population of 25,000 (although this quickly grew to 100,000). The site covers over two square kilometres and straddles the main route south out of Mexico City, from which service roads feed into the different sections of the campus.[87] While there is no east–west axis equivalent to the north–south highway, the area can conveniently be described as being quartered according to function. The great public stadium is in the north-west, the administrative and teaching buildings are in the north-east, the students' sporting facilities and halls of residence are in the south-east, and an area designated for staff accommodation and gardens is to the south-west. This was envisaged as a complete city with all the attendant services, where all staff and students were expected to live. In practice, the staff, not surprisingly preferred – and continue to prefer – to live elsewhere, and the construction of the planned student residences was delayed and in the end never fully realized, so the residential aspect of this city was not fulfilled. Otherwise it is much as originally conceived.

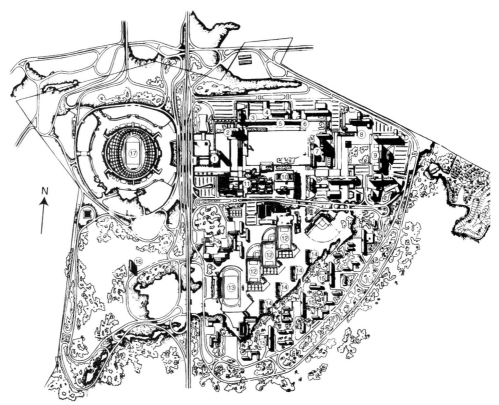

1 Rectorate
2 Library
3 Philosophy Faculty
4 School of Political and Social Science

5 School of Law
6 School of Economics
7 Science Faculty
8 Cosmic Ray pavilion

9 School of Medicine
10 School of Engineering
11 School of Architecture
12 Football pitches

13 Training stadium
14 Frontón courts
15 Student residences
16 Staff residences
17 Stadium

City University, UNAM (Universidad Nacional Autónoma de México),
Mexico City, 1950–52, plan.

View of the Philosophy, Law and Social Science Faculties, CU, Mexico City, 1952.

Of the CIAM's four functions, traffic circulation received special attention. Although the city is divided by the Avenida Insurgentes highway, the main university activities take place in the easterly half – the areas of teaching and administration, and student sport and residences, the central areas of which are entirely traffic-free. Goods and services are delivered to the main buildings from a route which circulates around behind them, leaving the centre as, in effect, a city without streets. Le Corbusier would have approved. Instead of streets, the main academic and administrative complex is grouped around two large squares, and with many buildings raised on *pilotis* the ground is freed up to create a variety of pedestrian through-routes and framed vistas. Many of the buildings are interconnected or linked by covered walkways, so that although the individual buildings are architecturally different in character there is a sense of a continuous whole. This is reinforced by the use of the local dark-grey volcanic stone for innumerable walls, flights of steps, paths and paved areas. The stone is cut into a multiplicity of different sizes and forms: large blocks set in cement like crazy paving, or – vice versa – bands of small chips set in cement to frame large concrete paving slabs, rough-hewn and irregular as coarse-surfaced walling, smooth and tight-fitting as stairways and pavements. The site itself was the quarry for this stone, the jagged surface of the landscape broken down into usable pieces by cheap local labour (presumably including the dispossessed shepherds) in an almost medieval system of community involvement in a gigantic cultural enterprise equivalent to that of building a cathedral – except that the Mexicans could be proud of the fact that the CU took barely four years, rather than a hundred.[88] It is this sense of the continuity of the landscape surface, tamed and rationalized but still clearly continuous with the untamed Pedregal topography round about and the volcanoes beyond, that makes the site unique.

The frontón courts and the stadium

But what of the buildings? The most successful, certainly from this point of view of integrating the university with the landscape and its history, are those which are outside the main north-east teaching and administrative quarter: the national stadium in the north-west quarter, and the *frontón* courts in the south-east. The handball *frontones* by Alberto Arai are open-air three-sided structures with trapezoidal profiles, the outer walls faced with volcanic stone. The view down the row of these staggered *frontones* is now masked by trees, but the intended effect was like that of the great avenue of truncated pyramids of the Street of the Dead at Teotihuacan, a few kilometres to the north-east of

Alberto T. Arai, frontón courts, CU, Mexico City, 1952 (photograph c. 1960).

Mexico City. Villagrán described how a visiting US architect had 'waited, horrified, half expecting to see warm human blood trickling down the walls'.[89] The stadium, too, is a striking building, where the past is again present. The architects Augusto Pérez Palacio, Raúl Salinas Moro and Jorge Bravo Jiménez began with a scheme for a structure in reinforced concrete, but a stadium to seat 110,000 spectators would have been too expensive and would have 'strained the capacity of the Mexican concrete industry at the time'.[90] On the other hand, there was an almost limitless supply of cheap labour and local stone: the solution was to excavate the centre and use this as a quarry for the earth and stone to create the terraced layers of seating.[91] The outer walls are also sloped, and with the western side elevated to provide more shaded seating for afternoon events, the profile of the stadium has the sweeping curves of a

Teotihuacan, Valley of Mexico, c. 100 AD.

volcano, and, although it is man-made, in effect the constructional technique
is analogous. There are also visual references to pre-Columbian architecture,
to the ramps and terraces and sloping *talud*, or wall, of traditional Mesoamerican
pyramids, and in particular to the circular pyramid of nearby Cuicuilco. The
outer wall of the stadium is decorated with a huge mosaic relief by Rivera
representing sporting figures, ancient and modern (Plate 4).

In the stadium and the *frontones* the landscape and the pre-Hispanic past are
suggested within the twentieth-century architecture in an exceptionally satisfying

Augusto Pérez Palacios, Jorge Bravo and Raúl Salinas, Olympic Stadium, CU, Mexico City, 1952 (photograph *c.* 1960).

way, and can be said to represent an architecture that is both modern and Mexican, geographically and historically rooted. Rivera and O'Gorman had experimented in this vein in the Anahuacalli, but this stylistic synthesis is inevitably much easier to achieve in buildings – or, rather, structures – which define external space and are open to the elements. Pre-Columbian monumental architecture, especially in the Valley of Mexico, was above all an architecture of exteriors, of pyramids the shape and sometimes the size of mountains, of terraces, plazas and ballcourts. Rituals were performed on top of pyramids in or in front of small temple-sanctuaries; ceremonies were held in the plazas and ball games in the ballcourts, with spectators gathered on the terraces around – public life was conducted in the open air, while internal spaces were not an architectural priority and were generally small and dark, reserved for private activities whether the occupants were priests, royalty or subjects. Pre-Hispanic architectural space can therefore be characterized without too much distortion as external public space, internal private space; and related to this is a lack of concern for windows, so that – to generalize further – we might say that external space is the realm of daylight, internal space the realm of darkness. This is in absolute contrast to the traditional European preoccupation with huge covered spaces – basilicae and cathedrals, castle great halls, theatres, railway stations, courtrooms, the Millennium Dome – which goes hand in hand with the West's persistent preoccupation with technology, especially with technology that enables large areas of the skin of such spaces to be glazed – from the rib vaulting of Gothic cathedrals to the iron-framed structures of nineteenth-century railway stations and beyond. In the twentieth century this teleology led to a taste for buildings encased almost entirely in glass, the antithesis of pre-Columbian architecture.[92]

The stadium and the *frontones* are, in this sense, exceptional in the degree to which their function conforms to pre-Columbian architectural norms: they are open-air public spaces dedicated to sporting activities, and in the case of the stadium to sport as ritualized public spectacle, with a minimum of internal covered areas reserved for services and changing rooms. The exterior spaces of the rest of the university city make use of a number of related devices to emphasize that this is a national project, a symbol of modern Mexico but rooted in history. This was achieved by organizing buildings around huge pedestrian plazas, with changing levels and flights of steps that evoke pre-Columbian ceremonial centres such as Teotihuacan or the newly popular (because newly accessible) site of Palenque, by the use of the local volcanic *tezontle* stone, and by the incorporation of local trees and shrubs.[93]

Teaching and administration buildings

For the teaching and administration buildings, however, the requirements were for large areas of well-lit interior space, for offices, lecture rooms and laboratories, where the solid volumes of pre-Columbian architecture were inappropriate. Although the different units were designed by different architectural teams, the overall language is uniformly that of the International Style, with clean lines and cubic volumes – vertical blocks, such as the Rectorate; more four-square, such as the Science Faculty; or horizontal, such as the History Faculty and the Law School. Most of the buildings are raised on *pilotis*, and reinforced concrete skeletons, and all have very large areas of glazing.[94] By and large the architecture of the CU announced the modernity of the project in an unequivocal formal and technical language: there is none of the rough-and-ready quality of Pani's Centro Urbano Miguel Alemán.

The University City was modern in design but not in function, except in so far as it provided wider access to a university education. With hindsight it is possible to see that with more time the CU could have offered an opportunity for reconsidering the nature of a university and a university education, as well as the forms the buildings might take in any radical new scheme. As it was, however, the administrative buildings, academic faculties and institutes of the north-west quarter of the campus were grouped around the two main squares in a way which was conceptually quite traditional. At the west end the fifteen-storey Rectorate, designed by Pani, Enrique del Moral and Salvador Ortega Flores, presides over the teaching blocks, and it is possible to see an almost Aristotelian anthropomorphism in the disposition of the different faculties. Working from west to east, the two ranges of buildings flanking the main square immediately below the Rectorate are, to the north, first the humanities block, followed by philosophy and geology, with the architectural faculty to the south. The main science block faces the Rectorate and closes the end of the main square, with the various mathematical and scientific institutes and finally the schools of medicine and dentistry grouped around the second, smaller square to the east. Therefore, if the layout of this complex is read as a metaphor for the body, which in turn is a metaphor for the educational and social structure, it is possible to see the administration as the brain; the library, flanked by the humanities and architecture, as the heart; the disciplines of law, economics and engineering as the essential functions, the mechanics of the body politic; supported in turn by the natural sciences and medicine.

Muralism at the CU

Apart from the setting, this is not an architecture in which it is easy to introduce formal, material or technical references to much that is distinctively Mexican.[95] There is perhaps an echo of pre-Columbian sites like Monte Albán in what has been called the 'asymmetrical harmony' of the plan,[96] and of the arcades and porticoes of colonial architecture in the rows of supporting columns, covered walkways and open ground floors, but these are very general similarities. The established method of 'Mexicanizing' modern architecture – as used by O'Gorman in his schools, Pani in his housing developments and Villagrán García in his hospitals – was, of course, to incorporate murals. The muralists, not surprisingly, had identified the new university city as a project of supreme importance for creating a new sort of visual environment, but they failed to persuade Lazo and his team to involve them from the outset. Indeed, the layout of the campus suggests that the architects chose to reinforce their primary role in relation to the other arts by spatial means too: the museum, the art institute and the theatre are hidden away within the plan, all incorporated into and accessible only via the Architecture Faculty.

One of the recurrent themes in the discussion of modern Latin American architecture is that of 'plastic integration': the integration of visual arts, especially painting and sculpture, into a building to create a composite unity. This idea had been promoted in Europe in the first decades of the century by several different theorists and was, for example, a central part of Bauhaus theory. In their *New Ideas on Architecture* (1919), Walter Gropius and Bruno

Taut declared: 'Artists, let us at last break down the walls erected by our deforming academic training between the "arts" *and all of us become builders again*! Let us together will, think out, create the new idea of architecture.'[97] The muralists, and Siqueiros in particular, argued vociferously in favour of a plan in which art was fully integrated into the architecture from the beginning.[98] In an impassioned address to architects and engineers at the Casa del Arquitecto in 1954, Siqueiros referred to the Mexican origins of a theory of plastic integration, quoting a radical art student leader who, before the Revolution of 1910, had declared: 'Painting separated from architecture is like a dead organ ripped out of a vital body. And architecture without painting and sculpture is a body without a voice.'[99] Of the muralists only Rivera had any active interest in architecture; Siqueiros certainly saw it only as a vehicle for his art. Most architects, on the other hand, continued to think within the traditional academic boundaries, and saw themselves as producing buildings first and inviting artists to contribute a relief or a mural as appropriate afterwards.

The CU could have been a great opportunity for exploring the possibilities of integrating art into a whole new urban environment, but – perhaps for a variety of reasons – the campus remains supremely architectural, and most of the murals are incursions, even intrusions, rather than fully integrated with the architecture. One reason, perhaps, was the lack of an eloquent sponsor in government on a par with Vasconcelos in the earlier years, and there were constraints of time and money. More important, however, was the architects' own traditional compartmentalized perception of the arts, partly established by the early functionalist rhetoric of O'Gorman and Villagrán, which made it hard for them to see art as other than an add-on extra, something which could be attended to after a building was completed. And if not on an individual, certainly on a collective, institutional level, the sense of architecture as playing a real part in the social and political transformation of Mexico is missing from the CU. Siqueiros believed that the problems lay with the architects, who were not interested in politics:

How is it possible to integrate political content when collaborating with architects who are against all political content? Furthermore, in University City there was no common theme… because the painters were denied the opportunity to participate with the engineers and architects…. We had to work where the architects wanted us to… I would have urged that the walls be made convex with their upper part forward. The surfaces I was offered did not correspond to my theories of composition and perspective in the exterior.[100]

There is a further problem. Murals of the sort Siqueiros had in mind are not easily compatible with an architecture dominated, as architecture so often is, by an essentially abstract aesthetic. The Renaissance theorist Leon Battista Alberti had recognized the contradiction between an architecture designed around ideas of the harmonious relationship between solids and voids, walls, columns and intercolumnar spaces, and a representational art where the intention is to create an illusion of a three-dimensional space, to deny the solidity of the surface. In the early twentieth century, abstract painting provided a way in which architects could accommodate art without disrupting the purity of their designs, but the muralists were not interested in accommodation. The other problem with the sort of buildings that were being designed for the CU was the predominance of external surfaces of glass. Modern architecture does not have to be like this – O'Gorman's schools, for example, included large areas of plain concrete that were ideal for murals – but in the 1950s, for the CU, the design of choice was an internal skeleton supporting a variety of glass boxes.

One of the most prominent CU buildings is the Rectorate, located at the head of the teaching and administrative sector. The four sides of the main block are almost entirely uninterrupted glass, with the result that the three areas allocated to Siqueiros to paint seem at odds with the rest of the building.[101] On the north wing he produced *The Right to Learning* – 130 metres square, it represents a huge arm, the hand pointing with a pencil to an open book in which are written key dates in Mexican history: Independence (1810), Revo-

Mario Pani, Enrique del Moral and Salvador Ortega Flores, murals by David Alfaro Siqueiros, Rectorate, CU, Mexico City, 1952.

lution (1910), and then an open-ended '19??' indicating Siqueiros's uncertainty about the future. Five storeys up on the east façade of the main multistorey block, a concrete cube projects out into the main university plaza, enclosing a small lecture theatre. This is painted with Siqueiros's version of the university crest, which brings the Mexican eagle and the Andean condor together into an allegory of Latin American unity. From close to it appears incongruous either as art or as architecture – a strange box stuck on to the flat *pan-verre* façade – but from the main plaza it is much more satisfying, and in a way that was perhaps not intended by either Pani and his colleagues, or by Siqueiros, it is like a modernized version of the crests and coats of arms which played so dominant a role on otherwise relatively plain masonry façades of colonial architecture, and which Vasconcelos had admired in the old houses of Oaxaca.

Roberto Álvarez Espinoza, Pedrio Ramírez Vázquez, Ramón Torres and Héctor Velázquez; mural by Frank Eppens, Faculty of Medicine, CU, Mexico City, 1952.

Siqueiros's most ambitious mural, however, is on the end of the long low south wing: a 'sculpture-painting' of modelled cement, covered with a mosaic of glazed ceramic, entitled, long-windedly, *From the People to the University – From the University to the People: for a New Humanist National Culture of Universal Profundity* (Plate 5). Siqueiros had his wife Angelica drive him up and down Avenida Insurgentes at 60 miles an hour in order to assess how the figures would indeed reach out in a forceful and dynamic way to those passing on the highway. The intention was to integrate the 'sculpture-painting' with the architecture, and the university with the people; and although the result is perhaps bizarre (and has been described as like extruded toothpaste), it is still startling in its originality and its attempt to investigate the possibility of a truly new form and function for the visual arts as a part of a genuine struggle for a new type of social order.

A few other walls in the main compound were assigned to muralists. The Faculty of Medicine by Roberto Álvarez Espinosa, Pedro Ramírez Vázquez and Ramón Torres – an interesting articulated building, permeable by stairs and walkways at different levels – has a large mosaic by Frank Eppens on the slightly convex end wall that faces west over the smaller plaza. With its over-sized vigorous figures, this is a bit like a drive-in movie screen, suggesting an element of the sort of popular entertainment that was not provided for in the plans for the CU campus. The auditorium of the Science Faculty at the end of the main square by Raúl Cacho, Eugenio Peschard and Félix Sánchez Baylón – another elegant building which counteracts the rather more rigid cubic geometry of the Rectorate – has a mosaic on the upper part of the façade: again a convex curve, by José Chávez Morado. Entitled *The Conquest of Energy*, this is an allegory of the pursuit and conquest of scientific knowledge, which ends on a slightly ambivalent note with the discovery of nuclear power. Again, this is not so much integration as incongruity, like a billboard that has strayed in from the 'real' city outside.

The library

The most famous and certainly the most prominent of these experiments with plastic integration, however, was the university library building, designed by O'Gorman, Gustavo M. Saavedra and Juan Martínez de Velasco (Plate 6). The final design was for a solid windowless cube housing the book stacks, above two storeys of reading rooms illuminated by continuous horizontal bands of windows, which in turn are partially supported on *pilotis*. The stack and the reading rooms therefore combine the solid and apparently weightless in dramatic dialogue: perhaps only the presence of the ever-changing student body in the reading rooms can justify the preservation of the body of knowledge above? The most striking feature of the library, however, is that the entire surface of the book-stack block is covered with intricate murals in mosaic by Juan O'Gorman. Siqueiros had tried in vain to find a modern alternative to the traditional glazed ceramic of Mediterranean origins for his 'sculpture-painting'. O'Gorman, on the other hand, scoured Mexico in search of coloured rocks which could be broken into suitable fragments in order to create the 4,000 square metres of images[102] (Plate 7). The theme, realized in immense detail, is the history and cosmology of Mexico, with the history of modern Mexico and the Revolution on the shorter walls to the west and east, pre-Hispanic cosmology on the north façade, and Western cosmology on the south. In style, and in their interlinking formal and intellectual intricacy, the designs resemble that of pre-Cortesian iconic manuscripts such as the Borgia Codex or the Coixtlahuaca map; at a distance, however, the detail is lost, and the overall design of the north and south faces resolves into two gigantic oculi reminiscent of the mask of Tlatloc, the goggle-eyed Aztec rain god.

O'Gorman's first proposal for the architecture was for a stepped structure reminiscent of an Aztec pyramid, but this was rejected as being insufficiently 'international'[103] – an interesting insight into the stylistic intentions for the central campus. The solution O'Gorman eventually found was to give the Aztec past iconographic rather than formal or structural primacy. This building can stand as a metaphor for O'Gorman's own professional development, since by this date painting had replaced architecture as his chosen medium – just as in the university library the architecture is subordinated to the mosaic surface. This is perhaps not so much a case of plastic integration as of architecture dissolving away. It is as if the contents of the books enclosed within the stack are revealed on the painted walls: the painted walls become the books, a part of the library's contents. O'Gorman's design represents a serious attempt to rethink not just what architecture – and especially monumental architecture – might or might not be, but also the function of a university library. By representing in visual form on the outside what is contained in the books inside, O'Gorman makes permeable, democratizes, the traditional ivory tower of the academic world, making it accessible to all Mexicans, whether or not, in fact, they can read.

The library building is unique. O'Gorman worked both on the design of the building and on the murals, and was fully competent to do so. As the work of both an architect and an artist – but one who had come to incline more towards the latter – it is unique among the administrative and teaching buildings in that, by its very nature, the main volume is without windows. In this way it is closer to the massed windowless volumes of pre-Columbian architecture, and therefore provides more opportunities for decorating the exterior surfaces. The intentions of art and architecture cohere. As I say, however, it is more than a neo-pre-Hispanic style but something which, while it makes reference to pre-Columbian culture in a number of ways, is nevertheless trying to do something new and different, exploring the boundaries between architecture and painting, between interior and exterior, between space and thought, and integrating images and ideas into space and volume. It rightly takes pride of place on the university campus.

The Cosmic Ray pavilion

The University City was a one-off, but it brings together a number of different strands in Mexican modernist architecture. O'Gorman provides a direct link with the early radicalism of the late 1920s and early 1930s, and although his library is far removed from the plain functionalism of his early schools, it is in some ways a logical outcome of his own political beliefs and his long association with the muralists. The stadium is unique in the way in which form and function successfully bring the ancient and the modern together. The main teaching and administrative buildings are more conventional, represent-ing the application of a modern architectural language as a style rather than an ideology, but saved from mere banality by the setting and overall layout, and

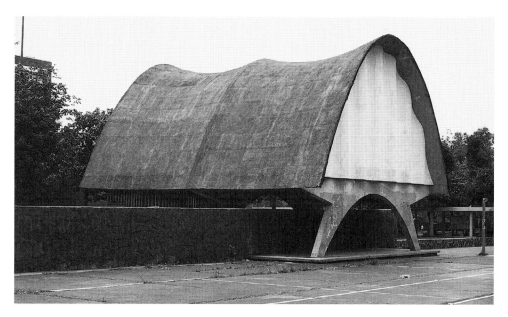

Jorge González Reyna and Félix Candela, Cosmic Ray pavilion, CU, Mexico City, 1952.

the startling intrusions of the murals. One further building, however, needs comment: the Cosmic Ray pavilion, which represents a rather different architectural direction. This dainty little structure interrupts the rectilinear geometry and glazed façades of the rest of the campus, and makes a dramatic statement about the formal and technical possibilities of reinforced concrete. The roof is a thin parabolic curve, like starched linen; the end walls ripple like curtains, and the whole dances on arched supports that echo the roof line above. The architect was Jorge González Reyna (1929–69), but the name more commonly associated with it is that of Félix Candela (1910–97), without whose technical expertise such a structure could not have been conceived, let alone built. Candela arrived in Mexico in 1939, a refugee from the Spanish Civil War, and developed the use of reinforced concrete to extraordinary ends. He was essentially a structural engineer who treated architecture as a mathematical challenge, and although more often than not he engineered buildings which were designed by others, the designs are dependent upon, derived from, the engineering. Thus Candela's work is an interesting example of form driven by technique – something for which O'Gorman had argued but which in Candela's case, despite his purely scientific starting point, does not produce purely efficient, rational results. Candela began with careful mathematical calculations, which were then converted into reinforced concrete structures using wooden form work – structures full of sweeping curves and arching vaults. As with so much of early-twentieth-century Mexican architecture, the construction techniques were unsophisticated: all that was required was plentiful supplies of cement and steel reinforcing rods, and a large workforce. Candela is especially remembered for elegant vaulted churches, designed by himself and by others, where the natural forms of the wood are preserved in the surface of the modern concrete: a witty play on the common metaphor of the column as tree, the vaulting above fanning out like branches (Plate 8). This is a modern version of Gothic, well suited to religious architecture, and the Cosmic Ray pavilion resembles nothing so much as a little chapel, a shrine to the science of the future.[104]

Parallel currents

A final word must be said about two figures who, from our own perspective, loom large in the history of Mexican architecture: Barragán and Goeritz. Just as the anti-muralist strand in Mexican painting is personified by Rufino Tamayo, so the alternative to mainstream government-funded architecture is personified by Luis Barragán (1902–88).[105] Barragán is seen as representing a countercurrent to the dominance of functionalism, both that of the early radicals and the later, more conventional, 'International Style' functionalism of Villagrán and Pani, and is now celebrated as the creator of a more acceptable 'Mexican' style of architecture which continues to flourish through the work of his disciples, particularly Ricardo Legorreta (b. 1931).[106] In fact, although Barragán subsequently took a different path, there are significant parallels between his earlier work and the 'official' Mexican architecture which has formed the core of this chapter. He was only slightly younger than O'Gorman and Legarreta, but in the late 1920s his first designs were in a neocolonial mode. His work became increasingly simple, so that ten years later the transition to a Le Corbusian rationalism was very smooth, and his houses and apartment blocks during this phase are close relatives of those built by O'Gorman a few years earlier. Then, as we have seen, in 1945 – at El Pedregal, on a site adjoining the future University City – he began working with architecture and landscape, placing International Style private houses in among the rocks and indigenous flora. He developed the style for which he is now recognized by building on the points of contact between traditional Mexican architecture and modernism – the simple, cubic volumes; the flat, undecorated surfaces painted in bright colours – in ways which are not so far removed from the early radical rationalism of O'Gorman and Legarreta. It is more accurate to see Barragán and others as complementing rather than opposing the mainstream of Mexican modernist architecture as it evolved up to the CU in the 1950s.

Mathias Goeritz (1915–90), like Barragán, received few public commissions.[107] He was interested in challenging convention, and in particular the boundaries between architecture and the other arts. In 1952 he worked on the short-lived Experimental Museum 'El Eco', and in 1957 he collaborated with Barragán on five gigantic brightly coloured towers at the entrance to the site of the new, futuristically named Satellite City urban development being designed by Pani (Plate 9). These towers are in fact sculpture on the scale of architecture, like megalithic standing stones, and are again made of the ubiquitous shuttered concrete, where the rough texture of the wood creates a nice tension with the abstract geometric forms. This sort of reference to the crude, the simple, the cheap, the popular (not something the architecture of the CU

Brickstacks on the site of the future Satellite City, Mexico City, with Mathias Goeritz and Henry Moore (in the hat), 1953.

chose to exploit) is reinforced by a historical reference to the extraordinary brick stacks of the brickmakers' yards which occupied the site before it became Satellite City. In this sense the towers are a tribute to the Mexican building worker, without whom they would not exist.

TWO

VENEZUELA

Venezuelan modernist architecture took a different route from the one we have traced in Mexico, despite the many historical and cultural parallels between the two countries. Oil provided both countries with the resources to fund national development. During the 1940s and 1950s both governments invested in large-scale, high-density housing developments, and new medical and educational facilities. In particular, both countries simultaneously initiated a major *ex novo* campus-style national university intended as a showpiece of economic, educational and general cultural progress. In both countries, after a period of architectural eclecticism, European modernism had a powerful impact, in particular the ideas of Le Corbusier and the CIAM. In both countries there was considerable interest in the role of painting and sculpture in an architectural context.

As with other Spanish American countries, Mexico and Venezuela share a history of European conquest and colonization which gave them a common language, a common religion and a common experience of political and economic control from abroad, as well as a legacy of racial contradictions which, in Venezuela, included African as well as Indian components. After a period of bloody struggle in the early nineteenth century, both achieved political independence (Mexico in 1810 and Venezuela in 1821), but exchanged Spanish domination for cultural and intellectual dependence on France. In both countries the post-Independence period was characterized by a succession of military dictators, the most powerful of whom – Porfirio Díaz in Mexico (president from 1876 to 1911) and Antonio Guzmán Blanco (1873–88) in Venezuela – were modernizers in so far as they welcomed foreign investment and readily gave concessions to foreign companies to extract their countries' natural resources. In the later nineteenth century, modernity in Latin America tended to refer to everything that related to the outside world, to the export of raw materials and to the import of culture, in contrast to tradition, which referred to everything internal.[1]

In terms of national cultural heritage, however, the two countries are rather different. The Mexican architect looking for historical roots on which to build a national identity was spoilt for choice: a pre-Columbian heritage unrivalled in the Americas, as well as plenty of examples of a lavish colonial tradition. Venezuela, by contrast, has no significant pre-Columbian architecture, and was never an important part of the Spanish Empire. Unlike the Aztecs of Mexico, the Inca of Peru, or even the Chibcha of Colombia, the way of life of the native Carib and Arawak peoples of the coastal region did not interest the conquerors: they had little in the way of culture or natural resources which the Spaniards regarded as of any value; they did not live in large-scale permanent settlements which, to the invaders, denoted the sort of organized society that would offer easy possibilities for the exploitation of native labour; and their extensive trade routes – around the Caribbean coast, down the Andean chain to the west and south, and into the Amazonian hinterland – seem not to have attracted attention or interest.[2] Caracas was founded in 1567, nearly half a century later than Mexico City, and the sparse population of European settlers that gathered there and along the coast was under the administrative control of the city of Santo Domingo on Hispaniola. Only in the eighteenth century was the province elevated to the status of an Audiencia, or seat of colonial authority subordinate to a Viceregal centre, with the little city of Caracas as its capital. Colonial architecture in the region was modest. The settlers lived in simple, single-storey houses of whitewashed adobe with roofs of tile or thatch, few external windows, and a private interior courtyard in the Andalusian tradition. Colonial churches, few dating from before the eighteenth century, were of the same materials, mainly single-nave in plan, with perhaps a little stone detailing around the main façade.

The cultural differences between Mexico and Venezuela were perhaps less marked in the nineteenth century. The struggle for independence follows a parallel course, with advances and failures between 1810 and 1821. In both countries the political discourse was influenced by the French Revolution, and cultural institutions and attitudes were shaped by those of the French Academy, although for geographical and political reasons Mexico was more closely involved with the USA than was Venezuela. They differed in that while the geographical limits of newly independent Mexico corresponded to those of the colonial viceroyalty, Venezuela, with no distinct geographical identity in the pre-conquest period and very little during the colonial regime, was initially part of Bolívar's utopian Gran Colombia, which fragmented into three separate countries only in 1830, on the death of Bolívar himself. Both countries, however, lost territory to their neighbours: under Guzmán Blanco Venezuela lost land to Colombia to the west, and to the British in Guyana to the east; while in 1848 Mexico lost nearly half its geographical area to the USA.

Guzmán Blanco, like all dictators, wanted to leave his architectural mark on the capital city, and he revitalized the old colonial centre with a number of major urban projects. As a modernizer he despised the architectural reminders of the colonial past and had many of them torn down, to be replaced by buildings in an eclectic range of styles – neo-Gothic, neo-Renaissance and neoclassical.[3] In Venezuela, only the less conspicuous provincial examples of colonial architecture survived. For government buildings the favoured style in the nineteenth century, as in Mexico, was neoclassical, and Guzmán Blanco's Capitol, completed in 1877 by Luciano Urdaneta, is no exception: columns, grand porticoes and plenty of classical mouldings, no doubt with half an eye on Washington. For non-governmental buildings, however, neo-Gothic was particularly popular: the old university opposite the Capitol was remodelled by Juan Hurtado de Manrique in 1878 into 'a beautiful structure of pure Gothic', as a US visitor, William Curtis, described it some few years later.[4] As part of the process of transforming Bolívar into a secular saint, the colonial church of Santisima Trinidad was rebuilt in neo-Gothic style and converted into the national Pantheon in 1874, ready to receive Bolívar's bones. And in 1883 Manrique fulfilled Guzmán Blanco's wish and had another old colonial church replaced with a new, Gothicized version within a period of three months, in time for the celebrations to mark the centenary of Bolívar's birth. The result was the Santa Capilla – inspired, as the name suggests, by the Sainte Chapelle in Paris.[5] The centenary celebrations were also the trigger for a number of other modernizing measures. The train service linking La Guaira with Caracas was inaugurated just in time, and Guzmán Blanco had electric lights installed (driven by a special steam-powered generator) to illuminate the main square and some of his new buildings and urban improvements: the Capitol, the main square, various Parisian-style tree-lined boulevards and gardens, the new Teatro Guzmán Blanco (1879), and a number of heroic statues – many of them commissioned for the occasion – located at important points in the city, including one of himself at the top of the Calvario hill, an area Guzmán had had landscaped to create a public park.[6]

Eclecticism under Gómez and beyond

With the Mexican Revolution (1910–17), the historical trajectories of the two countries inevitably diverged. The Revolution opened the door to a profound review of all aspects of social, political and cultural life, and enabled Mexicans to see themselves in the modernist vanguard. Mexico became a mecca for displaced radicals, refugees from Franco's Spain, or from Hitler's Germany. Venezuela, meanwhile, remained locked into the myopic world of one of Latin America's more brutal dictatorships. President Juan Vicente Gómez assumed power in 1908 and ruled until his death in 1935: in other words, for precisely the period during which other more open countries in Latin America were exploring both the stylistic and the ideological implications of modernism. None of this touched Venezuela. Gómez discouraged debate of any sort by, among other things, shutting down the university for ten years, between 1912 and 1922.

As we have seen, in Mexico the Revolutionary government initially flirted with neocolonial architecture as a radical, Mexican, even modern style, but the Venezuelan case demonstrates just how different the roots of this Pan-American enthusiasm could be. As elsewhere in Latin America, high culture in nineteenth-century Venezuela was Francophile: Guzmán Blanco had rejected both the colonial and the Spanish heritage, preferring wherever possible to promote French tastes and ideas. Gómez, however, built bridges with Spain, and encouraged the revalorization of Spanish culture.[7] Unlike in Mexico, where the colonial period came to be seen as genuinely national in contrast to the imported styles of the nineteenth century, in Venezuela the colonial past provided a link with the grand old culture of Spain. This shift had racist implications, allowing the oligarchy to distance themselves both from the Indian and – even more importantly – from the African elements in society (black immigration was banned under Gómez), so reclaiming for themselves the role of white civilizers. This opened the way for a new appreciation of colonial architecture or, in practice, the reinvention of an architectural past.

Gómez promoted an image of a Hispanic Venezuela, personified by the ever-popular Bolívar, whose house in the centre of Caracas was remodelled into a pseudo-colonial mansion complete with a brand-new coat of arms. Appropriately enough, the architect who did most to reinforce this ideology in concrete terms was a Spaniard. Manuel Mujica Millán (1897–1963) emigrated to Venezuela in 1927, and found favour with both the government and private patrons from the moment he arrived. One of his first tasks was to remodel the Pantheon, home to Bolívar's bones, back into an apparently colonial building, with towers imitating those of Coro Cathedral, one of the few

Gustavo Wallis, Palacio de Gobierno, Caracas, 1933 (photograph *c.* 1935).

significant colonial churches to have survived the nineteenth-century purges. After the neo-Gothic extravagances of the nineteenth century, the return to a more Hispanic/nationalist architecture was enthusiastically embraced in religious buildings. Mujica was a versatile and intelligent architect, and his Nuestra Señora del Carmen in Caracas (1935) and the cathedral in Mérida (1945) remain grand examples of a reinvented baroque (Plate 10).[8] He made good use of modern materials – steel and concrete – and borrowed freely from various Hispanic sources to create a world that succeeded in suggesting both tradition and modernity – both of which, in Venezuela, were more or less illusory. Mujica went some way towards filling the historical void which Venezuelans experienced when they compared their own city centres with those of their nearer neighbours in Colombia, Central America and Mexico.

But Venezuelan taste remained fundamentally eclectic. While neocolonial was popular for religious architecture, in the last years of his life Gómez rather suddenly commissioned some major new public buildings, and for this the favoured style was Art Deco. In Mexico City, Obregón Santacilia had won government commissions for Deco buildings including, as we have seen, his Ministry of Health and Social Security (1926), and by the mid-1930s Deco was widely associated with government buildings as an indicator of modernity, and so appropriate to self-styled modern regimes. Venezuela followed suit, and the Palacio de la Gobernación de Caracas (the City Hall) by Gustavo Wallis (1897–1979) of 1933 and the Ministerio de Fomento (Ministry of Public Works) by Carlos Guinand Sandoz (1889–1963) of 1934–35 are elegant examples.[9] Deco provided architects with a way of adapting their classical Beaux-Arts type of training to new ends, and it provided governments with several advantages: it could not be accused of being an imitation of the past; it could be monumental in its symmetry and rigour; and it implied classical order in the disposition of the spaces and volumes and in the frequent use of full-height, flattened pilaster-like panels on the façades. In other words, it lent itself to a sort of understated grandeur: large areas of smooth, undecorated wall surface, but with extravagant detailing such as doors, floors, light-fittings and stained-glass windows, all crafted by experts (often in Europe) and of the highest-quality materials.

On the other hand, the Museo Nacional de Bellas Artes, founded by Gómez in 1935 shortly before his death, was designed by Carlos Raúl Villanueva (1900–75) in a neoclassical mode, albeit with some subtle Deco undertones (Plate 11). Here it was not so much modernity as antiquity that was required. The world's great art museums traditionally used the classical architectural language, so Villanueva's porticoed colonnades demonstrated that Venezuela's museum belonged to this venerable family, implying that the building and its contents were descended from the great artistic traditions of classical Greece and Rome. This new museum is also significant in that it was situated not in the city centre but in the Parque de los Caobos on the eastern outskirts, suggesting that even the urbanistically *laissez faire* Gómez administration recognized that if the government was to have any control over the way the city was expanding, it had to make certain interventions. The introduction of a major new cultural institution provided a focus which, as we shall see, had a bearing on future urban developments.[10]

Evolutionary change

Commentators see Gómez's death as the moment when Venezuela changed course, when new ideas could be discussed openly, a time of new energy and optimism. Rómulo Gallego's novel *Canaima* (1935) is full of 'images of open doors and open books, deeds waiting to be done and histories waiting to be written'.[11] But in real terms Venezuela's progress towards full democracy was slow and erratic, and in architecture, too, Gómez's death was followed by a gradual evolution rather than a revolution. In fact, the last years of his rule were characterized by an increasing eclecticism in architectural taste, which was to persist for many years. This was most obvious in private housing. Since the First World War Venezuela's middle class had been expanding along with the oil revenue – a middle class with a generous disposable income, and cultural and social ambitions. The new housing which created the Caracas suburbs of Campo Alegre and La Florida in the 1930s and 1940s demonstrates a relaxed attitude to style. Architects became adept at producing houses in versions of neocolonial or neo-Hispanic – indeed, neo-almost-anything – but it is not the stylistic top dressing which is interesting in Venezuelan private housing during this period, but the more fundamental change by which the family dwelling became an index of social status.

The traditional town house or *casona*, the house type of the Spanish colonial elite, was characterized above all by understatement, its very plain street façade continuous with and largely indistinguishable from others on the block. The interior was another matter. William Curtis describes the effect of entering one such house in 1896:

> When you have passed through the wide-arched gateway, and reached the patio with its bronze fountain and tessellated corridors, its palms and roses, its orange trees

Manuel Mujica Millán, neo-colonial town
house, or *quinta*, Campo Alegre, Caracas,
1935 (photograph *c.* 1940).

and oleanders, you realize that the habit of South American millionaires is not to
spend their money beautifying their streets, but to use it entirely within their
dwellings.[12]

The houses of the Venezuelan *nouveaux riches* from the 1930s onwards were the
inverse of this.[13] Following the example of the Californian neocolonial villa
introduced into Venezuela by oil workers from the United States – and, to a
lesser extent, the English garden city model of the late nineteenth century –
these new houses, termed *quintas*, marked a break with the old style. They were
free-standing single dwellings, each in its own garden plot, the corridors, patios,
balconies and gardens of the old *casona* transposed to the outside of the houses,
their wealth and their individuality displayed to their neighbours and to the
street. They are modern in the sense that they represent a rejection of the old
city centre and its discreet, enclosed town-house model. The *quinta* was a form
of conspicuous consumption, and any meaning attributed to a particular style
was largely of individual rather than collective significance.

Architectural eclecticism in Venezuela in the 1930s was a sort of habit of
mind, and although the more neo-baroque-style *quintas* can be seen as a way

of laying claim to Spanish descent and to a significant colonial past, generally speaking a particular architectural style had little in the way of political resonance. Eclecticism in domestic architecture was not so much an anxious search for national identity as an individualistic desire for self-expression. This was partly, no doubt, because with little or no tradition of political debate there was no framework for considering culture in political or ideological terms. This is not to say that the choice of style was arbitrary, but that it was conditioned by the tradition of architectural decorum by which certain styles were considered appropriate for certain functions: houses were a matter of personal choice, while neocolonial was suitable for churches, and Deco for government ministries and banks. Guillermo Salas's Ministry of Education building (1938) is, if anything, even more lavish and exuberant than the Deco of the late Gómez era, while Wallis's Banco Central de Venezuela (1942) is a grander, more sober version, a no-risk investment.

Transition to modernity

There is no clear break with Gómez's death, just gradual shifts within the prevailing eclecticism, but one example that has been identified as marking a change of mood is the Venezuelan pavilion at the Paris World's Fair of 1937.[14] This does suggest some sort of political agenda, perhaps because this was easier to do in Paris than at home. In contrast to Brazil's 100-foot-high, flag-like façade, the Venezuelan building opposite was a low, distinctly domestic-looking block which the official guide described as 'a harmonization of Spanish buildings with roofs of red tiles and Indian buildings covered with thatch. The pavilion extends around a great patio, such as can be seen in all Venezuelan houses' – adding, perhaps in case business visitors should be put off by such modesty, that 'Venezuela is the greatest exporter of petroleum in the entire world'.[15] In Venezuelan terms, however, this understated building is quite radical: the racially exclusive arrogance of the reinvented baroque has been replaced by a building which draws on popular and more genuinely Venezuelan

Luis Malaussena Pimentel and Carlos Raúl Villanueva, Venezuelan pavilion, Paris World's Fair, 1937, interior court (photograph 1937).

architectural traditions, a building which suggests social inclusion in its stylistic hybridity. This building was designed by two young Venezuelan architects, both of whom had been trained in Paris: Luis Malaussena Pimentel (1900–63) and Carlos Raúl Villanueva; both of them went on to develop this less ostentatious, more widely acceptable version of Venezuelan architecture – more neo-traditional than neocolonial – in a variety of ways. Malaussena excelled in adapting it to schools, airports and medical centres, including the Sede de la Dirección de Malariología (Malarial Studies Institute) in Maracay (1942–45).[16] We shall return to Villanueva's subsequent work.

Carlos Guinand Sandoz, Club Alemán,
Caracas, 1935 (photograph c. 1940).

The appearance of a more characteristically modern aesthetic is gradual and
almost covert in Venezuela. The tendency towards simplification, where the
interest in ornament makes way for an interest in volume and plane, can be
traced in the various different styles – Deco, neocolonial, neo-Hispanic, neo-
Moorish, neo-traditional. Except in a few cases this is not so much a matter
of political commitment as of fashion – fashion loosely influenced by ideas
about the machine aesthetic, about health, hygiene and progress, and about the
decadence of ornament or its irrelevance to modern life. This means that it
makes little sense to try to place buildings in distinct stylistic categories. Generally speaking, perhaps, the simplification of neocolonial tends to a sort of
neo-traditional, which in turn converges with a sense of modernity (as with

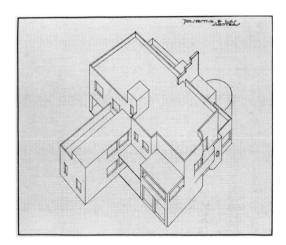

Manuel Mujica Millán, isometric drawing of
modernist house, c. 1930.

Barragán's mature work in Mexico); while simplified Deco remains rather more
foreign. The Venezuelan pavilion for Paris in 1937 is an example of the former.
An example of the latter is Guinand's Club Alemán (1935).[17] This was an
institution for those who valued their German roots and, to judge by their
chosen style of architecture, thought of themselves as very up to date. Spatially
it is quite traditional, and in detailing it is Deco, but the structure is of concrete, and the overall appearance is of a fashionably modern simplicity.

Even under Gómez this architectural eclecticism occasionally extended to
buildings which were much closer to the sort of *modernist* modernity of Le
Corbusier and the Bauhaus, where the decorative elements have been pared
away to almost nothing. In such cases the driving force came from the architects. Manuel Mujica is best remembered for his neocolonial work, but he was
aware of the European trend away from ornament. He was quite capable of
producing buildings that were stripped of all the neocolonial top dressing, and
so were therefore visually very modern in the sense that they combine a
number of cubic volumes articulated by frameless windows and doors, cement
render and metal.[18] In the early 1930s Mujica constructed three such houses,

not to commission but as speculative ventures, living in each himself before selling it.[19] In terms of the asymmetry of the façade, the irregularity of the footprint, the multiple internal levels and diversity of volumes, these 'modern' houses were identical to the more popular *quinta*, the only difference being the lack of ornament. In 1934 Villanueva built for himself in the La Florida district a house which is more genuinely modernist, a rationalist architecture of pure cubic volumes, with less of the busy asymmetry, and no trace of a moulding or decorative detail. But these are isolated examples, and in this sort of context 'modern' is more of a style than a challenge to any established order. It is a far cry from O'Gorman's Rivera–Kahlo house, for example.

But as in Mexico, Le Corbusier was to become a significant influence, and in January 1936 Cipriano Domínguez – who, as a postgraduate student of architecture in Paris in the early 1930s, had worked in Le Corbusier's studio – lectured to the Venezuelan College of Engineers on Le Corbusier and his 'Five Points towards a New Architecture'.[20] Domínguez was not alone, however: all of the younger generation of architects who had been trained in Paris had come across Le Corbusier and his ideas. The year 1936 also saw the first rumbles of unrest among the workers, and the increasingly liberal military government of López Contreras (1935–40) did not need Le Corbusier's declamatory warning 'Architecture or Revolution!' to realize that something had to be done. Conveniently, as we have seen in the case of Mexico, modern European architectural theory offered an economic justification for a functionalist plain style – 'maximum efficiency for minimum effort and expenditure' – so it is not surprising that in the immediate post-Gómez years the Venezuelan government, like the Mexican, embraced the new architecture as a style suitable for public schools and hospitals.

In Caracas, one of the first projects to make use of the new style was a school by Le Corbusier's disciple Cipriano Domínguez, the Liceo Fermín Toro (1936), which – although it does not make use of the 'Five Points' – accords with Le Corbusier's general ethos. It used reinforced concrete to produce a flat-roofed, cubic design without decorative detailing, just generous, clearly

Cipriano Domínguez, Liceo Fermín Toro, Caracas, 1936.

legible spaces: broad corridors and stairwells, internal courtyards and gardens and, above all, plenty of light and ventilation. And as if all this does not sound healthy enough, it was located opposite the Calvario park. This style was admirably suited to educational buildings, since it seemed so self-evidently 'rational', a metaphor for enlightenment. Similarly hospitals and clinics could benefit from the same style because it could be equally easily read in terms of cleanliness, hygiene and health. Early examples of this sort of rational simplicity are a maternity hospital, the Maternidad Concepción Palacios (1936) by William Ossott, and Guinand's Sanitorio Antituberculoso (1939).[21] In other words, the style could be interpreted as appropriate to the function, and adopted for reasons of expediency, without necessarily taking on board the political rhetoric with which it was invested in Mexico.

The Gómez administration had recognized that national development and progress entailed – indeed, were contingent upon – urban growth, and that it was the government's duty to oversee and control such growth. The Banco Obrero had been set up in 1928 as a State Housing Institute answerable to the Ministerio de Fomento, the Ministry of Public Works; it was a non-profitmaking corporation founded to provide leasehold housing for lower- and middle-income families in a number of major cities.[22] It achieved little under Gómez, but in 1936 it commissioned the architect González Méndez to build a small group of multi-dwelling blocks in the Bella Vista district of Caracas.[23] Up to this time Venezuela had had no real apartment blocks; rich and poor lived in single-family, largely single-storey units. González Méndez designed a complex of six blocks, each comprising several modest flats of considerable diversity. At one level these are in a thoroughly modern idiom – smooth surfaces, recessed, frameless windows and doors, flat roofs – and they imply a new set of social relations; but their spatial interest – the irregularity of the plans, the balconies and external stairs, and the juxtaposition of semicircular and cubic bays – is not dissimilar to that of the *quinta*. Perhaps this was intentional, and González Méndez wanted the inhabitants to enjoy the same sense of pride and domestic distinction as their richer neighbours. Unlike the handful of modern-style schools and medical centres built around this time, there was no pretence at mass-production or prefabrication in this housing development.

The Rotival Plan

It was not piecemeal housing developments that Caracas needed, however, but radical rethinking of the urban plan if it was to address the problems of expanding population, traffic congestion and the resulting degradation of the city centre. President López Contreras was an enthusiastic Francophile who dreamed of turning his capital into a new-world Paris. It was fashionable during this period for Latin American governments to employ French town planners. Jean-Claude Forestier had been employed in Buenos Aires and

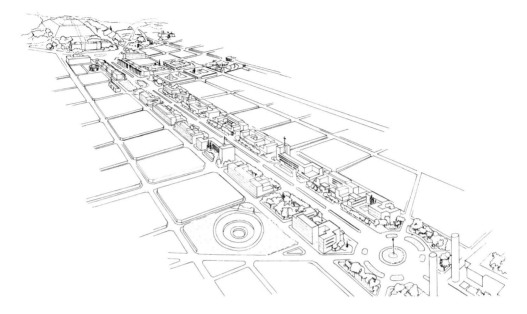

Maurice Rotival, plan for the urban development of Caracas, showing the projected central avenue linking El Calvario (upper left, landscaped to look like a Mexican pyramid) and the Plaza Caobos (lower right), 1939.

Havana in the 1920s, while in Brazil during the 1930s Alfred Agache worked on a new city plan for Rio de Janeiro.[24] In 1937 the Venezuelan government approached the office of the French town planner Maurice Rotival. They recognized that what was urgently needed was a city plan which would halt the flight of the moneyed classes out into the new suburbs – a plan which would include a system of roads to facilitate movement, and a new monumental centre suited to the growing economic importance of Venezuela and its capital.

Two years later, Rotival and a team of French and Venezuelan architects – including Carlos Raúl Villanueva, Carlos Guinand, Cipriano Domínguez,

Enrique García Maldonado and Gustavo Wallis – presented the Plan Regulador, more commonly known as the Plan Rotival. The plan rationalized the tendency begun under Gómez for the city to expand eastwards. It proposed an entirely new network of roads, with a gigantic central boulevard leading from a relocated Plaza Mayor – complete with new Capitol – at the foot of El Calvario, via another new focal point three blocks to the south of the old city centre, to a big arterial interchange near Villanueva's new Museo Nacional de Bellas Artes in the Caobos district, with the possibility of extending further east in the future. The planners envisaged that as business and commerce built premises along this central axis, so residential development would follow in an orderly fashion on the land immediately behind, and they included plenty of green spaces, gardens, parks and sports grounds. The plan was accepted, and although most of it remained on the drawing board it had the effect of forcing the government to take the urban development of Caracas seriously, and to set in place bureaucratic structures to monitor it. The one aspect that was eventually completed was the great central avenue, the Avenida Bolívar. As with the ambitious Avenida 9 de Julio begun in Buenos Aires in 1935, this involved levelling a path a whole block deep through the old city grid. In fact, in practice the effects of the Rotival Plan were other than those intended. The mess, the noise, and above all the traffic congestion caused by the demolition of the necessary swathes of buildings drove business out to the more peaceful suburbs.[25] Nevertheless, the Rotival Plan made it possible to think of the city as a whole, on a large scale, and in new and ambitious ways – ways in which architecture could play a crucial shaping and controlling role.

El Silencio

Villanueva, brought up in France, returned to Venezuela in 1928, so he was well placed to work with Rotival's team and to interpret their ideas. Shortly after his arrival from Paris, Villanueva was also appointed chief architect and adviser to the Banco Obrero. At first this body had been concerned with lending money to support private construction, but in 1941 it undertook the first of its own rehabilitation projects aimed at eradicating 'all slums in the metropolitan area of Caracas'.[26] Guinand and Villanueva were invited to submit plans for the redevelopment of a very run-down quarter known as El Silencio, situated at the extreme westerly end of Caracas. This area was the point at which the regular colonial grid began to break up as the town expanded past the River Caraota and up the lower slopes of the steep El Calvario Hill. There had already been some improvements to the district, including the Domínguez school, the Liceo Fermín Toro (1936), and it had been identified in the Rotival Plan as the starting point for the new avenue. It is a measure of the lack of administrative clarity concerning the city at the time that, although the Rotival Plan had been accepted, the architects were not required to take this into account. The decision to renovate El Silencio, of course, precluded the construction of a monumental governmental centre on the site, as proposed in the Rotival Plan, but the monumental axis was still firmly a part of future plans. In the event, Guinand did incorporate it into his proposal, but the commission was awarded to Villanueva, who did not. The terms of the commission then required Villanueva to adapt his original scheme along the lines of Guinand's, and take the future grand avenue into account, which he accordingly did.

Villanueva was nothing if not flexible. It has been suggested that he was ambitious and astute, and that on his arrival from Paris he recognized that he would have to play his cards very carefully in order to establish a safe reputation; only then would he be able to do what he wanted.[27] Perhaps he learnt the art of diplomacy from his father, who had been Venezuela's ambassador to England, and no doubt through his father he would also have had a good understanding of the political lie of the land under Gómez. His tactful eclecticism is evident in his work during the 1930s. His first major commission under Gómez was for a Moorish-style bullring in Maracay in 1931; as we have seen, he also designed the neoclassical National Museum in 1935; in 1937 he was involved in the neo-traditional Venezuelan pavilion at the Paris World's Fair; and in 1939 he designed a Deco-modernist-style school, the Escuela Gran Colombia.

The instructions from the commission set up to oversee the El Silencio project were quite specific, demonstrating that a lot of thought had gone into it.[28] They included instructions about the internal layout of the apartments, with a requirement that each apartment should incorporate facilities for cooking and washing clothes, and a place to work, a 'sitio de trabajo', in a specially designed wide corridor; and that because washing was not to be dried on the roof, there should be adequate room in each flat. It was recommended that every flat should have direct ventilation, and that there should be internal patios, closed off from the street and accessible only to pedestrians. Villanueva's final submission conformed to all these requirements, including the wide corridor for washing and cooking, 'in conformity with the way of life of Caracas'. He also noted that 'special care had been taken with the ventilation of the dwellings, which will be by a system of cross-ventilation, and every bedroom will have daylight and a direct view on to the street or on to open spaces'.[29]

Villanueva's modified designs also took into account the intended shape of the fast-growing city. This was the first such government-backed housing project in Latin America, and involved – controversially – the prior clearance of the whole area: a move of which modernist architects and town planners, particularly members of the CIAM, would have fully approved. Villanueva envisaged the district of El Silencio as an area of relative residential calm between the landscaped parkland of El Calvario on the one hand and the expanding city of commerce and business on the other, the point at which the new grand axis, proposed in Rotival's plan, would open out and cut through the colonial grid three blocks to the south of the Plaza Bolívar. Instead of the traditional, approximately concentric growth around the old centre, the Avenida Bolívar therefore indicated that the future of the city lay in a more linear expansion along the valley to the east.

Villanueva's redevelopment of El Silencio matches this in a very simple metaphorical way. The blocks are grouped at the bottom of El Calvario hill around the large rectangular Plaza O'Leary, which marks the beginning of the new Avenida Bolívar. At street level they use a neocolonial vocabulary: they are linked by colonial-style arcades with fat-bellied *panzuda* columns of a type found in the surviving architecture of Coro, Caracas's predecessor as the provincial capital – and, incidentally, very similar in shape to the distinctive pear-shaped trunks of a local type of palm (Plate 12). The main doorways are framed with neocolonial polylobed arches with decorative stone mouldings. To emphasize this sense of history, the plaza has two monumental fountains designed by Francisco Narváez, with dolphins and reclining water nymphs, deliberately evocative of the grand European urban squares of the baroque era, and in particular of Bernini's fountains in the Piazza Navona in Rome (Plate 13). In other words, tucked under El Calvario Hill and opening out towards the future, and to the rising sun to the east, El Silencio suggests the grand colonial city Caracas never was. The 'colonial' arcades create a sense of old-world intimacy, providing shelter from the sun and rain; the street named La Subida al Calvario, the Ascent to Calvary, climbs up the lower slope of the hill in a picturesque curve more associated with old European city centres than with those of colonial Spanish America. In inventing a historic centre for Caracas, Villanueva manages to combine elements from Venezuelan tradition (the distinctive squat columns, the baroque mouldings, the blue-and-white paintwork) with elements from the European past (the grand baroque plaza and ostentatious fountains, the winding, apparently unplanned streets, the general irregularity of the plan).

As a functional housing development, however, El Silencio looks forward as well as back. The illusion of being in a colonial centre is in fact quite superficial, because above the level of the arcades some of the blocks rise to seven storeys (unusually high for Caracas at this time) with flat white façades and carefully asymmetrical patterns of frameless windows and balconies reminiscent of the Art Deco work of Mallet-Stevens, which Villanueva would

Carlos Raúl Villanueva, El Silencio, Caracas, 1941, view of interior court (photograph c. 1955).

certainly have known from his time in Paris.[30] More interesting still, in order to create the atmosphere of a traditional neighbourhood the blocks back on to inner courts with gardens and playgrounds to which only the residents have access. The inward-facing elevations, in striking contrast to the neocolonial public face, are bold, plain and functional, with no superfluous ornament. Balconies and room-sized loggias jut out at regular intervals to create geometric patterns of light and shade in a thoroughly modern idiom. This is a remarkably successful idea, providing Caracas with a sturdy sense of history while also – gently – introducing a modernism that is both 'honest' in the sense promoted by modernist architects in Europe and visually interesting. El

President Isaias Medina inaugurating the demolition of the old El Silencio district, Caracas, 25 July 1942.

Silencio is extremely well adapted to the climate, with effective cross-ventilation and plenty of shade provided by the balconies and by the trees in the inner courtyards; it is also socially modernizing in that it included schools and health centres for the 747 families that were rehoused there in 1945. Like Villanueva and Malaussena's Pavilion for the 1937 Paris World's Fair, the architecture of El Silencio implies a move towards a more inclusive society, but it also suggests another reconciliation, this time between past and present.

The government used the demolition of the existing houses and small businesses in the area as a moment for celebration. President Isaias Medina Angarita (1940–45) exploited the propaganda potential, and chose the feast of Santiago, 25 July 1942, the 375th anniversary of the founding of the colonial city of Santiago de León de Caracas, on which to have himself photographed with a pickaxe applying the first blow to a tyre-repair workshop. This is suggestively similar to photographs of Mussolini, who, as a part of his plans for the renovation of Rome in the 1930s, had promoted an image of himself wielding a pickaxe, 'an effective means of projecting the demolition of the old Rome as a "revolutionary" Fascist act'.[31] In Caracas, after the photograph was published in the papers the next morning, hundreds of men turned up on the site in search of employment, and although in this case it was not immediately available, as those required had already been hired, this and subsequent Banco Obrero housing schemes did provide employment for enormous numbers.

The social organization of the El Silencio urbanization was – perhaps inevitably – paternalistic. The first block of the seven was completed in July 1944, and the Junta Directiva of the Banco Obrero laid out an elaborate tenant's agreement with twenty-six clauses covering the respective responsibilities of the Bank and the tenant in considerable detail.[32] Some of these clauses read rather like rules for good behaviour in the school dormitory, highlighting the fact that neither the Bank nor the inhabitants had much experience of such high-density housing: it was a real social experiment for all concerned. So, for example, tenants were fully responsible for maintenance of plumbing and electrics, children were not allowed to play on the stairs, no radios were permitted between 11 p.m. and 8 a.m., and only the superintendent was allowed to put in nails to hang things on the walls. And the inhabitants were required to comport themselves in such a way as not to annoy their neighbours. El Silencio's significance as a part of the development of the city centre, as well as a one-off housing development, is reflected in its relative cost. In 1945 it provided 747 living units in seven blocks for between three and four thousand residents. Figures from a report published by the Banco Obrero in 1968 show that the price per unit was over five times that of the 1,219 units built under the organization's aegis in 1946, and nine times as much as the 848 units of 1937.[33]

Centro Bolívar

As work began on El Silencio, the government turned its attention to the great central avenue that Rotival and his team had recommended, and which Villanueva's plan now clearly anticipated. The development of El Silencio precluded the new government centre Rotival had wanted at the head of this

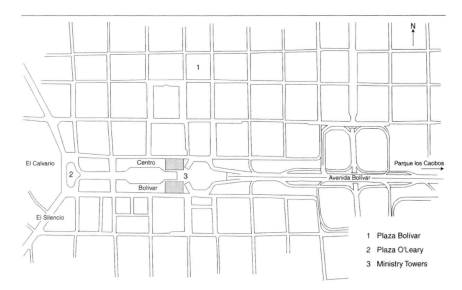

El Silencio and central Caracas, as of about 1960.

avenue; instead, the Le Corbusian enthusiast Cipriano Domínguez was commissioned to design an urban and ministerial complex, the confusingly named Centro Bolívar, which would straddle the new Avenida Bolívar just to the south of the colonial central sqaure, the Plaza Bolívar. The Centro Bolívar marked a completely new approach to the city; indeed, it was designed to be a city in itself, and in some ways prefigures Brasília. It comprised not only the offices of all the major government ministries but also residential blocks, shops, restaurants, galleries, garden terraces and pedestrian precincts on several levels, with car parking and the central bus station below. The design was deliberately monumental, symmetrically arranged either side of the Avenida Bolívar, which itself ran through an underpass between the two blocks.[34] Demolition work for the avenue began in the mid 1940s, and the construction of the Centro Bolívar itself started in 1947. Building on the implications of Villanueva's 'colonial' residential area of El Silencio to the west, Domínguez's new development grows gradually in height along horizontal ranges of high-density housing and offices up to the main complex and its two twenty-storey ministerial towers. These form a veritable gateway to the future (Plate 14).

This architecture explores a visual language which is Le Corbusian, but filtered through recent Brazilian practice. The Brazilian government's new Ministry of Education and Health building in Rio de Janeiro, on which Le Corbusier had acted as consultant, was completed in 1942, and provided an obvious starting point for Domínguez's design. This much-celebrated building was ostentatiously modern, a huge rectangular block towering above everything around it, and it demonstrated the practical application of Le Corbusier's 'Five Points towards a New Architecture' on which Domínguez had lectured in 1936: *pilotis*, free design of the ground plan and of the façade, curtain windows and rooftop gardens and terraces – all, of course, made possible by the use of modern materials and techniques, glass, steel and reinforced concrete. As with the Rio Ministry building, Domínguez's Centro Bolívar develops these Le Corbusian elements in distinctive ways, adding features demanded by the climate: deeply set windows, movable sun-screens and louvres to deflect the sun and the fierce midsummer heat, openwork grilles of cast concrete to create through-draughts (Plate 15). The main public concourse is above the level of the surrounding city, and the use of *pilotis* provides shady pedestrian areas as well as a view of the expanding city below.

Geographically, the Centro Bolívar takes into account the city past, present and future. As in Rio, the *pilotis* frame – and so, in a sense, incorporate – these different aspects: El Silencio and El Calvario to the west, the expanding city to the east, but also the nineteenth-century church of Santa Teresa in its shadow.[35] The use of the strong colours of popular traditional architecture – dark reds and greens, and a vivid yellow ochre – adds a regional accent. At the same time, it retains the profile and general effect of the classic modernist vertical tower block, with curtain walls. The Centro Bolívar can be seen as a sort of riposte on the part of the Venezuelan government to Brazil's new ministerial building, in that instead of Rio's single tower, Caracas has two. Now, of course, these examples of early modernist high-rises are dwarfed by other, higher buildings round about, but at the time they heralded the future, emphatic statements of their governments' ambitions for their respective cities, and of the high-profile, expanding role which they saw for the state in the provision, via the various ministries, of the necessary forms of welfare for the people. Today the south-facing windows are marred by air-conditioning units, the ministries have moved further east, and the implied open gateway to the future has been challenged by the monumental arch of Gómez de Llerena's 1990s' Palacio de Justicia beyond (this time a more literal as well as a more threatening city gate, complete with portcullis), but the Centro Bolívar is still an impressive manifestation of the sense of optimism characteristic of Latin America at the time.

The Banco Obrero superblocks of the 1950s

The Centro Bolívar may have been symbolic of the government's intentions to reshape Caracas into a modern capital, but the slums represented a more serious challenge. In terms of housing the onus lay, as we have seen, with the Banco Obrero. Neither El Silencio nor any of the other projects it sponsored in the 1930s and 1940s was really intended to address the much more serious problem of the mushrooming *ranchos* on the hills around the city.[36] In 1936 the population of Caracas was around 400,000; by 1950 rural migration had doubled this to 800,000. Accordingly, the Banco Obrero had to scale up its operations dramatically to finance much larger housing schemes, but it is significant that it could do so only under the dictatorship of Pérez Jiménez, who came to power in 1948. Work began in 1951 on a series of gigantic housing schemes on the hills around Caracas with the intention of eradicating all slums – not out of the goodness of Pérez Jiménez's heart, but because they were unsightly and gave the lie to his slogan that Venezuela was uniformly happy and prosperous. By 1956 about 180,000 people had been rehoused into 33,462 units.[37]

Villanueva headed teams of architects on a number of these Banco Obrero projects during this period, especially in the Catia district to the west of the city, including the Cerro Piloto and El Paraiso housing developments. These were – and continue to be – controversial, but at the time the weight of contemporary town planning and architectural theory in Europe and the USA was behind them. Everyone agreed that drastic action was required. Le Corbusier's 1929 Plan Voisin for Paris argued passionately for demolishing the centre of the city, with its dilapidated housing and networks of narrow streets choked with traffic, and replacing it with wide traffic arteries and 'a *vertical* city, a city which will pile up the cells which have for so long been crushed on the ground, and set them high above the earth, bathed in light and air'.[38] The received wisdom was that the only solution to the crisis facing the rapidly expanding cities of the world, especially the Third World, was to build high. Only by building high could you free up lots of ground space for healthy activities, and also provide every apartment with plenty of daylight and fresh air. The CIAM Charter of Athens (1933) had declared: 'it is by making use of height that town planning will recover the free areas of land necessary to communications and the spaces to be used for leisure'.[39] Gropius helpfully provided useful calculations which demonstrated that the higher the blocks, the better the results – up to his ideal of ten to twelve storeys.[40]

This aggressive approach to urban problems was not easy to realize in the middle of cities, especially well-established cities with historical centres like Paris, but in Caracas a number of factors coincided to make major urban intervention seem possible as well as highly desirable. For a start, the Rotival Plan had provided politicians and practitioners with experience in thinking of the city as a whole. From the government's point of view, large-scale building projects would stimulate the construction industry and provide employment beyond the city centre, while also eliminating the unsightly shantytowns. From

Le Corbusier, design for 'A Contemporary City', from
The City of Tomorrow and its Planning, 1929.

the point of view of socially concerned architects and town planners, these
schemes afforded them an opportunity to realize some of the theorists' visionary ideals. They offered a chance to provide large numbers of Venezuela's
poorest citizens with a better standard of living, and it was believed that, if
properly planned, this in turn could lead to political change. José Luis Sert, for
example, who worked on projects in Latin America from 1943, argued that the
new type of urban environment proposed by the CIAM would encourage new,
more democratic forms of civic interaction:

Human contacts, now limited by social barriers, would easily expand in a city where everyday life was harmoniously conceived, within a planned frame. Greater possibilities of collaboration would arise from these more frequent and direct contacts. Open discussion ... would stimulate political, scientific, artistic and social awareness; for this would come to many of us not only through lectures in classrooms, radio speeches, and books, but through opportunities for meeting our fellow citizens under conditions favoring an exchange of ideas.[41]

As Juan Pedro Posani points out, for a group of enthusiastic and idealistic young architects, steeped in this sort of rhetoric, with the government pushing them on to speedy results and throwing money their way as an added incentive, what could be more natural than to forge ahead, to put the theory into practice?[42]

The need for decent housing had been a preoccupation among Latin American architects since 1923, when the Congreso Panamericano de Arquitectos, at their meeting in Santiago de Chile, declared that it was a 'primordial duty' of the state to provide its citizens with cheap, healthy habitation.[43] By 1950 there were already small-scale examples under construction elsewhere in Latin America. The Mexicans had made a start with Pani's Miguel Alemán development in 1947, and the Brazilians with Affonso Reidy's project in Pedregulho, begun in 1949, but Venezuela was rapidly to outstrip such examples with a massive building programme which, within a few years, was to create a cityscape of a type that until then existed only on the pages of Le Corbusier- or CIAM-influenced theoretical texts. Of the Cerro Piloto development, Henry-Russell Hitchcock wrote: 'The result seems almost the equivalent of a complete city and the vision of these loose groups of blocks set against the splendid landscape seems to realize one of the recurrent dreams of twentieth century urbanism.'[44]

This was achieved by forcibly sweeping the *ranchos* off the land and building high-rise, high-density blocks set in spacious grounds, with – in theory, at least – schools, shops, social and health centres, sports facilities, a church on site and, of course, all necessary roads and services. The architectural prototype

Carlos Raúl Villanueva, consultant architect, 23 de Enero urbanization, Caracas, completed 1957 (photograph c. 1960).

usually cited for these Caracas housing schemes of the 1950s is Le Corbusier's superblock in Marseille, the Unité d'Habitation (1947–52), which was designed as a self-contained village for 1,600 inhabitants, complete with shopping centre, swimming pool, gym and child-care facilities.[45] The best of the Caracas developments are more like the Mexican and Brazilian examples, however, in their use of blocks of differing heights and in the grouping of several superblocks around a core of low-rise detached or semi-detached central services, so that there is more potential for ground-level, outdoor interchange. Villanueva, as the Banco Obrero's consultant architect, oversaw the projects and was actively involved in the designs for the first few, the Cerro Piloto and El Paraíso, both completed in 1954, and the 23 de Enero, which was completed by 1957. These early schemes became prototypes for later developments in Caracas and elsewhere.

For El Paraíso, Villanueva collaborated with Carlos Celis Cepero and José Manuel Mijares. It comprises one fifteen-storey and two three-storey blocks, with a freestanding commercial centre, a social and sports club, and a kindergarten. The main block is raised on *pilotis* to provide car parking below; the second-floor level was designed to have shops, a 'soda fountain' and restaurant, and a day nursery, all of which open on to a wide terrace partially covered by an undulating concrete canopy, so providing a communal social space equivalent to a traditional town square.[46] Flats are typically duplex, with kitchen and living/dining room on the lower floor, and bathroom and three or four bedrooms on the upper. The façades are set back behind grid-like skeletons of concrete to create strong textures, while brightly painted wall panels scattered asymmetrically across the surface suggest a monumental mosaic. Pedestrian precincts were to be landscaped and planted with trees and shrubs as appropriate, and the plans included reforestation of some of the land freed up by replacing the *ranchos* with high-density high-rise housing.

The Cerro Piloto and 23 de Enero schemes were on a much larger scale, and were built at breakneck speed: sixteen superblocks were completed within the first year, and the remaining thirty-two took only another couple of years

Carlos Raúl Villanueva, consultant architect, El Paraíso urbanization, Caracas,
completed 1954, detail (photograph c. 1960).

or so. They were designed by Guido Bermúdez with a team that included
Mijares, Carlos Brando, Juan Centellas and José Hoffmann, with Villanueva
again as consultant architect. In 1955 Hitchcock noted the lack of finish of
these speedily erected blocks (a point he also made in relation to Pani's housing developments in Mexico City) but he was impressed by the spectacular
setting and overall visual impact:

The plans incorporate with great ingenuity dwelling units of many different sizes serviced by skip-floor elevators. Construction is rather rough and ready but standardization has allowed serial production of the blocks and the colored rendering happily continues a Venezuelan tradition. The wooded mountains serve as a splendid background for the very tall blocks and the rising terrain on both sides to the valley has necessitated much variety in the grouping of the nearly identical blocks. Wide spacing generally provides magnificent views from all windows and the finish, inside and out, if rather crude is at least direct and unpretentious. The scale and pace of the operation justify on the whole the lack of finish in the execution.[47]

The more serious problem with the superblocks, however, was rather different: while the pace of the operation might justify the lack of finish in the execution in architectural terms, it could not justify the lack of social consideration. The shantytown dwellers for whom these blocks were intended were for the most part recent rural migrants. Not only were they quite unprepared for high-rise living, they did not even come from the traditional small-town environment which these 'unidad'-type blocks were designed to replace in vertical form. One of the criticisms regularly repeated by foreigners and middle-class Venezuelans alike was (and is) that the inhabitants had no notion what a bathroom was for, and would use it as a place to keep livestock – just as rehoused slum-dwellers in Victorian London were always said to keep coal in the bath. The problem in Caracas was not, of course, that these people were unwashed ignorant savages, as such criticism implies, but that households were still very dependent on a traditional subsistence type of economy. It is interesting in this respect that in 1947, in his plans for the new town of Chimbote on the north coast of Peru, José Luis Sert had already recognized this problem, abandoning the high-rise schemes of his earlier developments in favour of low-rise housing with special provision for animals.[48]

From a rather different perspective, the architecture rather than the inhabitants came to be seen as the problem. By the 1960s, sociologists and urban planners were becoming interested in the social life of slum-dwellers in Latin America. In 1969, in the editorial to a special feature on Caracas in *Architectural Design*, Walter Bor commented:

Emilio Duhart, CEPAL building, Santiago, Chile, 1960–66.   1

Juan O'Gorman, Rivera/Kahlo house, San Angel, Mexico City, 1931–32.   **2**

3   Juan O'Gorman, Melchor Ocampo school, Coyoacán, Mexico City, 1932; playground.

4   Diego Rivera, relief, Olympic Stadium, CU, Mexico City, 1950–52.

David Alfaro Siqueiros, 'sculpture-painting', south wing of Rectorate,   **5**
CU, Mexico City, 1952–56.

Juan O'Gorman, Gustavo Saavedra and Juan Martínez de Velasco;   **6**
mosaics by Juan O'Gorman, Library, CU, Mexico City, 1952.

7 Juan O'Gorman, Gustavo Saavedra and Juan Martínez de Velasco; mosaics by Juan O'Gorman, Library, CU, Mexico City, detail, 1952.

8 Félix Candela, church of the Miraculous Virgin, Mexico City, 1953.

Mathias Goeritz and
Luis Barragán, Satellite
towers, Satellite City,
State of Mexico, 1957.

9

Manuel Mujica Millán,
Cathedral, Mérida,
Venezuela, 1945.

10

11   Carlos Raúl Villanueva, Museo de Bellas Artes,
      Caracas, 1935.

12   Carlos Raúl Villanueva, El Silencio, Caracas,
      1941, colonnade.

Carlos Raúl Villanueva,
El Silencio, Caracas, 1941,
Plaza O'Leary, fountain
by Francisco Narváez.

13

Cipriano Dominguéz,
Centro Bolívar, Caracas,
postcard, c. 1970.

14

15 Cipriano Dominguéz, Centro Bolivar, Caracas, detail of ministry towers, 1947–50.

16 Carlos Raúl Villanueva, Olympic Stadium, CU, Caracas, 1950–51, detail grandstand.

Carlos Raúl Villanueva, Rectorate with Museum to the left, Caracas CU, 1952–53; mosaic mural by Osvaldo Vigas 1954.

Carlos Raúl Villanueva, Plaza Cubierta, Caracas CU, 1952–53.

19   Carlos Raúl Villanueva, Plaza Cubierta, Caracas CU, 1952–53; *Cloud Shepherd* sculpture by Hans Arp, 1953; mural by Mateo Manaure, 1953.

20   Carlos Raúl Villanueva, Plaza Cubierta, Caracas CU, 1952–53; Fernand Léger, *Bi-Mural*, 1954.

Chacaito Metro station, Caracas, mobile by Fernando de Soto, *Cubo virtual azul y negro*, 1979.

21

Carlos Cruz-Diez, painted wall and grain silos, La Guaira, Venezuela, 1975. These murals were damaged in the floods of 1999.

22

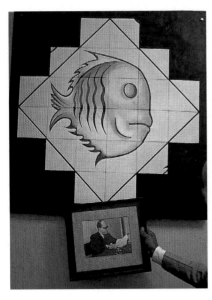

23 MES building, Rio de Janeiro, detail of tiles with portrait of Gustavo Capanema as a fish, Cândido Portinari, c. 1942.

24 Attílio Corrêa Lima, Seaplane Station, Rio de Janeiro, 1937–38.

Roberto brothers, Santos Dumont airport, Rio de Janeiro, 1937–44.   **25**

Oscar Niemeyer, Palácio do Planalto, Praça dos Três Poderes
(Plaza of the Three Powers), Brasília, 1958–60.   **26**

27   Oscar Niemeyer, National Congress, Brasília: the twin towers of the Secretariat, concave cupola of the Chamber of Deputies, and convex cupola of the Senate, 1958–60.

28   Oscar Niemeyer, Palácio de Itamaraty (Foreign Ministry), Brasília, 1962.

Oscar Niemeyer, **29**
Cathedral, Brasília,
1959–70, statues by
Alfredo Ceschiatti.

Oscar Niemeyer, **30**
Cathedral, Brasília,
interior; stained glass
by Marianne Peretti,
sculptures by Alfredo
Ceschiatti

31 Church of Bom Jesus
do Matosinhos,
Congonhas do Campo,
Minas Gerais, 1757–71;
statues of Old Testament
prophets by Aleijadinho,
1800–05.

32 Ricardo Porro,
School of Plastic Arts,
Cubanacán, Havana, Cuba,
1962–65.

The remarkable initiative of the poor to build make-shift accommodation on the steep slopes overlooking the city and to improve them as their incomes rise represents hitherto insufficiently tapped human resourcefulness; this, given more positive guidance, could prove an enormous asset in the mammoth task of housing the poorer section of the community. As it is, the only alternative offered to them are the Banco Obrero flats, usually in the form of high density highrise slabs, equipped with sanitary facilities, but otherwise restricted in floorspace and social amenities.[49]

'Monumentality, even veiled in contemporary design, is often given higher priority than socially oriented public need and serviceability', wrote Francis Violich of government housing projects in Venezuela and elsewhere in Latin America, contrasting their 'sterility' with the dynamism and diversity of the *ranchos* of Caracas and the *barriadas* of Peru.[50] The self-build *pueblos jóvenes* which replaced the shantytown *barriadas* in Peru were often cited as offering an alternative route: here the authorities simultaneously legalized and controlled squatters by laying out whole districts of the coastal desert on the outskirts of Lima with water, sanitation, electricity and street lighting before allowing the settlers in. These were seen as a more humane alternative: a compromise between insanitary but sociable slums, and sanitary but inhospitable high-rises.[51]

The Banco Obrero solutions to the housing problems of Caracas in the 1950s were fundamentally architectural, based on utopian architectural and urban theory with very little regard to the real needs and conditions of the inhabitants. The government wanted quick, visible results, not protracted, expensive research into the social and economic issues. Once the schemes were under way, funds often ran out before the social infrastructure incorporated into the architects' plans – the schools, health centres, social and sports facilities, and transport systems – could be completed. In some ways this is not dissimilar to the resettlement schemes of the sixteenth-century colonizing Spaniards who imposed a new spatial and social order on the indigenous population. There were those among the Spanish administrators and missionaries who genuinely believed that the native population would willingly embrace and benefit from the new order; while there were others for whom the compliance of or benefit to those involved was irrelevant: the economic, political and aesthetic benefits to the Spanish conquerors were what mattered. The government of Pérez Jiménez was similarly cynical in its motives. The Banco Obrero was itself among the first to recognize the shortcomings, and in an evaluation of 1961 the 23 de Enero development and its extension, Atlántico Norte, housing a total population of 105,000 people, were described as 'without the basic services for such a conglomerate: neither the public administration, nor the schools, the open spaces, markets, entertainments, supplies, nor medical centres etc. none of these functions in sufficient quantity for their needs.'[52] The truth of the matter is that the government was not prepared to invest in the necessary infrastructure to support them. These huge modern blocks served their purpose: from a distance they were a great improvement on the ramshackle disorder of the *ranchos*, presenting foreign visitors and Venezuela's own middle classes with an image of a modern city, sweeping the poor out of sight and out of mind.

It is difficult now to imagine undertaking such an enterprise. It is so hard to reconstruct the sense of self-confidence and clarity of purpose promoted so eloquently above all by Le Corbusier, by which progress was unidimensional, unidirectional and unquestionably beneficial. It was perhaps almost inconceivable that people who had only recently moved in from the country into shacks of mud, tin and cardboard, without electricity, water or sanitation, precariously and arbitrarily ranged up the mountainsides, would not immediately be grateful for a brand-new home in a high-rise block with glass windows and a bathroom, and with access to schools, clinics and public transport. And from the perspective of the times, even if they did not immediately appreciate it, part of the function of such architecture was, of course, to educate people out of a state of underdevelopment and into the modern world, as a part of a more general process of modernization. Sibyl Moholy-Nagy's attitude was probably not untypical: 'The mere effort of facing the resistance of the slum dwellers, of organizing the enormous financial outlay, and of settling a population that knew nothing of urban life, was in itself admirable, and offers an object lesson in urbanism to every other country.'[53] Dictatorships like that of Pérez Jiménez, which became increasingly oppressive during the 1950s, promoted housing projects such as these in order to promote both wealth and prosperity in the way that Renaissance princes patronized big building projects: as a demonstration of their own political and economic achievements, and as a visible sign of their country's progress. Liberals and philanthropists supported such measures for different reasons.

What role did the architects play within such a system? Villanueva's position seems to have been non-political. At least, he recognized that the government would pay for large-scale urban projects which could contribute to the city; he believed that the city was the 'supreme cultural creation', and that it was an architect's responsibility to tackle its problems by means of planning.[54] In 1962 – speaking in general terms, but inevitably with his own experience in mind – he acknowledged that architecture, more than any other art, is hugely constrained by external circumstances – by the client, the budget, the technical means available, and by society – so that the question of the architect's own creative freedom is also a difficult one. His view was that architects had to live in the real world; there was no point in feigning an imagined creative autonomy, nor of dreaming up perfect but unrealizable projects; but also the architect had a responsibility always to criticize and challenge, not to be what he called 'a mere translator, mechanical and passive'. He argued that artistic achievement was directly related to the degree to which it was involved with the historical situation; that an understanding of the social context in which he had to work was the architect's first and most important duty, and 'the reason for his very existence'.[55] The architects of the superblocks were indeed highly constrained, but in the long term the results do not look so bad. The population has adapted to high-rise living, the infrastructure has generally improved, and some at least of the superblocks are now considered desirable places to live. They certainly provided a more secure environment than the *ranchos* during the floods of late 1999.

There may be a further factor in the change from encomium to opprobrium in the critical responses to the Caracas superblocks – a factor which, as we shall see, was to play its part in the criticism of Brasília at about the same time. The emergence of negative comments from US and European critics, to be picked up later by parts of the Venezuelan middle class, can be seen as part of a larger ideological issue: that of the traditional assumption that Latin America's role was to follow the cultural lead of Europe. To forge ahead and put the CIAM theories into practice on such an ambitious scale – to create, as in Caracas, the appearance, however superficial, of so uniquely modern a city – was welcomed by Hitchcock in 1955 as a model from which the USA could learn. But as the superblocks proved not to be a panacea for urban problems, as the theoretical tide turned, and as the USA grew in strength and self-confidence in the late 1950s, so Latin America's efforts came increasingly to be seen as immature or ill-considered.

The Ciudad Universitaria

Villanueva's greatest architectural achievement – and, indeed, Venezuela's too, during the period under consideration – was not the superblocks but the Ciudad Universitaria (CU). Planning began in 1944 under the democratic regime of President Isaias Medina, and the campus evolved gradually over the next twenty years, but the period of most rapid development was the early 1950s, during Pérez Jiménez's dictatorship. It is thus contemporaneous with the construction of the UNAM campus in Mexico, and it is fascinating to compare the two projects, if for no other reason than to highlight the astonishingly fertile diversity of modern architecture in Latin America at this time. Mexico City and Caracas were both expanding fast, and their university cities were both located close to new, fashionable middle-class districts. Here, however, the similarities end. In Mexico, as we have seen, the chosen site was redolent of history, and indeed of the drama of history: a place where the history and culture, archaeology, geology and landscape were of mythical importance, a place where the future of Mexico could grow out of the volcanic rock and the prehistoric past lying beneath it. The CU in Caracas, by contrast, was allocated an old hacienda, a fertile farm in gently rolling countryside within the lush valley of the Guaire river, a place hovering somewhere between past and present, evocative of vaguely provincial rural gentility.

In Mexico the new university campus was planned and almost completed between 1950 and 1954, within the presidential term of Miguel Alemán; while in Venezuela construction continued over many years after a significant early peak of activity before the official inauguration on 2 March 1954, an event timed to coincide with the tenth Iberoamerican conference, which was held in Caracas in that year.[56] Mexico's university was designed for 25,000 students, and the first stage was the site plan laid out under the overall direction of Carlos Lazo, Enrique del Moral and Mario Pani, after which different architectural teams were appointed to design the individual buildings. Venezuela's campus was intended for a mere 5,000 students, and very early on Villanueva came in as the controlling architect throughout: the plan and his own architectural language developed gradually over time, with – as we shall see – very different results from those in Mexico.

Villanueva's first idea was for a grand Beaux-Arts-style university. This was to have had a monumental axis with the Medical School at one end, a great oval circus at the heart, symmetrically arranged faculty blocks on either side, and a centrally placed Rectorate complete with colonnaded portico.[57] Indeed, before Villanueva became involved, work had already begun on the hospital and the medical schools as the focal point of the campus. The hospital had been begun in a strangely functional way, with North American experts commissioned 'to organize the interior of the building, regardless of its architectural form'. The result was 'a towering mass of uncertain proportions', which it was Villanueva's uncomfortable task to try to rationalize.[58] The façade that fronts on to the main campus is articulated in a four-armed E formation. Each of the long protruding wings or pavilions has a broad corridor along either side that opens on to spacious semicircular balconies on the ends, like passenger decks on an ocean liner. This Art-Deco-ish nautical language is functional: it makes for rooms which are bright and breezy and enjoy good views – ideal for the health and comfort of the convalescent patients – while also breaking up the façade of what could easily have been too dominant a presence in the campus as a whole.

The first part of the new campus over which Villanueva had full control was the Escuela Técnica Industrial, a technical high school for pre-university students. Begun in 1947, it is tucked down in the south-west corner of the site and comprises classrooms, laboratories and workshops, an auditorium, a café and student residences, administrative offices and sports facilities. Instead of a single building Villanueva designed a series of low-level blocks around interior courts, linked by covered walkways – a self-contained environment almost in the manner of a small village, or indeed a miniature university city. Here Villanueva experimented with a functionalist aesthetic appropriate to the school's purpose: no curves, no Deco echoes, just the increasingly international modernist language, with neat concrete elevations, ribbon windows (standardized units with metal frames) and extensive use of *pilotis* to provide continuous interlinked spaces between the buildings and the walkways. Spatially and volumetrically the Escuela Técnica Industrial is rather more complex than O'Gorman's schools, but it makes use of the same basic elements, with the exception of a very individual use of horizontal concrete panels projecting out from the wall over those windows exposed to direct sun. Although the internal spaces of the Escuela Técnica Industrial and the hospital are relatively conventional, these projects provided Villanueva with a chance to explore the technical possibilities of reinforced concrete, and to experiment with ways of creating breeze and shade that are practically as well as aesthetically satisfying.

Villanueva's working process throughout was to tackle the campus in discrete zones, and his next major project, apart from student residences (1948), was the Olympic Stadium (1950–51). Its positioning at the opposite side of the

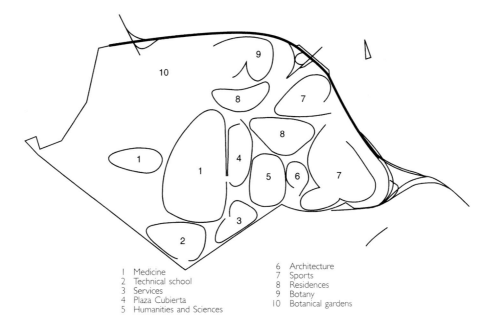

1 Medicine
2 Technical school
3 Services
4 Plaza Cubierta
5 Humanities and Sciences

6 Architecture
7 Sports
8 Residences
9 Botany
10 Botanical gardens

Carlos Raúl Villanueva, schematic plan, University City (CU), Universidad Central de Venezuela, Caracas, c. 1950.

site from the hospital effectively blocked the possibility of a monumental axis with the hospital at its apex. As in Mexico, however, it is tempting to see these two areas as deliberately juxtaposed: the sick and the healthy body on the outer limits of the site, leaving the centre as the province of the mind. The Olympic Stadium – so called because it was completed in time to host the Pan-American heats for the 1952 Olympics – is necessarily a traditional sweeping oval, but absolutely different from the massive, geological nature of the stadium in Mexico. In Caracas it is light and elegant, the uncovered seating

Carlos Raúl Villanueva, Olympic Swimming Pool, CU, Caracas, 1956 (photograph c. 1960).

opens up like the rim of a deep china plate, cantilevered out beyond unobtrusive concrete piers. The covered grandstand in particular marks a clear departure from the tasteful stylishness of the hospital: the seats and roof are supported by gigantic concrete ribs which curve up and over so that it opens out like a great mouth towards the arena, amplifying the cheering crowd both acoustically and visually (Plate 16). It is not just that the structure is laid bare; the structure *is* the aesthetic, a powerful industrial aesthetic that celebrates the possibilities of modern technology, as taut and supple as a gymnast.

In the slightly later Olympic swimming pool (1956), again located in the easterly quarter of the campus, Villanueva takes this idea of giant concrete ribs more literally. The overall shape is that of the hull of a great ship, the spectators' seating supported on curving members like the timber skeleton of a ship's hull, complete with the suggestion of a prow at one end and a stern at the other; and, of course, the water of the swimming pool contained within it. It is almost as if Villanueva were making a deliberate, witty comparison between this architectural ship on one side of the campus and his own earlier, much more conventional use of nautical stylistic devices on the hospital wings on the other.

The Plaza Cubierta

Before he built the swimming pool, Villanueva had already built the famous core of the campus, so he could afford to make fun of his earlier work. Between 1952 and 1953 he designed and built the administrative and cultural centre. A three-sided trapezoidal plaza provides an entrance to the university that is at once open-armed and architecturally unostentatious: announcing in understated fashion the non-hierarchical, permeable spaces the visitor will find further in, and implying too, perhaps, the egalitarian, permeable nature of the ideal education (Plate 17). The three-storey Rectorate is flanked by the two-storey Student Union building and the single-storey Museum. All three are simple, rectangular blocks raised on *pilotis*, and the only real suggestions of the architectural (and intellectual) pleasures to which they provide the gateway are the twisted clock tower, an unstable-looking constructivist fantasy (which Sibyl Moholy-Nagy patronizingly describes as 'playful and permissive, befitting the easy intellectual burden placed on the shoulders of Latin American students'[59]), and the curved concrete canopies, one stretching asymmetrically out and up from the entrance to the Rectorate, another forming an arch linking the Rectorate to the Museum.

Beyond the Rectorate are the buildings of the Aula Magna or main auditorium, the small concert hall and the main university library. The Aula Magna has the same inside-out feel as the swimming pool, with exposed concrete ribs. These protrude high above the roof line, and from the air the hall looks like something exotic and weightless – a fan, or an elaborately pleated cap; a design which owes something to Le Corbusier's 1931 designs for the great hall of the Palace of the Soviets. Villanueva avoids monumental entrances wherever possible, and the Aula Magna is an extreme example of this, having no obvious entrance at all. Instead it is linked to the smaller hall and the library by what must be one of the world's most imaginative environments. Known as the Plaza Cubierta, or Covered Plaza, this sinuous interlinked set of spaces, mostly covered but with occasional irregular openings to the sun and rain, is both inside and outside, street and garden, room and patio (Plate 18). The area is broken by openwork screens, freestanding segments of wall, works of art and clumps of tropical vegetation. Enclosed within this is the Aula Magna, its access ramps a smooth continuation of the curving spaces of the Plaza Cubierta, a lecture and concert hall which itself is also a work of art, so placing the arts at the literal and metaphorical heart of the campus. It has been said that while the hospital assumes a spectator, the Plaza Cubierta assumes an actor: it can be experienced only by moving in and through it.[60] This is not an architecture which announces a unilateral path to a clearly defined educational goal but implies, in a Hogarthian sense, that the intricacies, the twists and turns of the pursuit, are what give pleasure to the mind, and lead ultimately to genuine personal fulfilment and moral purpose.[61]

The location of the arts at the heart of the CU marks a rejection of the CIAM's ideas on town planning as formulated in the Charter of Athens in 1933. The Charter's widely accepted four functions – housing, work, recreation and traffic – in effect prioritized housing and work, and the efficient traffic flow between them. Recreation was understood almost entirely in terms of sport, which could conveniently be slotted into the green spaces between the workplaces, dwellings and roads. Other urban activities – most notably education and the arts, which do not fit tidily into one of the four functions – scarcely feature. In his plans for the Ville Radieuse (1931), before the four functions had acquired their totemic status, Le Corbusier did include a cultural zone at the centre (although in fact the real centre or spine of the design is a giant highway through the middle), but the educational zone, which might be thought to benefit from contact with the cultural zone, is relegated to the outlying satellite cities. By 1944, however, in his extended exposition of the proposals contained in the Charter of Athens, *Can Our Cities Survive?*, José Luis Sert makes only the briefest of gestures in the direction of the cultural or educational needs of the citizens. The Plaza Cubierta at the centre of the Caracas CU emphatically prioritizes the arts, as indeed does the campus as a whole.

Just as the Plaza Cubierta cannot be defined by reference to traditional categories of architecture or town planning, so too it disrupts the traditional role of the architect as single controlling force. In the Covered Plaza, Villanueva was able to realize a genuine 'plastic integration' of the arts, because here he was able to work with a number of artists to produce an environment that incorporates works of art seamlessly into the architecture. This, perhaps the best-known aspect of the Ciudad Universitaria campus, was again Villanueva's idea. At earlier points in his career he had used works of art as additions to his architectural schemes, as in the fountains by Narváez in the Plaza O'Leary in El Silencio, but just as his architectural style had evolved from modernism as something of an optional stylistic extra to more of an ideology, a belief in the transformative power of modern architecture, so his ideas about the relationship between architecture and the other arts changed too. He was to define the freestanding work of art as 'a superimposition, and as such, useless and even hostile to the goals of architecture', while his idea of integration

is the product not only of understanding common purposes, but of the necessary subordination between the different expressions as well. It is the creation of an architectural-sculptural-pictorial organism, in which not even the smallest indecision is evident, where there is no visible gap between the different artistic genres.[62]

Artistic integration and the politics of style

Villanueva's success in integrating works of art into the CU campus in the early 1950s is especially significant in view of the appearance of a political strand to artistic debate in Venezuela at the time in relation to the relative merits of figurative and abstract art. The problem was that while in Mexico the Revolution had encouraged a break with the past, enabling artists to embrace socialist realism as a modern means of expression in a new political context, in Venezuela there had been no such break. Representation was the rule across the political spectrum. Even in the late 1940s, art education was firmly rooted in the figurative tradition of the late nineteenth century. This suited the conservatives, of course, but paradoxically it also made Venezuelan-educated artists with left-wing inclinations well equipped to embrace the more politically aware Mexican model, even if the opportunities for doing so under the Pérez Jiménez regime were limited. There were those who argued force-fully that abstraction was alien and inimical to democracy. As the artist Pedro León Castro put it in an interview published in 1949, before Pérez Jiménez came to power:

> At present, two art trends are struggling in the world: abstractionism, defended by the forces of a bankrupt imperialism, and on the opposing side, realism, on behalf of which worthy figures of the democratic movement wage action, new men who want better destinies for humanity. I must reassert that this struggle is taking place not just in Venezuela, where isolated native existentialists try to justify their ideas. This is a universal struggle between two separate philosophies, between two differ-ent classes and two completely opposed forms of art.[63]

On the other hand, in 1950 a group of young Venezuelan abstract artists, working in Paris and calling themselves 'Los Disidentes', produced a journal of the same name in which they attacked the conservatism of the art education they had experienced in Caracas, which, they said, taught nothing but a 'pseudo-impresionismo bastardo'.[64] In an article entitled 'Anacronismo e irresponsabilidad', specifically about an exhibition of León Castro's work, Pascual Navarro urged him (and others like him) to be honest with himself and break away from the past – the past was useful only as a point of departure towards the future: 'Why give history the force of the present? Our problems and uncertainties are different. To shelter beneath tradition as a way of disengaging with the present is nowadays one of the most common ways of being irresponsible.'[65] In a later issue, in response to those Venezuelans who were urging the Disidentes to reintegrate themselves back into Venezuelan reality and escape from the exotic influences of Paris, Pascual Navarro argued that it was only by reacting against this 'reality', and against established tradition, that they would be able to make real progress.[66]

Villanueva – who was born and educated in Paris and had returned to settle in Venezuela only at the age of twenty-eight, and always spoke Spanish with a French accent[67] – understood both sides of the argument, but as an architect he was more sympathetic to the position of the Disidentes. He knew that the early theorists of modern architecture had, in their different ways, argued for an abstract art to match their ornament-free style of building. For Le Corbusier, abstract art – and he mentions Cubism in particular – was the only appropriate style of painting for the new architecture; indeed, that style had led the way:

> Today, painting has outsped the other arts. It is the first to have attained attunement with the epoch. Modern painting has left on one side wall decoration, tapestry and the ornamental urn and has sequestered itself in a frame – flourishing, full of matter, far removed from a distracting realism; it lends itself to meditation. Art is no longer anecdotal, it is a source of meditation.[68]

In other words, Le Corbusier saw painting as something apart from architecture, something that could enhance a space; but at the same time he urges painters, 'Do not forget the problem of architecture', and asks for their help, 'that we may reconstruct our towns. Your works will then be able to take their place in the framework of the period and you will everywhere be admitted and understood.'[69]

Theo van Doesburg's position was slightly different. In 1924 he had declared architecture to be 'a synthesis of Neo-Plasticism': 'Building is a part of the new architecture which, by combining together all the arts in their elemental manifestation, discloses their true nature.' He includes painters in his 'architects of plasticism', but 'the new architecture permits no images (such as paintings or sculptures as separate elements)'; it does, however, permit 'colour organically as a direct means of expressing its relationships within space and time'. This is where the painter fits in: 'The modern painter's task consists in creating with the aid of colour a harmonious whole in the new four-dimensional realm of space–time – not a surface in two dimensions.'[70] In the De Stijl manifesto of 1923 he, Gerrit Rietveld and Cor van Eesteren had expressed a similar idea: 'We have given colour its rightful place in architecture and we assert that painting separated from the architectonic construction (i.e. the picture) has no right to exist.'[71] Gropius's position in 1919 was somewhere between the two. He, like others (Le Corbusier, Lúcio Costa), looked back enviously to the Gothic cathedrals as collective creative projects apparently unparalleled in their unity of purpose and design. Gropius argued for the primacy of architecture, of course, but he wanted to see painting and sculpture incorporated into a unified architectonic whole:

> Painters and sculptors, become craftsmen again, smash the frame of salon art that is round your pictures, go into buildings, bless them with fairy tales of colour, chisel ideas into the bare walls – and *build in imagination*, unconcerned about technical difficulties.[72]

And in the Bauhaus manifesto and programme (also 1919), he declared:

> The ultimate aim of all visual arts is the complete building! To embellish buildings was once the noblest function of the fine arts; they were the indispensable components of great architecture. Today the arts exist in isolation, from which they can be rescued only through the conscious, co-operative effort of all craftsmen. Architects,

painters and sculptors must recognize anew and learn to grasp the composite character of a building both as an entity and in its separate parts.[73]

Villanueva's position was closest to that of Gropius, but as with all these theorists it is very clear that his preference was for abstract art. In 1945 he had expressed his ideas about plastic integration:

> In the field of the plastic arts the necessity for an integration of painting and sculpture with architecture is being formulated, the return of the ancient elements of colour and volume to the white architectonic organism, using the proper language of the major arts purified through a long evolutionary process.
>
> To limit oneself to mere wall decoration, or to place paintings and sculptures in improvised sites, has no more value, in terms of the integration of the arts, than a museum collection could have. The idea of integration can crystallize into positive results only when painting and sculpture meet the architectonic reasons for their incorporation into a constructed environment. That is to say, only when they are painted or sculpted in relation to the spatial elements which make up the architectural work.
>
> This, properly regarded, is the spirit of the synthesis of the arts: to corroborate, to accentuate, and to enhance the space–form reality of the architectural design; or in a reverse process, to disperse, transform the actual volumes into purely spatial relations, if this is the architect's intention.[74]

There can be no doubt that even if there were a Venezuelan school of social realist art equivalent in stature to that of Mexico, and even if it were conceivable that the right-wing government of Pérez Jiménez would have financed murals of this type in their showpiece new university, Villanueva would not have wanted his walls dominated by figurative art.

Architecture and abstraction in the CU

While the Disidentes were complaining about the conservative nature of the art establishment in Caracas, Villanueva was planning to make the university into a sort of Trojan Horse which would introduce the abstract enemy into the heart of the city, in a bolder but not dissimilar strategy to the one he had used in El Silencio, when he had discreetly introduced a modern architectural aesthetic behind a neocolonial façade. A central reason for Villanueva's success was that Pérez Jiménez trusted him. He had little sympathy for avant-garde art, but he was persuaded that Villanueva could create a university campus that would impress the delegates to the Iberoamerican International Conference in 1954, and he provided the funds for Villanueva's ambitious plans. A crucially important element in this story is Villanueva's decision not to rely on Venezuelan artists alone. With help, advice and introductions from the influential Venezuelan critic Sofia Imbert, Villanueva approached a number of well-established artists in Europe and North America, with Paris as the connecting element between all those involved.

The timescale for the first and most important wave of commissions was very tight. Villanueva wrote to a number of artists sometime early in 1952, and once he had an expression of interest he would send sketches of the architecture and details of the proposed location.[75] When he had a concrete proposal from an artist, it had to be vetted by university officials and a price approved.[76] He worked tirelessly. He visited the artists and discussed their contributions in detail. In the case of the sculptures by Laurens and Arp, he visited the artists' studios in France, seeking works he already knew from earlier visits, and suggesting that small-scale sculptures could be enlarged to a size appropriate to the spaces available. In the case of the Pevsner, he bought the sculpture outright. Many other works arrived in Venezuela as sketches or small-scale models, and were realized on site, under Villanueva's direction. As a result, between 1950 and 1954 sixty-four works of art were installed on the campus, so that it became, in effect, a gallery of modern art.

If the architecture of the Plaza Cubierta can be seen as a metaphor for intellectual exploration and discovery, the integration of the arts is a metaphor for the cultural integration of Venezuela into the wider modern world. Villanueva incorporated works by high-profile foreign artists – Arp, Léger, Pevsner, Vasarely, Laurens, Calder and Lam – alongside works by Venezuelans, most of whom, like Villanueva himself, had lived and worked in Paris and so, in effect, had European modernism in their blood. This is not to say that there are no figurative works, but they are assigned carefully chosen sites and are primarily sculptural. Villanueva's old friend Narváez executed a number of pieces for the campus – female nudes personifying Education and Science for the Faculty of Education in 1950, and a male Athlete in 1951 outside the Olympic Stadium, for example, all three in the warm creamy Cumarebo stone he had used earlier for the El Silencio fountains. His bronze *Sculpture* (1954) for the Plaza del Rectorado is already less literal, suggesting that his style changed with exposure to that of the Europeans. The monumental bronzes by Henri Laurens (*Amphion*) and Hans Arp (*Cloud Shepherd*), both 1953, are also anthropomorphic, freestanding, detached from the architecture, taking their places alongside the pedestrians who move through the interlinking paths and patios (Plate 19). *La Maternidad* (1954), by the Spaniard Baltasar Lobo, is similarly anthropomorphic, suggesting a mother playing with her child. Generally speaking, there is a transition from the more or less figurative freestanding work to the pure geometrical abstraction of the works which are fully integrated into the architectural fabric. Léger's *Bi-Mural* (1954), with its glyph-like eagle and serpent motifs, is a freestanding wall that curves across one of the open areas of the Plaza Cubierta (Plate 20); while Otero's joyful stained-glass wall-window (1954) in the Faculty of Engineering library is made up of clear glass bricks with occasional inserts in primary colours, the dominant gridlike pattern of the metal frame superimposed over zigzagging diagonals, combining – integrating – wall, window and work of art.

Elsewhere, Vasarely's *Positive–Negative* (also 1954), a screening wall of aluminium slats, is very closely related in form and function to the other openwork screens of the Plaza Cubierta: breaking up the sunlight into ever-changing dappled patterns, and allowing the air to circulate. The three panels of his *Sofia* (a tribute to Sofia Imbert, also 1954), on the air-conditioning tower of the Aula Magna, a pattern of black lines vibrating across a white ground, are a sort of airy version of the functional grilles below. Similarly, Valera's geometric mosaic murals in the Facultad de Ciencias Jurídicas y Políticas (1955 and 1956) animate large plain walls with geometric designs that echo the patterns of the openwork screens; and Mateo Manaure's aluminium and glass mosaic wall panels in the Facultad de Arquitectura y Urbanismo have a whimsical architectural character, suggesting doors or windows to imaginary workshops. Most famously, Alexander Calder's bright-coloured flying saucers which float under the great curving roof of the Aula Magna are integrated into the architectural design; they are essential, functional elements in the acoustics of the hall, and they are sculptures in the manner of his stabiles.

Villanueva's campus provides a context in which college students could be introduced into an entirely new type of spatial and cultural environment. It integrated Venezuela into the visual culture of the modern world, and – perhaps more importantly – it integrated modernism and, more specifically, abstraction into Venezuela. Here, aspects of Parisian modernism are translated into a Venezuelan environment where brilliant sunshine falls through screens and tropical vegetation to create endlessly moving, changing patterns, and bold panels in primary colours contrast with raw concrete to provide a backdrop for dark-green foliage, so integrating elements associated with the landscape and traditional architecture of Venezuela into new works of art.

It is interesting to compare Villanueva's achievement in the Ciudad Universitaria with Le Corbusier's views on architecture as expressed in *Vers une Architecture*. The famous passage where he affirms his belief in architecture as an essentially abstract and aesthetic medium – 'Architecture is the masterly, correct and magnificent play of masses brought together in light' – continues:

> Our eyes are made to see forms in light; light and shade reveal these forms; cubes, cones, spheres, cylinders or pyramids are the great primary forms which light reveals to advantage; the image of these is distinct and tangible within us and without ambiguity. It is for this reason that these are *beautiful forms, the most beautiful forms*. Everybody is agreed as to that, the child, the savage and the metaphysician. It is the very nature of the plastic arts.[77]

Pure primary forms are revealed to us by light. Because they are so tangible and unambiguous (and comprehensible), they are beautiful. This beauty is universally recognized, and is therefore 'the very nature of the plastic arts'. Villanueva incorporated abstract art into his architecture in a way that enhances both: the architecture is adapted to the individual work of art, and the art is adapted to the architecture. There is no battle of styles between a representational art and the essentially abstract, mathematical nature of architecture, nor any battle of wills, as there was between Siqueiros and the UNAM authorities in Mexico.

There seems to be an obvious, logical division between the use of abstract art in the more 'architectural' contexts and figurative works as the more independent organic elements that, along with the people and the plants, occupy the spaces rather than being fused to the fabric of the architectural structures, but this division emerged only gradually, as the CU evolved. In 1950, for the Institutes of Experimental Medicine and Anatomy, as well as the sculptures of Education and Science, Francisco Narváez also produced figurative allegorical murals in glazed tiles, which suggest a knowledge of similar developments in Brazil. And as late as 1954, for similar reasons of friendship and national loyalty, Villanueva commissioned murals from the same Pedro León Castro who wrote the anti-abstraction polemic in 1949, and from Héctor Poleo, who had trained with the muralists in Mexico. Both these murals, however, were for formal meeting rooms within the Rectorate building – in other words, out of sight of the public while at the same time in positions of central importance from the point of view of the administrative structure of the university. Just as the Rectorate building itself is safely but unadventurously modern, so these murals are suited to the conservative artistic tastes of university bureaucrats. Neither Castro nor Poleo had the status, the confidence or the sheer artistic power to produce works that presented a challenge to the university government in the way in which Rivera, for example, managed so often to challenge his patrons.

The question of the relationship between Villanueva and the other Venezuelan artists – many of whom were outspokenly socialist and most of whom had been members of the radical Disidentes group in Paris in 1950, which had attacked everything that smelled of tradition – and the government of Pérez Jiménez has been little explored.[78] Pérez Jiménez was a fierce nationalist, but he was supportive of Villanueva's determination to involve foreign artists in the decorative programme – his government, of course, had to fund it – and he was not hostile to its predominantly abstract character, perhaps because he recognized that an unmistakably modern art, as with modern architecture, gave an impression of a modernizing country in political and economic terms, even though the main point was to bolster his own military regime. It has been suggested that Villanueva and Pérez Jiménez were in effect playing a sort of game of chess with each other, each dependent on the other's moves.[79] The president's close association with the campus provoked a reaction after his fall from power. In the later 1960s students attacked the works of art as the hugely expensive product of a corrupt regime; in response, the artists themselves produced an 'Intellectuals' Manifesto' justifying their work and distancing themselves from Pérez Jiménez's government.[80] For several years the deteriorating condition of the campus was a cause for concern; then, in 1982, a unit was established with responsibility for its protection and conservation. It is now well maintained, and – at least in Venezuela – is acknowledged as a central feature of the twentieth-century architectural canon.

The Caracas Metro: urban integration

One of Villaneuva's greatest achievements in the CU was to create a very particular type of urban environment in which modern architecture and abstract art are handled in a matter-of-fact way, so that they seem natural rather than difficult and alienating. They help to establish an urban character for the CU that is special and welcoming, but at the same time almost ordinary. A university campus is, of course, a small, rather particular type of urban unit which is not easy to duplicate in a different context and for a different purpose, but its ideology was crucial to the planning behind a project which, strictly speaking, falls outside the chronological limits of the present study: the Caracas Metro.

The idea of a metro for Caracas dates back to the mid 1940s, when French companies offered to build a system in exchange, of course, for very lucrative deals.[81] The idea continued to crop up periodically,[82] and with increasing urgency, as the city mushroomed out into the neighbouring hills and valleys until finally, in 1976, a law was passed authorizing the necessary funding. In 1977 the Compañía Metro de Caracas was created, a public company with legal responsibility for the planning, design, construction and operation of the metro system. The Metro began commercial operations in 1983, with further sections opening throughout the rest of the 1980s, and Caracas now has a network of over 42 kilometres serving 39 stations.

By the late 1970s Caracas was urbanistically incoherent, sprawling and socially fragmented, with working-class areas of tower blocks like the 23 de Enero housing development (mentioned above), and of shantytowns or *ranchos* – both, in their different ways, lawless no-go areas for non-residents – and middle-class enclaves isolated from each other and from the main financial and commercial centres of the city by acres of motorway, often gridlocked with traffic. The new Metro was promoted under the slogan 'La Gran Solución para Caracas' ('Caracas's big solution'): as well as facilitating movement within the city, it was designed to address the problem of social disunity and urban degradation, and plans for the public architectural face of the Metro went on alongside the engineering works under the direction of Max Pedemonte. It is interesting how often in the literature describing the intentions behind the design of the Metro the word 'integration' occurs: the designers aimed for spatial continuity by means of 'the physical and visual integration of the different levels which made up each station'. For stations at ground level, or only partially subterranean, 'this integration also involved the use of natural light and incorporated the immediate urban context, making the transition between open exterior and confined interior spaces less brusque.'[83]

The idea that the architecture of the Metro could be used to create a sense of at least visual urban cohesion was not new: it was already present in Hector Guimard's Art Nouveau designs for the Paris Métro (around 1900), which in turn are descended from the mid-nineteenth-century ideas of Baron Hauss-mann, whose standardizing measures included benches, lampposts and clocks as well as street façades. In Caracas the designers decided to go for a high level of homogeneity in terms of the finish, the associated street furniture and the interior equipment in order to make metro stations easily identifiable and to make the traveller feel at home even when visiting new parts of the city, but to combine this with diversity in terms of the actual architectural designs. Thus such things as bollards, benches and signage are standardized and announce the Metro even before the station itself is visible; while the architecture is heterogeneous and often site-specific. The station at Parque del Este, for example, is a part-greenhouse, where exhibitions of plants are held. Where possible the character of the station entrance is established by means of land-scaping as much as architecture. In the up-market district of Altamira, an existing ornamental pond was adapted to form a noisy waterfall that rushes down into the station entrance on one side of Avenida Francisco de Miranda while the entrance on the opposite side forms part of an open-air amphi-theatre. The emphasis is always on space, both at street level and in the various intermediate levels and halls between the street entrance and the platforms.

Just as the Plaza Cubierta area in the heart of the CU comprises archi-tecture and art in a sequence of interlinked exterior and interior spaces which coincide around the university auditoria, so too the plans for the Metro in-volved the integration of the visual arts with small amphitheatres (as at Altamira) or other similar areas for the dramatic and musical arts as well, and, in an extension of the CU ethos, with spaces for temporary exhibitions, so that many of the stations also function as the local cultural centre. A special cultural division of the Metro management was set up to commission the art and organize exhibitions and other cultural events for the different locations. Funds were set aside to commission for the stations works of art that would bear in mind some aspect of the local community, the history, the architectural space of each station, or the character of the plazas, boulevards and pedestrian precincts of the neighbouring area. Among the most striking examples is Fernando de Soto's *Cubo virtual azul y negro/Virtual Blue and Black Cube* at the busy Chacaito station, a forest of black, blue and silver metal rods suspended from a steel frame over the entrance, where they ripple and sway in the wind (Plate 21). The big interchange of La Hoyada includes works by Gego (Gertrudis Goldschmidt), Francisco Narvaéz and Mercedes Pardo, and the one at Plaza Venezuela by Alejandro Otero and Carlos Cruz-Diez, but even lesser stations have works of art, freestanding or built into the structure in some way.

The launch of the Metro in Caracas was preceded by a comprehensive propaganda programme to encourage in *caraqueños* a sense of ownership and pride in their new transport system.[84] Schoolchildren were given educational tours of the tunnels while they were under construction; there were public lectures explaining the process and posters announcing progress. And in the main, this was effective; even in the poorer parts of town the precinct of the Metro station is generally free from litter, flyposting and graffiti, and the cultural events are well attended. The Metro provides an urban identity – not for the whole city, of course, but certainly for those areas it serves – while at the same time it emphasizes the characteristics of the different districts. The many-faceted ideas of integration implied in the CU laid the foundations for an understanding of an environment as multifunctional. The Metro is not just a system of transportation, any more than the CU is just a degree factory – both are conceived as part of a broader educational programme: 'We are absolutely convinced that with the fundamental, permanent support … of all the institutions which produce and encourage creative work, the Metro is a good road for culture.'[85]

Villanueva's work at the CU sowed seeds which have borne a variety of fruits, of which the Metro is but one. Above all, perhaps, it naturalized modern architecture and abstract art in Venezuela, making it seem normal and acceptable to an unusual degree. In his novel *Rite of Spring*, set in the late 1950s, Alejo Carpentier – who lived in Caracas from 1945 to 1959 – draws comparisons between Caracas and Havana. Enrique the architect, who finds that he cannot get interesting commissions in Cuba because he is not one of Dictator Batista's cronies, decides to go to Venezuela, where he knows that architecture is enjoying a boom.[86] Once in Caracas he is astonished to find himself in such a rich and cosmopolitan environment, where wealthy connoisseurs collect works by Renoir, Picasso, Klee and Vasarely, and where people like Alexander Calder, Francis Poulenc, Wifredo Lam and Heitor Villa-Lobos have visited and left their mark.[87] There are few places in Latin America of which the same could be said. In a less intense way – but on a much larger scale than in the CU – the Metro does the same thing. It is still astonishing, even today, to find works by Soto, Cruz-Diez and Otero, not as isolated 'works of art' but as part of the urban texture. If there is a particularly national character to Venezuelan modern architecture, it is precisely the way in which it has integrated high culture into the local environment, the cosmopolitan into the domestic, without diminishing or compromising either (Plate 22).

THREE

BRAZIL

RIO DE JANEIRO AND BEYOND

If any one building was responsible for placing Latin America on the international map of modern architecture, it was the Ministério da Educação e Saúde (Ministry of Education and Health) in Rio de Janeiro, designed in 1936 by a team of young Brazilians in consultation with Le Corbusier, and constructed between 1937 and 1942. It was the building which alerted the USA to the fact that Brazil had seized the initiative in terms of modern architecture. Americans in the States were keen to identify continental 'American' traits, and anxious – where appropriate – to see what could be learnt from their southerly neighbours, with the result that the Museum of Modern Art in New York, one of the cultural arms of Nelson Rockefeller's Office of the Co-ordinator of Inter-American Affairs, dispatched Philip Goodwin and the photographer G.E. Kidder Smith to find out more. The result was the Brazil Builds exhibition at MOMA in 1943, and in the bilingual catalogue Philip Goodwin wrote:

> [The MES building] has set free the creative spirit of design and put a depth charge under the antiquated routine of governmental thought. While Federal classic in Washington, Royal Academy archaeology in London and Nazi classic in Munich are still triumphant, Brazil has had the courage to break away from the safe and easy path with the result that Rio can boast of the most beautiful government building in the Western hemisphere.[1]

Other US critics followed suit. In 1958 Henry-Russell Hitchcock confidently described it as the 'great building which opened so brilliantly the story of new architecture in Brazil',[2] and in 1960 Sigfried Giedion said that it was with this building that 'Brazil took her place in the history of modern art'.[3] This is the paradigmatic example of the way in which Latin American architects used European ideas as a basis for an alternative modernism, and those outside Latin America sat up and took notice.

The urban evolution of Rio de Janeiro

Among capital cities Rio de Janeiro is unusual in the degree to which the geographical centre of power has shifted with the changes in political power.[4] In the sixteenth century, after an initial fortress on a more westerly headland, the little settlement moved to the top of the fortified hill of Castelo, near where the national Santos Dumont Airport is now situated. Only in 1720, after the discovery of gold in the state of Minas Gerais, was the Portuguese dependency elevated to the status of a Viceroyalty, and only in 1763 did Rio replace Salvador as the viceregal capital. As the colony became more secure, the expanding city moved down to the flat plain to the north, with its centrepiece the Paço Real, the Viceregal palace, facing out to sea about midway between the site of the old Castelo fortress to the south and the Benedictine monastery on the promontory to the north.[5] With the transfer of the Portuguese imperial court to Brazil in 1808, the heart of the city shifted inland to the area around the large park, the Campo de Santana. This is perhaps symptomatic of the government's shift of attention towards the Brazilian interior and away from the sea and the (abandoned) European country, which in effect became more like a province of Brazil. At this point there emerges a dual-centred city governed from the Santana district, where most of the social elite lived, with the business district at the portside, around the Paço Real, now renamed the Paço Imperial.

Castelo hill   1
Santo Antônio hill   2
São Bento hill   3
Nossa Senhora
da Conceição hill   4
Livramento hill   5
Imperial Palace   6
Campo de Santana   7
Praça Floriano   8
Avenida Beira-Mar   9
Gloria Bay   10

Plan to show the hills and coastline of central Rio de Janeiro in 1910; dotted coastline indicates the results of landfill by 1965.

The topography of Rio, however, was the constraining factor. The solid wall of mountains to the west meant that there was nowhere for the city to expand further in that direction, and when Brazil declared itself a Republic in 1889, the nerve centre shifted back towards the coast, this time to the south around the Praça Floriano at the base of the Castelo hill. Here a theatre, a museum and the national library, all built in the first decade of the twentieth century, created a cultural focus nearer the beach and the new Avenida Beira-Mar. The Monroe Palace, a copy of the Brazilian pavilion for the 1904 St Louis Expo, housed the Senate, and the various elite clubs (the Jockey club, the Naval club, the Military club) were also here. This Praça Floriano nucleus reoriented the city back to an expanded north–south axis, and the Avenida Central (later Rio Branco), inaugurated in 1906 as the central pillar of the Haussmannization programme of the city's prefect, Francisco de Pereira Passos, linked the sophisticated districts of the cultured and pleasure-loving classes in the south with the recently established new docks on the bay to the north of São Bento, where another gigantic new Avenida was constructed, the Avenida Rodrigues Alves. The Avenida Central thus became the real commercial and financial spine of the city, linking the port to the business, administrative and cultural districts.

During the 1920s, urban restructuring continued with major earth-moving projects and slum clearances. In particular the Castelo hill, which blocked expansion to the sea to the south-east, was removed, and some of the material used to fill in part of Gloria Bay and create a large, flat headland.[6] In 1927 the French town planner Alfred Agache (1875–1959) was called in to advise, and he and his team identified three key problems: a lack of urban focus, a lack of architectural and scenic interest, and the overly dispersed nature of the government buildings. Agache's proposals were published in 1930, and although they are visually pompous and conventional they do address these problems.[7] The focus of the modernized Rio was to be a range of vaguely authoritarian-looking buildings forming a crescent around a gigantic plaza which was to open out, via two monumental columns, to Guanabara Bay and

View of old Rio with levelling of Castelo hill, 29 October 1921.

the sea. Thus the government buildings would be grouped together around a suitably imposing open space, and the columns would mark the entrance to the country as a whole, as well as to the capital city and, specifically, the seat of power. Significantly, Agache proposed that this complex should be built on landfill in Gloria Bay, well to the south of the old city centre. Agache is important for recognizing that the city needed a new focus away from the densely overcrowded area around the port, and that the Avenida Central/Rio Branco should have somewhere significant to go to rather than just to the beach. The MES building was to fulfil these needs.

Origins of the Ministério da Educação e Saúde (MES) building

The Revolution of 1930 brought Getúlio Vargas to power, and during his fifteen-year presidency the government introduced a whole range of social reforms, including labour laws and compulsory education. As in Mexico and Venezuela, the inexorable growth in population of the capital city was a constant reminder of the need for urban planning and social welfare schemes. Vargas created a new joint Ministry of Health and Education, and appointed Gustavo Capanema, as ardent a modernizer as himself, to head it. As with Vasconcelos in Mexico a dozen years earlier, Capanema needed a building to house his new ministry, a building which would announce the significance of an institution charged with overseeing the two key engines of social reform and modernization. The government identified a site at the southerly end of the city centre, one block away from the Museo Nacional de Belas Artes and the Biblioteca Nacional, in the area known as Castelo after the recently levelled hill. With the little colonial church of Santa Luzia on one side, the Ministério do Trabalho, the Ministry of Labour (the only other relatively high building in the area) on the other, plenty of room for further building nearby, with good views of the bay and within walking distance of the airport, the new Ministry building would play an important part in the evolving urban fabric.

Capanema wanted a building that would include all the necessary offices and facilities, but as well as an administrative institution it was to be a centre for the arts with an exhibition wing, a lecture room and an auditorium. The Brazilian constitution required that the design of all public buildings should be decided by open competition, but Capanema, 'inspired by the mixture of vision, audacity and common sense that characterized him',[8] paid off the prizewinners of the 1935 competition for the MES building and got a special dispensation from President Vargas to ask one of the young architects whose work had been disqualified by the judges as too radical to submit a new project.[9] This man was Lúcio Costa, well known for his political radicalism, his love of

Brazilian baroque architecture (in 1933 he had been a key figure in the move to get the whole centre of the colonial goldmining city of Ouro Preto in Minas Gerais declared a national monument), his modernist architecture and his interest in contemporary architectural theory.

Costa insisted that the other young architects who had been excluded from the competition should also be included, and so a group was established comprising Carlos Leão, Jorge Moreira and Affonso Reidy. Ernani Vasconcelos and Oscar Niemeyer were invited to join shortly afterwards; every one of them was an enthusiast of modernist functionalist architecture and an admirer of Le Corbusier, and they convinced Capanema that the only way to ensure that the Ministry would be a major work of modern architecture would be to invite Le Corbusier himself to be involved. He came for six weeks, from the beginning of July to mid August 1936. He worked on alternate days on the MES project and on a project for a university city for Rio, and because he could not be paid for any of this he also delivered a series of six (very expensive) lectures.[10]

Le Corbusier's visit was enormously important for all the young architects involved in these schemes, and for the subsequent history of modern architecture in Brazil, but it was not a simple teacher–pupil relationship.[11] Those present at the time, who attended his lectures and worked with him on the MES and university city projects, describe it as one of intense excitement and creativity. Le Corbusier was 'the spark which kindled talents to find their own way of expression', as Sigfried Giedion put it,[12] and at the time that was how Le Corbusier saw himself. In one of his lectures in Rio he addressed the issue of architectural education, and argued that if the master–pupil relationship were too rigid the results would be very limited. For his own part, he said, he never wanted to correct students' projects, nor to take on educational responsibilities.[13] It was only later – when he himself had not had as much success as he felt he deserved, and when the MES building had achieved international recognition – that he claimed a more dominant role in the design process.

The design of the MES building

Le Corbusier did not find the Brazilians to be passive disciples. For a start, there was the question of the siting of the new MES building, which, as we have seen, the government had already determined. Le Corbusier had visited Rio before, on his return from a lecture tour in Buenos Aires in 1929, and on that occasion he had been inspired by the spectacular landscape to devise a utopian scheme for the city that solved the problems of traffic congestion and overcrowding in one go. His proposal was for a superhighway supported on a gigantic, extended high-rise housing block that would curve gracefully along the coast while also describing a 'faultless horizontal' against which the mountains around could be seen to advantage.[14] Or at least this is how it would be perceived from out at sea. In other words, Le Corbusier's image of the city is from the outside, and when he was invited back to advise on the new ministry building he already had an idea in his mind, a development of his earlier, much more ambitious urban plan.

While he was in Rio in July 1936 he identified a site on the coast beside the airport which conformed to his pre-existing image and which, he argued, was much better suited than the town centre to a large, path-breaking building. He designed a long horizontal building facing out across Gloria Bay, set up on *pilotis* in its own landscaped grounds, with the auditorium and exhibition hall projecting at either side. Vehicular traffic and parking was largely restricted to the landward side of the building, so that those within could enjoy undisturbed views of the spectacular coastline.[15] So, too, visitors arriving by sea could appreciate the showpiece building against the backdrop of Rio's distinctive mountains. In other words, Le Corbusier wanted his building to turn its back on the city, and this was emphasized in his sketches by the way the huge *Man of Brazil* statue in front of the main entrance lobby was to be seated facing out across the bay. As in Agache's earlier plan for urban renewal, the emphasis was on the non-Brazilian world, with the government buildings of the capital city oriented towards the Atlantic, designed to welcome foreigners, a sort of frontier-cum-gateway.[16] At least Agache's design was part of a larger urban

Le Corbusier, sketch for a master plan for Rio de Janeiro, 1929, from
Precisions on the Present State of Architecture and City Planning, 1930.

plan; Le Corbusier's building was for a stand-alone showpiece, within easy
reach of the airport, isolated from the city and from Brazil.

As far as Capanema and the Brazilian government were concerned, however, they were not interested: they had already decided on the location, and
this was not negotiable. Le Corbusier grumbled, but had to put his mind to

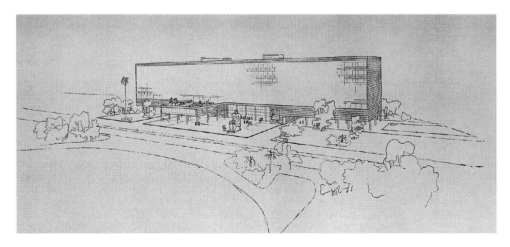

Le Corbusier, first proposal for the MES building, Rio de Janeiro, 1936.

a very different site, and thus a very different sort of building. The result was what he called 'une grande innovation urbanistique'.[17] Instead of the traditional urban practice whereby the footprint of the building coincides with the limits of the city block and, space allowing, opens on to an enclosed interior courtyard, the main block, raised on *pilotis*, is placed in the middle of the square, freeing up the rest of the ground in an unprecedented way. Nowadays this arrangement is common in city centres, but at the time it was indeed revolutionary.

The question of the origins of this 'great innovation' is not entirely clear. It certainly seems Le Corbusian but, unusually, Le Corbusier does not explicitly claim it as his in the *Complete Works*; while Henrique Mindlin, in his detailed survey of modern Brazilian architecture (1956), presents a sequence of designs which begins with an innovative U-shaped plan which he credits to the Brazilian team.[18] It seems certain, however, that the design went through several stages, that Le Corbusier returned to France before the final form was decided, and

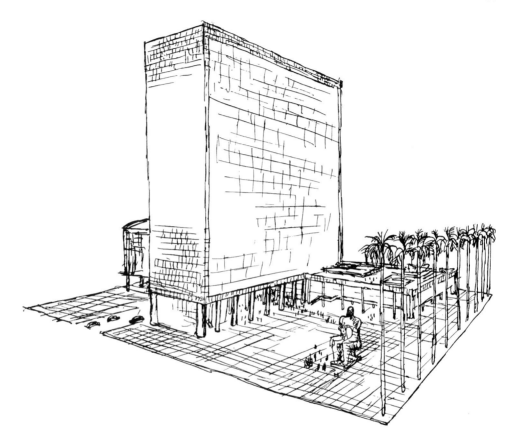

Le Corbusier, second proposal for the MES building, Rio de Janeiro, 1936.

that he continued to work on a series of drawings for his own chosen site, presumably in the hope that the authorities would change their minds.[19] The team of Brazilian architects, meanwhile, were working on a T-square plan for a much taller block, and at this point the young Oscar Niemeyer is credited with making some crucial modifications that were incorporated into the final design.[20] This was then sent to Le Corbusier in Paris; he gave his approval, and construction began in 1937.

The Brazilian modifications included giving the building a more nearly north–south orientation than east–west, so setting it at right angles to the main avenues of the city. This gave it greater prominence, facing up to the old centre and the port, and, on the other side, with a spectacular view down to the airport and the coastal beaches beyond, thus also avoiding Le Corbusier's implications of a gateway between the interior and the exterior, the Brazilian and the foreign. The orientation also means that the sun, a major consideration in Rio, strikes the windowed north façade at midday rather than in the later afternoon, and, although this may seem paradoxical, at this latitude the sun at midday is near the zenith, making screening possible without loss of view; while the full force of the lower, but still very hot, afternoon sun strikes the windowless west wall.

The MES was one of the first slab-block high-rises of its kind to be built anywhere, and it incorporates all of Le Corbusier's 'Five Points towards a New Architecture': *pilotis*, free façade, free plan, glazed walls and rooftop gardens. The main fourteen-storey block is raised on *pilotis* ten metres high, leaving most of the block open at street level; the skeleton structure allows for the flexible plan, the free façade and the two *pan-verre* walls. There are roof gardens: one on top of the main block, where there was also a restaurant; and one above the exhibition wing, accessible from the ministerial offices. But more than these Le Corbusian features, the MES building was where commentators, especially from the USA, first identified features that they saw as distinctively Brazilian or Latin American, related to popular or colonial forms, and conditioned by local climate and geography. This was the area where the collaboration with the Brazilian team was especially fruitful. In his enthusiasm for Brazil and for Brazilian culture Le Corbusier served as a catalyst, encouraging the architects to identify national or regional characteristics which could be adapted to enhance their designs.

MES building, Rio de Janeiro, 1936–42, south elevation (photograph c. 1950).

Take the example of the *pilotis*. *Pilotis* were, of course, a key feature of Le Corbusier's theory, on which he had waxed lyrical a few years earlier in his lectures in Buenos Aires, especially in describing his ill-fated project for the League of Nations building in Geneva.[21] By means of *pilotis* he envisaged separating the buildings from the landscape:

> What happens on the ground concerns circulation, mobility, and what happens above, inside the building, is work, is motionless. This will presently become an important principle in city planning. I conserve the grass and the herds, the old trees, as well as the ravishing views of landscape, and above them, at a certain level, on a horizontal slab of concrete, on top of the *pilotis* descending to their foundations, I raise the limpid and pure prisms of utilitarian buildings;… I compose in the atmosphere. Everything counts: the herds, the grass, the flowers in the foreground on which one walks caressing them with one's eyes, the lake, the Alps, the sky … and the divine proportions. And thanks to the *pilotis*, on this acropolis destined for meditation and for intellectual work, the natural ground remains, the poetry is intact.[22]

I quote this at length because we can recognize in Le Corbusier's vision for the League of Nations building much of what lay behind his idea for the MES project in Rio de Janeiro, where, similarly, he envisaged creating a pure prism floating above a ravishing landscape.

But Le Corbusier's importance in the history of modern architecture in Brazil is not just a matter of the introduction of a new aesthetic. He pointed to ways in which the modern could also be Brazilian. His identification of and enthusiasm for distinctive local traits coincided with ideas that had been voiced by Brazilian intellectuals from the 1920s on. He noticed, for example, that the use of *pilotis* was well established in Rio:

> [T]he black has his house almost always on the edge of the cliff, raised on pilotis in front, the door is at the back toward the hillside; from up in the *favellas* [sic] one always has a view of the sea, the harbors, the ports, the islands, the ocean, the mountains, the estuaries; the black sees all that; the wind reigns, useful in the tropics, there is pride in the eye of the black who sees all that; the eye of the man who sees wide horizons is prouder, wide horizons confer dignity; that is the thought of a planner.[23]

Of course the stilts on the houses of the *favelas* are, as Le Corbusier recognizes, a practical necessity on steep hillsides, but by using the term *pilotis* and by extending his discussion to include the mind-expanding effects of a good view, he is making a link between traditional Brazilian building techniques and modern architecture which others were to make subsequently; one of which the younger generation of Brazilian architects were themselves acutely aware. As Le Corbusier also recognized, the positioning and construction of houses in the *favelas* made them pleasantly breezy. In Europe and the USA at the time, contemporary architectural theory was preoccupied with the idea of ventilation as part of a general concern for health and hygiene, with the circulation of air as a means of dispersing smog, smells and germs. In the tropical climate of Rio ventilation is primarily a matter of climate control.

Le Corbusier promoted *pilotis* on the grounds that they released space for pedestrians to move freely about underneath a building, and that in his ideal park-like urban environment they could provide uninterrupted views of the surrounding landscape and vegetation. In Rio, of course, they do both these things: in the MES building the plaza and gardens extend underneath the building between the columns, providing a vista from one street across to another and, for example, a view of the Santa Luzia church, so that although it is dwarfed this little fragment of colonial Rio is at least not boxed in. *Pilotis*, in creating shady areas, also encourage the circulation of air at ground level, so that instead of buildings creating wells of heat between them, they stimulate breezes between and around them.

Another Le Corbusian feature which comes into its own in tropical America is the *brise-soleil*. The MES building incorporated a revolutionary system of movable louvres across the entire sunny north façade in order to mitigate the heat and the full force of the sun. The glazing is set back between deep vertical jambs and behind these adjustable louvres, so that it is protected from direct sunlight, a system much admired by Philip Goodwin. In the light of the Brazilian precedent Goodwin criticized the way that the question of sunscreening had been 'blandly ignored' in North America, where in summer 'the

MES building, Rio de Janeiro, 1936–42,
north elevation (photograph c. 1944)

average office building is like a hot-house', where 'the miserable office workers
either roast or hide behind airless awnings'.[24] Le Corbusier had proposed a
similar system of sunbreaks or *brise-soleils* in his projects for Algiers in 1933,
but these were to be fixed, whereas those of the MES building could be
adjusted according to the season and the time of day.[25] It is their mobility
which animates the vast flat façade, changing its expression from hour to hour
and from day to day. Over the years, the Cariocans have exploited this façade
as a sort of giant billboard, with the louvres arranged to spell out simple
slogans.

But the *brise-soleil*, like the *piloti*, is not an invention of modernist architects.
In colonial Brazil, as in the Iberian peninsula, the use of grilles, screens, lat-

MES building, Rio de Janeiro, azulejos
by Cândido Portinari c. 1942
(photograph c. 1944).

ticework and shutters with movable slats to shield the interior of a building while still allowing for light and air, as well as a view, is entirely traditional. Air conditioning had perhaps first been used by Frank Lloyd Wright in the Larkin Building in Buffalo in 1904, and Le Corbusier had included it in his plans for the Assembly Hall at the League of Nations in 1927, but its use was not common, and it was expensive. In 1937, when the MES building was being discussed, the idea of an isolated high building with the north façade completely protected from direct sun by movable louvres, and both this and the southerly façade made up of curtain walls of openable windows to allow for cross-ventilation through the then-fashionable fully open-plan interior, must have seemed entirely manageable. Today much of the interior has been divided up into smaller units which limit the effectiveness of the cross-ventilation; the smog and noise from the surrounding city have increased enormously, so that working with the windows open is less attractive; and – perhaps most importantly – people's expectations of a comfortable ambient temperature have changed, making air conditioning seem indispensable.

Another much-commented-on feature of the MES building attributed to the influence of Le Corbusier is the use of decorative glazed tiles on the curving walls enclosing the ground-floor entrance lobby and services. Henrique Mindlin observed that as well as encouraging the use of *pilotis* and *brise-soleils*, 'Le Corbusier did us still another service when he suggested that the *azulejos* should be revived.'[26] In colonial buildings, particularly churches, walls were often decorated with panels of blue-and-white tiles painted with scenes both edifying and entertaining.[27] The tiles on the MES building were designed by the artist Cândido Portinari, painted by Paulo Rossi (who later worked under the name Osirarte) and made by Matarazzo & Co. of São Paulo, all Brazilians.[28] They are surprisingly baroque: fish, sea shells, seahorses and mermaids form a flat pattern over undulating background shapes in white and various shades of blue. The local, site-specific nature of these tiles is confirmed in a witty tile of a fat-bodied fish with Capanema's distinctive jowly profile, removed at an early date at the Minister's behest and now preserved inside the building (Plate 23).[29] A further innovation by Le Corbusier was the use of Brazilian stone for the walls, the plaza, and the veneer on the *pilotis*. Astonished that public buildings in Rio were still being built of stone shipped in from France, he recommended that the Brazilians make use not of exposed concrete, as one might expect, but of their own pinkish local granite.[30]

Capanema – no doubt with half an eye on Mexico – wanted to complement his new Ministry with works of art, and Pietro Maria Bardi relates a nice anecdote which demonstrates the high-level interest in the building during its construction and decoration: the US painter George Biddle arrived in Rio with a letter from none other than President Roosevelt himself, requesting that Capanema allocate him some walls to paint. Capanema, who was passionately interested in every detail of his new Ministry building, was not prepared to oblige, but instead sent Biddle off to the Biblioteca Nacional to paint scenes of 'War' and 'Peace' in the entrance hall.[31] Capanema commissioned Portinari to do some murals for the conference room and the main ministerial reception area, as well as commissioning work from the sculptors Bruno Giorgi and Antônio Celso. And in a move which could be seen as establishing a precedent for Villanueva's patronage of important foreign artists at the CU in Caracas, Capanema commissioned Jacques Lipschitz to design a sculpture for the exterior wall of the Auditorium. Lipschitz sent plans for a piece on the aspirational theme of Prometheus Unbound, but financial constraints meant that it was cast to one-third of the intended dimensions and so looks a little lost beneath the huge façade.[32]

The other striking feature of the MES building is the garden. Here, too, Le Corbusier's ideas are in evidence: time and again in his writings he stressed the value of the roof garden. The flat roofs made possible by modern technology meant, for Le Corbusier, that all the space – the best part of the city, which had previously been left to 'sparrows and alley-cat dating' – is made available to its inhabitants.[33] In one of his lectures in Buenos Aires in 1929 he described the roof of an imaginary modern house with a garden

> full of flowers, of ivy, of arbor vitae, of Chinese laurels, of okubas, of spindle-tress, of lilacs, of fruit trees [and where] covered shelters allow a siesta in hammocks. A solarium brings health. In the evening we dance to a gramophone. The air is clean, noise is smothered, views are distant, the street is far away. If there are trees nearby, you are above the tops. The sky sparkles with stars.[34]

He also argued that in a hot climate the roof garden was the best practical way of protecting the flat roof surface from cracking up in the heat.[35]

Modified and neglected now, the MES gardens were designed by Roberto Burle Marx, and were an integral part of the original design. At street level a series of irregularly shaped beds break up the plaza and spread in under the building, so that the *pilotis* rise up from the vegetation like smooth pink tree trunks. On the top of the main block the gardens are contained within deep-sided concrete forms – like architectural planters – which complement the larger shapes protecting the lift housings and services. On the roof of the two-storey exhibition hall, the rooftop garden is accessible only to the Minister and his immediate staff, whose offices it adjoins, but those working in the offices above could at least look down on this pleasant island of green below them. When the building was still new, but the gardens were well established, the effect greatly impressed the Brazilian correspondent of the *Architectural Review* in 1947:

> As for the roof garden of the Ministerio, it has now grown so high that, looking up at the building from below, you have the mysterious feeling of some jungle rising fantastically into the sky and bringing the rainclouds down to the level of the two blue funnels which enclose the lift shafts and the water cisterns of what is still the most beautiful skyscraper in Rio.[36]

The origins of modernism in Brazil

The MES building did not occur in a vacuum. The first co-ordinated response to the modern movements of Europe was the Week of Modern Art in São Paulo in 1922, and although the architectural contributions tended towards the neocolonial style favoured, as we have seen, elsewhere in Latin America during the 1920s, the event served to stimulate debate about the relationship between Brazilian culture and that of Europe. In 1924 this was articulated by Mário de Andrade, a leading member of the São Paulo avant-garde, in the Pau–Brazil poetry manifesto, which was an appeal for an authentically Brazilian form of modernism, one that could mix both superstition and rationality, 'medicine men and military airfields', 'the jungle and the school'.[37] In architecture, however, the first moves were not overtly Brazilian.[38] In the mid 1920s, as with O'Gorman and others in Mexico, modern architecture was embraced in Brazil in its 'pure' form, as a style-less style, and there was an influential group of young artists who had understood the theory and learnt the rules of functionalist building. Commentators identify the MES building as the moment when, with Le Corbusier's encouragement, they began to vary those rules.

Warchavchik

The foundations for Brazil's school of modern architecture were laid in 1925, when a young Russian émigré, Gregori Warchavchik, published a call for a new architecture, first in Italian in São Paulo and then in Portuguese in Rio de Janeiro.[39] Warchavchik's piece has the tone of a manifesto, ending with the declaration 'Down with absurd decoration and up with logical construction!', and it borrows freely from contemporary European theory, especially Le Corbusier and Futurism.[40] Much of it is close to ideas voiced by the Mexican modernists at the time. It calls for an aesthetic appropriate to the machine age, for the architect to eschew irrational ornament, to be an 'engineer-builder', not an 'architect-decorator', and to embrace modern materials, especially reinforced concrete, in the interests of economy and, through its purity and honesty, of beauty. Warchavchik differs from the Futurists in that he does not deny the past, arguing instead that modern architecture can learn from it, but like Le Corbusier he calls for a style-less style which will be true to its age.

In 1928 Warchavchik saw modern architecture as the solution to social housing on a large scale. In terms similar to those used by O'Gorman at about the same time, he argued that the ideal for modern architects, as for sociologists and urbanists, was to find a way of providing housing of 'maximum comfort for minimum cost', especially for 'the least favoured classes'. 'When industry is capable of supplying, without interruption and at low cost, the right sort of materials to architects, then they will achieve extraordinary results.' All that architects want is to be able to provide 'plenty of air, plenty of light, plenty of hygiene and a little simple elegance and very good taste to the inhabitant of each house'.[41] Warchavchik does not see palaces as important – 'the landowners have always had them and will continue to have them' – but in the twentieth century, he argues, everyone has the right to a house, to comfort and to hygiene.[42]

Warchavchik was an energetic self-publicist,[43] and between 1927 and 1934 he proceeded to build a series of houses in what he called the 'new' architecture, to distinguish it from 'modern' – by which, he said, people meant no more than a house with electricity and a bath.[44] The first of these houses, in Vila Mariana in São Paulo, was a remarkable piece of propagandistic subterfuge.[45] From the street the house has the appearance of a very symmetrical cubic design with flat white walls and simple, metal-framed windows. In order to get the plans accepted by the São Paulo city authorities the drawings Warchavchik submitted included traditional architectural mouldings around the door and windows, and a cornice across the top of the façade. When he built the house he included none of these, on the grounds that he had run out of money, leaving the house officially unfinished but in fact strikingly modern in appearance. The other problem he had to tackle was that the materials so celebrated by contemporary theorists as the rational answer to cheap, standardized housing were not yet available in São Paulo, so that although the house has every appearance of being constructed out of reinforced concrete, it is in fact of brick faced up with a cement render, and with a raised façade to hide the sloping tiled roofs behind. And so, by default, the first modern house in Brazil is also thoroughly traditional, thoroughly Brazilian, in its construction.

The other very important feature of this and Warchavchik's subsequent modern houses is the use of local Brazilian plants to offset the plain white walls. Warchavchik's wife, the landscape architect Mina Klabin, was responsible for designing the gardens and, presumably, for influencing Warchavchik's views on this issue.[46] The question of native plants as a potentially important element in the urban environment had first been recognized by Rino Levi in 1925:

> Because of our climate, because of our nature and customs, our cities ought to have a different character from those of Europe. I believe that our rich vegetation, and all our incomparable natural beauties can and must suggest to our artists something original – to give to our cities a touch of liveliness and colour unique in the world.[47]

Warchavchik himself said something similar the following year in an interview published in a periodical produced by the literary avant-garde who had been behind the Week of Modern Art in São Paulo. Here he argued that there were

Gregori Warchavchik, the architect's house, Rua Santa Cruz, Vila Mariana, São Paulo, 1927–28 (photograph c. 1930).

many reasons for adopting an ornament-free architecture, one of which was that the native flora provided an alternative to plaster mouldings. 'It is a shame that up to now no one of taste has thought of this splendid element, despite the inexaustible variety of climbers and shrubs, indigenous and foreign, which grow in the gardens of São Paulo', he said, and remarked how much it would benefit the city if the hideous and expensive façades of the houses on Avenida Paulista were covered with vegetation.[48]

The use of plants in Warchavchik's modern houses impressed Mário de Andrade, who enthused about his first house in the São Paulo *Diário Nacional* in June 1928. He admired the way true architectural beauty lay in the play of light on surfaces and volumes, and the effect of the plants: 'the smooth, flat dog-grass framed by cactus and palms is of a splendid originality, and gives to the whole a strong note of tropicalism and discipline'.[49] Andrade, in fact, sees architecture as the most advanced, the most modern of the arts, the most universal and most anonymous of artistic languages, and in this anonymity he sees a parallel with popular or traditional culture. This, he feels, will change to reflect the individual and race to whom it belongs, and he argues that it will be important in Brazil to try to prevent modern architecture degrading into arbitrary individualism by searching for genuinely Brazilian characteristics, the constant elements in Brazilian architecture.[50] Andrade, from his first exposure to modern architecture, is therefore predisposed to find ways in which it could be 'cannibalized' to become authentically Brazilian. Visitors to Warchavchik's Modernist House were alerted to this feature by the promotional leaflet accompanying the exhibition, in which the artist Anísio Teixeira discussed the way in which it was

> a work of collaboration with the new world. In this land we are all foreigners, it is simply a question of turning back time. Therefore the work of the son of a Portuguese will be just as Brazilian as of a Pole or an Italian or a Japanese. Warchavchik is Russian, and never have I had a stronger impression of a Brazilian house than when, with my modern, free spirit as the son of America, I visited his home with its strong clear lines, constructed completely in cement, iron and glass, within a frame of gigantic national cacti.[51]

During his first visit to Brazil, in 1929, Le Corbusier lectured in São Paulo and Rio de Janeiro, suggesting grand schemes to deal with their respective urban problems. In São Paulo he met Warchavchik, saw his work and was very impressed to find that the most up-to-date European ideas were being so intelligently developed in Brazil. Accordingly he invited him to represent South America on the committee of the recently formed CIAM. Warchavchik does not play a prominent part in the subsequent development of modernist architecture in Brazil.

One later incident, however, is interesting. In 1945 Warchavchik welcomed Richard Neutra to Brazil, then collaborated with him on a book of essays published in São Paulo in 1948 in a bilingual edition.[52] Neutra, who had worked for the US government building schools in California and Puerto Rico, was sent to Brazil by the US State Department to tell the Brazilians how to build cheaply and efficiently.[53] Unless his introduction is thoroughly disingenuous, Warchavchik was very impressed. He already knew of Neutra's work, but he found the man to be a 'deeply agreeable human being, irradiating his specific kind of sympathy, unselfishly helpful' – although, to judge from the book, Neutra was completely ignorant of Brazil, and of Brazil's previous architectural achievements. Other foreigners who descended on Brazil were often equally insensitive or unaware, but at least people like Le Corbusier or Lévi-Strauss were inspired by what they saw, and developed their own ideas as a result. Neutra, who came to advise on how to build schools and medical centres efficiently in rural areas, was a passionate believer in the universal benefits of technology and of capitalism: 'A modern technological civilization calls for [the] vigorous spread of consumership.' Architects must encourage this, because their job depends on it:

> Everything the modern architect depends on, from window operating hardware, applied finish material, bathroom fixtures, to any material and elements of sensible prefabrication; all of it comes into commercial existence only by substantial demand and cannot be developed without mass consumption.[54]

This involves 'a guerrilla warfare against backwardness',[55] combined with a total disregard for any existing social organization or culture among those whose lives he aims to improve, and a moral purpose very close to that of sixteenth-century missionaries. So, for example, girls should be taught some basic principles of home-making, and encouraged to create a pleasant domestic environment. To this end they should be taught to plant 'a few quick-growing tropical shrubs and perennials about the entrance and in the rear of the most modest dwelling', just as they should be taught how to make a bed and lay the table.[56] On the delicate question of rehousing the inhabitants of slums in more salubrious modern accommodation, he recognizes that this needs to be done with tact and gentleness, because it always causes 'psychological friction':

> [Slums are] highly reflective and re-influential; they condition the human mind in its plastic stage of infancy. Sometimes, of course, mentally powerful individuals might intensely react and make their personal escape, but slum dwellers at large are helpless like drug addicts, only often more innocent of their condition.[57]

Perhaps this sort of narrow, authoritarian view of the social benefits of modernity and modern architecture was shared by Warchavchik. In any case, his own output was largely in a very different direction; he was not involved in the MES building, nor was he to have anything to do with Brasília. In fact he received little government sponsorship, and spent most of his life producing houses for the rich. Bruand suggests that his architectural style became increasingly rigid as the technology caught up with his ambitions; perhaps this was matched by a parallel theoretical sterility.

Lúcio Costa's architectural theory

Lúcio Costa attended Le Corbusier's lecture in Rio in 1929, but – at least according to one account – he left before the end, unimpressed by Le Corbusier's self-importance and crazy schemes.[58] Up to this time Costa's architectural interests lay in a neocolonial direction. In 1930 – partly, no doubt, as a result of Le Corbusier's visit – he abruptly changed his mind. When President Getúlio Vargas (1930–45) first came to power, his various liberalizing measures included the reform of the Escola Nacional de Belas Artes (ENBA). Costa was appointed Director in place of his old mentor, the arch-conservative José Mariano Filho, and invited Warchavchik to join the teaching staff. Warchavchik has been credited with converting Costa into a modernist,[59] but the conversion was probably due to a combination of circumstances, not least his own intellectual openness to change. During his brief tenure as Director, before he was sacked following a revolt by the old guard among the professoriate, Costa persuaded a whole generation of young architects of the benefits of modern architecture. Sometime in 1930 he wrote an essay, *Arguments for a New Architecture*, which – although it was not published until 1936 – reads as if it originated as a public lecture, probably at the ENBA.[60] It makes a measured, eloquent case for change.

Costa avoids the polemical language of the machine aesthetic used by Warchavchik, and uses instead an argument based on history, on classical architectural theory and on aesthetic principles. Just as the architecture of the Greeks and Romans, and from the Renaissance to the eighteenth century, was determined by technology and material constraints, so too, he argues, must be the new architecture if it is to be true and honest. The nineteenth century had brought great changes, new materials and techniques, but a loss of aesthetic direction. Industrial production of decorative elements had replaced the traditional craftsman, opening the door to endlessly meaningless eclecticism. He singles out the USA for special criticism for its resistance to making the technological means of construction visible: 'As a respectful tribute to Art they religiously cover the purest structures in the world, from top to bottom with all the detritus from the past.'[61] In less Le Corbusian language than Warchavchik, he argues that architecture should be an art of construction, not an art of ornamentation, and that beauty will result from the satisfactory solution of technical problems; in concentrating on the fundamental questions of volume and space, architects will be able to raise architecture to a level of pure art never achieved before. To do so they can learn from the lessons of the past to create buildings of symmetry and harmony. Costa argues that this new architecture is a genuine style because it is applied to buildings of all types – from palaces to factories – but instead of making this into a democratic principle, he compares this 'style' with the widespread use of neoclassicism in all sorts of different buildings in the eighteenth and nineteenth centuries, in

Berlin, London, Washington and Buenos Aires. In fact, unlike so much of the rhetoric of modern architectural treatises and manifestoes, this is a defence of modernism predominantly on aesthetic and moral, not social, grounds. Costa does not use arguments about the economy of standardization or the possibilities it offers for providing decent cheap housing.

Costa regards the integration of architecture with the other arts as something only rarely achieved, and only briefly sustained. History suggests that painting and sculpture will tend once again to separate themselves from architecture, murals giving way to canvases and relief sculpture to sculpture in the round. Contemporary architecture does offer new possibilities, however, and the large areas of wall lend themselves to 'painterly expansion' and shallow relief sculpture – not, he stresses, in any regional or limited sense of ornament, but as a contribution to the overall purity of plastic expression. He implies that only very restrained, predominantly abstract works of art can blend with and contribute to the overall effect of the architecture.

The most Le Corbusian section of the *Arguments for a New Architecture* is Costa's discussion of the changing role of the wall.[62] The new architecture arose because the new technology made redundant the traditional function of the wall as the structural load-bearer in a building. With the use of an independent frame of steel or reinforced concrete, the wall can be light and positioned according to functional and aesthetic, not technical, criteria. This allows – following Le Corbusier – for the free plan and the free façade, and for walls entirely of glass. Costa is surely addressing a commonly voiced middle-class anxiety when he points out that this does not mean that *all* walls will be of glass: certain small rooms will have solid walls, so that dignity can be maintained. This sort of remark has the ring of live delivery, and suggests an audience of genteel doubters whom he is trying to persuade, rather than an eager band of student acolytes. Costa's *Arguments* make no reference to Brazil or to regionalism, but they do allow, as does Warchavchik, for the past to play a role in the architecture of the future. For Costa, the new architecture is a direct descendant of the Mediterranean architecture of Greece and Rome, and the Italian Renaissance: 'The forms vary but the spirit is still the same, and the same fundamental laws remain.'[63]

For Costa and his immediate circle in Rio, the early 1930s were a period of great architectural ferment. During his time at the ENBA, Warchavchik had attracted commissions for work in Rio, and in 1931, in order to complete these while commuting between this city and São Paulo, he and Costa established their own construction company. The buildings they produced are entirely in line with Warchavchik's work in São Paulo, suggesting that it was he who was the designer.[64] Costa certainly would have learnt much from the collaboration; he talks about how this was, for him, a time of intense immersion in the principles of modernism.[65]

Burle Marx and the modern Brazilian garden

Another figure who was later to play a central role in the evolution of Brazilian modern architecture was Roberto Burle Marx. Burle Marx is best known as a landscape gardener, and for that reason he has been categorized in recent years as apart from other aesthetic developments. During the mid twentieth century's enthusiasm for Latin American and especially Brazilian architecture, however, he was always incorporated, and treated on an equal footing, as an architect of landscape alongside other types of architecture. Even in Brazil his contribution to the evolution not just of architecture but of the visual arts has been ignored recently.[66] But Burle Marx was much more than a gardener: like Warchavchik, and especially Costa, he was a man of immense erudition, educated in Europe, multilingual, someone who respected the past but believed in the future. His output included not only gardens but also numerous murals, weavings, paintings, sculpture, furniture and architecture. He became friendly with Costa in the early 1930s, after his return from Europe, and one of his first commissions was from the Warchavchik–Costa construction company for the gardens of one of their new-style cubic houses in Copacabana, the house for Alfredo Schwarz (1932). Burle Marx would have known of Mina Klabin's contributions to Warchavchik's houses in São Paulo, and he designed a garden with raised concrete beds in simple geometric shapes, planted with native species, which – as with Klabin's work – complemented the smooth spare surfaces of the building.

In 1934 Burle Marx took a three-year appointment in Recife, with responsibility for refurbishing the city's various nineteenth-century parks and gardens. His significance was that unlike so many of his contemporaries – Costa included – who saw the relationship between Man and Nature in Euro-Christian terms, as a battle between opposing forces, with Man the conqueror who domesticates Nature, and submits her to his will, Burle Marx welcomed Nature as a friend. In this he is much closer to Native American beliefs, as well as being a genuine modernist, welcoming the Other as a source of subversion and revitalization. Here he is closer to the avant-garde intellectuals of São Paulo than to the modern-leaning architects. His position is that of the poet Mário de Andrade, who argued for the importance of accepting Brazil's many contradictions: the competing demands of modernization and tradition, of rationalism and superstition.

Burle Marx recognized that it was ridiculous to try to construct gardens in Brazil in the European manner, with mown lawns and neatly ordered shrubs: this would mean negating both Brazil's climate and its flora, as well as ignoring the degree to which the country as a whole was undomesticated, not 'civilized' in the snobbish Eurocentric way in which the wealthy urban elites wished it to be. In Recife, therefore, although he had little control over the general layout of the gardens, he introduced native Brazilian plants wherever possible. In particular he created a garden planted with the cacti typical of the local desert scrub, the *caatinga*. This distinctive arid landscape and the consequent poverty of the inhabitants had been publicized through novels such as Euclides Da Cunha's *Os sertões* (1904), so Burle Marx's *caatinga* garden had a deliberate political resonance. In subsequent work in Rio de Janeiro, where the climate is very different – the tropical vegetation threatens to invade at any moment; the city is always in danger of being swallowed up by the jungle – the deliberate

Roberto Burle Marx, roof garden of Exhibition Wing, MES building, Rio de Janeiro, 1938 (photograph c. 1950).

introduction of the enemy, in the form of exuberant tropical plants, into the midst of the city was deeply subversive.

From the time of the MES building, the success of Costa and the rest in Rio has been seen as due to their flexibility, their inventiveness and their deliberate adaptation of the imported modernist models to match their own circumstances and requirements. In this, I believe Burle Marx's contribution was of crucial importance. In 1938 Costa invited him to join the design team working on the MES building. He had three areas to work on: the street-level plaza, the roof of the second-storey exhibition hall, and the roof of the main sixteen-storey block. His solution for each was different, but all drew on the imagery of the landscape of Brazil's tropical wetlands. Le Corbusier had flown over such terrain in 1929, and referred to it repeatedly in the book of essays he produced in 1930 after his South American trip. He saw the sinuous water-courses and rampant vegetation with a mixture of horror and fascination typical of the foreign traveller. From the way the river would periodically break its banks and cut off a loop to create a stagnant oxbow lake he derived the 'Theorem of the Meander', a metaphor to illustrate the way innovation could be achieved when the human brain cut through all the convolutions of existing ideas to come up with a clear new route.[67] He repeatedly identified the wetland meanders with the irrational and the outmoded, an image of untamed nature in opposition to human rationality, geometry and modernity.

Burle Marx, in an inspired gesture of cultural independence from European norms, took the forms of this untamed landscape and brought them into the heart of Rio, incorporating them into the MES building, the very building which was designed to modernize standards of education and health care for the Brazilian people. The plaza is laid out like a river; the informal beds have undulating, liquid contours like small islands in shallow water, and where these penetrate under the building the *pilotis* rise up from the lower vegetation like gigantic tree trunks. On the roof of the main block, raised beds similarly project into the pedestrian terrace like occasional, irregular promontories along a river bank, while the roof of the exhibition wing is the most explicit in its riverine iconography. Seen from above, the path is exactly like a river that meanders unchecked, carving out bays and creating headlands as it goes. These beds were planted with tropical plants native to Brazil and, as in the quotation from Claude Vincent included above, made a major contribution to the effectiveness of the building. From the MES building on, the use of gardens became a mark of Brazilian architecture, a way of combining Costa's ideas of 'pure art' – pure, abstract beauty of volumes and planes, light and shade, created by the rational application of modern technology – with the irrational exuberance of nature. Burle Marx's gardens combine the potentially sterile with the infinitely fertile, order with chaos, international modernism with an unmistakably Brazilian reality – the 'jungle and the school', as Mário de Andrade had argued in 1924.

Burle Marx's work is also closely related to painting. He worked out his designs first as two-dimensional drawings, blocking out areas in strong, flat, often primary colours, before transforming them into three-dimensional gardens. Despite the vegetation they remain very abstract, and closely related in form and intention, although not in scale, to the floating forms of Hans Arp in the early 1930s. Costa also commented on the abstract nature of his work in 1951, in relation to the recent successes of Brazilian architecture,

> [which has been enriched] by the landscape contribution of the painter Roberto Burle Marx, who knew how to renew the art of gardening, introducing into it the conception, the choice and design, the principles of erudite plastic composition in an abstract sense.[68]

A British architect resident in Rio in 1954 recognized his 'considerable influence' on the other arts, especially architecture.[69]

Burle Marx's subsequent work included gardens for schools and hospitals, for government housing projects, for private owners and businesses, and for public parks. He has built gardens all around the world, but is perhaps best known for his designs for the gardens along the Rio waterfront, which provide a

Copacabana beachfront, Rio de Janeiro, pavements and planting by Burle Marx, 1970 (photograph c. 1975).

public space which serves to unite the city and its citizens with the beaches, the sea and the spectacular landscape behind. Miles of public space – sometimes little more than a decorative strip of mosaic pavement, sometimes a park with benches and ponds and statuary among the flowering plants and shrubs, sometimes more like a semi-wild area of woodland where birds can flourish in relative peace – Burle Marx's gardens are Brazil's finest contribution to the concept of plastic integration in Latin America, where gardens that are both aesthetic abstractions and untamed or barely controlled areas of wilderness bring life to modern architecture, saving it from itself. In the words of José Lins do Rego:

> Le Corbusier was … the point of departure that enabled the new school of Brazilian architecture to express itself with great spontaneity, and arrive at original solutions. Like the music of Villa Lobos, the expressive force of a Lúcio Costa and a Niemeyer was a creation intrinsically ours, something which sprang out of our own life. The return to nature, and the value which came to be given to landscape as a substantial element, saved our architects from what could be considered formal in Le Corbusier.[70]

This is not so much a case of integration in the aesthetic sense of blurring the distinctions between painting, sculpture and architecture as integration in a more ideological sense: integrating modernism into a Brazilian context.

During his long career, Burle Marx was so successful, and created so many gardens, that his designs have lost their power to shock; the subversive radicalism his work represented in the 1930s and 1940s has been forgotten. Burle Marx has come, like Barragán, to represent the acceptable face of Latin American modernism, as testified by aestheticizing exhibitions of their work in the Museum of Modern Art in New York.[71] He would not have wanted it this way: as a lifelong socialist he saw his gardens as playing a real social role. 'A garden must have didactic qualities,' he said in interview in 1977. 'From a garden one can teach many lessons, and encourage people to live better.'[72] In 1952 José Lins do Rego saw the importance of the landscape gardening movement Burle Marx had initiated:

The penetration of the *caatinga*, the Amazonian forests, the mountains of Minas Gerais, or the gaucho pampa into the heart of the city, even onto the skyscrapers, would help modern man to become more human, to belong to his land, to be more than a simple machine for living.... Man and house, man and forest, man and animal no longer confront one another like enemies, defending themselves from each other.... Europeans, who are fearful of the jungle, imagine that everything in it is dangerous. The Brazilian, who has conquered it, still retains elements of bitterness in relation to it, but this terrible resentment is disappearing.... Man and the landscape are not enemies any longer.... They used to say, when the city of Rio de Janeiro began to adopt European habits, that 'Rio is becoming civilized'. But that which is done in opposition to the landscape, which is what constitutes all our originality, that was not civilized. Our own civilization will perhaps be found in precisely that which we disparage.[73]

The evolution of modern architecture in Rio

The MES building was one of a series of major architectural projects in Rio in the later 1930s, designed as a part of the broader modernization programme of Getúlio Vargas's Estado Nôvo government, which from 1937 sought to unite the country around a strong central government, to promote industry, to improve communications and to boost national pride. Le Corbusier's 1936 visit and the debates surrounding the MES building served to validate the modern style. In 1937 competitions were held for two important adjoining transport facilities, the Seaplane Station and the National Airport, both named after Brazil's famous pioneer aviator Alberto Santos Dumont, and it is no coincidence that both the winning designs were for modern buildings: modern buildings for modern transport systems. Le Corbusier himself had commented in his lectures in Rio in 1936 that the French urbanist Agache, who had been working on Rio's city plan between 1927 and 1930, had recommended the future airport site as suitable for a new capitol for Rio; others wanted to put an airport there, and Le Corbusier strongly endorsed this, arguing that an airport belonged to the future, while a capitol represented the past.[74]

The Seaplane Station

The Seaplane Station by Attílio Corrêa Lima (1901–43) received the international flying boats, and was therefore given priority over the national airport. Completed in 1938, it is a clearly legible, compact design. The building economically combines all the necessary elements: baggage areas, Customs, administration, airline counter, restaurant and offices, and a spacious central waiting hall supplemented by a tropical garden complete with an aviary of tropical birds. It makes good use of the possibilities of reinforced concrete to open up the two opposite sides almost entirely to glass, allowing a view through at both ground- and first-floor levels. The two levels are linked by an elegant spiral staircase supported only on a single pillar, giving the upper storey a great sense of airy lightness, entirely appropriate to the function of the building (Plate 24). It is functional and modern but, as in the MES building, the reinforced concrete structure is clothed in stone, in this case yellow travertine from Argentina. This was Attílio Corrêa's only major work. He was killed in an air crash just offshore from the Seaplane Station in 1943; the history of Brazilian modern architecture might have been different had he lived.

Santos Dumont Airport

The national Santos Dumont Airport, although it was begun at the same time as the Seaplane Station, was completed only in 1944. It was designed by the Roberto brothers, Marcelo and Milton, and provides a gateway to the city just as, in a very different language, Agache's designs for a capitol would have done. The long horizontal block nicely illustrates Costa's argument that modern Brazilian architecture is a development of Mediterranean classicism, tracing its origins back, via the Italian Renaissance, to Roman and Greek antiquity. Its design is dominated by the full-height *pilotis* which encircle the building like the peristyle of columns around a temple, while on the interior they are used to create a high, open central space rather like a basilica (Plate 25). Just as in the nineteenth century people compared the arching iron structures of railway stations to cathedrals, so Santos Dumont Airport is the twentieth-century reinforced concrete equivalent. At the main, off-centre axis of the building the architecture allows for views right through – out to the runway, the aeroplanes and the sea on one side, and in the opposite direction, via a landscaped park by Burle Marx, to the city and (not coincidentally) towards the nascent MES building and the other new blocks of the city centre growing up around it. It is altogether a wonderfully spacious, light and calm sort of space, permeable and welcoming.[75]

Obra do Berço

Niemeyer's first solo architectural composition is another mark of the Brazilian government's acceptance of modern architecture as its public face. The Obra do Berço (1937) was in itself a new concept: a maternity clinic that provided social and medical support for working-class women and their babies, including pre- and postnatal consultations and advice, free milk, day-nursery facilities, a sewing room, a restaurant and a lecture hall. As Papadaki put it, 'this building with its bare contours satisfactorily reflects the modest financial means of the institution and the desire to obtain a friendly, anti-institutional atmosphere'.[76] It is very compact, very functional, and very much conditioned by the climate: it makes good use of open-air spaces both covered and open, and the main west-facing façade is protected – and enlivened – by movable *brise-soleils*. As first built these were rigid, but Niemeyer realized that they were not providing the necessary protection, and it is an interesting reflection on his determination to get it right that he replaced them with movable louvres at his own expense.

Brazil Pavilion, New York World's Fair

The most important building of the 1930s from the point of view of the international reputation of Brazilian architecture, however, was the Brazil Pavilion at the New York World's Fair in 1939. This was designed by Lúcio

Lúcio Costa and Oscar Niemeyer, Brazil pavilion, New York World's Fair 1939.

Costa and Oscar Niemeyer, with help from Paul Lester Wiener, whom we shall meet again in Brazil, where he worked on the Cidade dos Motores in 1943. The theme of the Fair was 'Tomorrow's World', and the Brazilian authorities organized a competition for a design for a building that would satisfy two criteria: it should be distinctively Brazilian, and it should fulfil its function as an exhibition space.[77] In the event, Costa was awarded first prize for a design that the jury considered met the first of these, and Niemeyer came second with his less Brazilian but more economical, practical proposal. Costa, with customary altruism, suggested they should collaborate on the project, and they ended up with a building which is different from either submission but draws on both, a building which is a very clear statement about Brazil as a country of the future. 'There were a number of excellent modern buildings at the Fair, but none was more light-heartedly elegant than the Brazilian Pavilion', wrote Goodwin, who placed it at the end of the Brazil Builds catalogue (1943) as a sort of herald of the future.[78]

The design shares a number of features with the Spanish Pavilion at the Paris World's Fair of two years earlier, by José Luis Sert and Luis Lacasa.[79] On a general level both have an open, welcoming, asymmetrical plan and a fluid treatment of space, especially the use of transitional areas that are neither inside nor out – covered patios, balconies and terraces; more specific similarities include the importance of trees in the architectural design, and the use of curving ramps giving direct access to an upper floor. Both stand out, and were deliberately designed to stand out, from the other buildings around by their wholehearted enthusiasm for modern materials and a modern aesthetic. Instead of an open-air auditorium, the Brazilian pavilion had a tropical garden in the internal court, complete with an orchid house, an aquarium and a snake pit, and a sinuous pool with huge, distinctive *Victoria Amazônica* waterlilies, a deliberate marketing of the touristic image of Brazil.

Niemeyer and Kubitschek at Pampulha

Meanwhile, Oscar Niemeyer was gaining experience. In 1940, in a partnership that prepared the ground for a later collaboration on Brasília, he began working with the mayor of Belo Horizonte, Juscelino Kubitschek, on a series of public buildings for a new development just outside the city. The garden designer was Roberto Burle Marx. Pampulha was intended as an elite urbanization around an artificial lake, and Kubitschek's carrot to encourage the *nouveaux riches* to buy plots and build in the area was to provide a Casino, a Dance Hall, a Yacht Club and a church on the lakeside, all in the most up-to-date architectural taste. This is a good example of the way modern architecture was seen

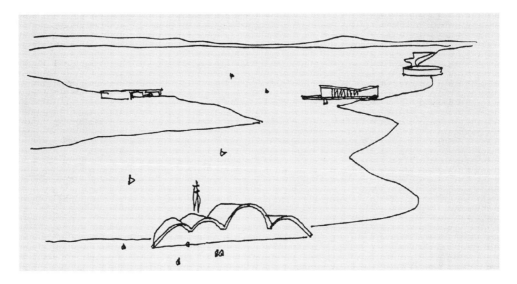

Oscar Niemeyer, sketch of lakeside development, Pampulha, Belo Horizonte, 1942, showing, clockwise from bottom, São Francisco, Casino, Casa do Baile (Dance Hall), Yacht Club.

as a way of promoting a region. Kubitschek wanted to provide entertainment in elegant surroundings to encourage the development of high-quality private housing, preferably in a similarly modern style. To this end he also commissioned Niemeyer to build him a country house at Pampulha – a simple villa with a shallow M-shaped profile produced by the two trapezoidal volumes that come together in the centre. The Pampulha buildings mark the point at which what David Underwood calls Niemeyer's 'free-form modernism' really comes into its own. In each case the design is explicitly related to function; the architectural forms are a metaphor for the activities they are intended to contain.

The Casino, the centrepiece, is raised on a slight promontory overlooking the lake, and contrasts the relatively static cube of the main block of the gaming room with the sweeping ellipse that encloses the dining room, stage

Oscar Niemeyer, Pampulha, Belo Horizonte, Casa do Baile (Dance Hall), 1942 (photograph c. 1945).

and central dance floor. The Casino, by definition, was aimed at those with money to spare; the 'Casa do Baile', House of Dance, on a small island on the opposite side of the lake, was intended to be a more popular dance hall and restaurant – a gesture, as Underwood puts it, to the working classes.[80] There is a smooth transition between interior and exterior space: the circular restaurant and dance hall are linked by a sinuous concrete canopy, balanced apparently precariously on single thin columns, to a smaller stage and dance area at the other end of the island. The House of Dance is shaped, in effect, like an undulating group of *sambistas*, echoing the outline of the island itself. The Yacht Club is not yacht-shaped (this would have been too close to the Deco enthusiasm for nautical imagery, and so not modern enough), but the balcony projects out over the water like a pier, and the zigzag roof line has been compared to sails. These are all explicitly playful, hedonistic buildings that

Oscar Niemeyer, Pampulha, Belo Horizonte,
São Francisco, 1942 (photograph c. 1945).

make full use of the possibilities for new and imaginative forms offered by
new technology; they are generously glazed to provide views of the lake shore
and surrounding hills, and include inviting and varied public spaces for dancing, flirting, drinking and gambling.

The evolution of Niemeyer's curvaceous 'free-form modernism' at Pampulha
surely owes something to Burle Marx's distinctive garden designs. At the time
they were both involved in the ongoing construction of the MES building,
where Burle Marx's designs are a deliberate counterpoint to the architecture.
Their work at Pampulha is very different, and suggests close collaboration to
produce this exceptionally intimate formal relationship between the gardens,
the architectural forms, and the lake and the wider landscape setting. In fact,
at Pampulha the distinction between architecture and garden becomes very
blurred in designs which involve paths, patios and covered walkways as features

of central importance; the functions of the buildings, too – relaxation and entertainment – encouraged the development of forms where the climate and the setting could contribute to the enjoyment. A decade later, in Batista's Cuba, Max Borges developed the idea of combining nature and architecture to pleasurable ends even further. In his Tropicana Night Club in Havana, the trees and plants invade the indefinite architectural spaces just as the cabaret dancers periodically invade the audience.

Niemeyer's fourth building at Pampulha is the church of São Francisco. Here he transforms the idea of sheets of flat concrete, which he had used to create the horizontal canopies at the Casa do Baile and over the entrance to the Casino, into a single parabolic curve to create the nave. This tunnel-like vault narrows towards the high altar, which slots inside a wider and higher-curving vault to create the chancel. The elements – vaults, nave, chancel and choir over the entrance opposite the altar – are entirely orthodox; the handling is entirely new. The inverted obelisk of the bell-tower reinforces the message that modern materials can defy conventional notions of architectural decorum. São Francisco also disturbs expectations in terms of orientation. It does not face the street or square, as would a conventional church, but across the lake. Traditionally the church façade is decorated, as in the west end of Gothic cathedrals, but here the façade faces east, and the back, west, street-facing wall is the decorated part: a series of scenes from the life of St Francis in blue and white *azulejos* by Cândido Portinari. At the same time the church is in sharp contrast to the other buildings at Pampulha: it is very gently lit by discreet sources, not by large picture windows; the space is not free-flowing but strictly disciplined, with attention focused on the high altar; and it is securely grounded like a traditional church, in contrast to the other buildings, which dance along on *pilotis* or reach out over the water. Nevertheless São Francisco was too radical for the Catholic Church, and has never been consecrated.

These buildings were all completed by 1944, but despite Niemeyer's extravagant architecture and Kubitschek's enthusiasm, the scheme failed to take off. The elite did not buy plots and build houses as quickly as expected; in

1946 a law was passed prohibiting gambling, which rendered the Casino obsolete; and the lake was found to be infested with parasites, and so unsuitable for water sports. More recently, Underwood reports that failure to invest in adequate sewerage facilities also means that the lake is now heavily polluted.[81] Pampulha was built on the myth that public money would pump-prime investment, which would in turn produce a middle-class utopia, but at least the architecture remains interesting, even if the social dimension of the project was not a success.

During the 1940s and early 1950s Niemeyer accepted commissions for all manner of buildings: hotels, houses, office and apartment blocks; hospitals, theatres, schools, museums and commercial premises. This was a period of expansive creativity, not all of it entirely successful. Niemeyer has come to exemplify modern Brazilian architecture. He has inspired a succession of monographs on his work.[82] He also exemplifies the contradictions inherent in architectural production, especially in a country like Brazil: the political and economic factors on which all architectural commissions depend, but which become more important and potentially more intrusive the larger the project concerned. Niemeyer joined the Communist Party in 1945 and has been, on occasion, very outspoken in his political views. On the other hand he has never let his politics stand in the way of a good commission, trying to find ways of challenging the status quo in the process. The church at Pampulha, for example, includes no confessional, as if he was unrepentant about the pleasures which the other buildings around the lake were designed to encourage:

> I have done very few projects of a social nature, and I must admit that whenever I do one, I feel like I'm conniving with the demagogic and paternalistic objective they stand for, fooling the working class that demands higher wages and the advantage of having better opportunities.… On the other hand, I never felt afraid of monumentality when the theme in itself demanded it. After all, what remained of architecture over the ages were the monumental works, those that represent the evolution of techniques – those which, fair or unfair from the social point of view, still manage to move us. Beauty imposes itself on the sensibility of men.[83]

Social housing in Rio de Janeiro

One reason why Niemeyer has undertaken few projects of a social nature is not just that he feels uncomfortable with them; it is also that Brazil has not commissioned very many. While in Mexico the government invested heavily in social housing, as did the Banco Obrero in Venezuela on the government's behalf, in Brazil there has been relatively little serious interest in solving the housing problem created by the enormously expanding urban populations. This was not an easy problem to solve, of course. In 1943 Philip Goodwin believed that progress was being made, but acknowledged that the new housing was not always welcomed:

> Rio has little flat or even rolling land near the center. If the people who perch in the huts on the adjoining mountainsides are to be moved, where can they go except for out on the dismal flat ground up the bay? They would prefer to hang by their teeth over the gay lights and lovely views of the city.[84]

Le Corbusier, too, had recognized the attractions of the vertiginous *favelas*. He took no notice of the 'important Brazilian personages' who were angry with him for climbing up into the *favelas* inhabited by black Brazilians to see the slums they, as 'civilized persons', were so ashamed of:

> I explained serenely that I found these blacks basically *good*: good-hearted. Then, beautiful, magnificent. Then, their carelessness, the limits they had learned to impose on their needs, their capacity for dreaming, their candidness resulted in their houses being always admirably sited, the windows opening astonishingly on magnificent spaces, the smallness of their rooms largely adequate.[85]

The resistance to forced slum clearances in Rio dates back to the beginning of the twentieth century, when the Avenida Central (now Avendia Rio Branco) was opened through in an effort to 'civilize' the city along the lines of Paris, Barcelona and, closer to home, Buenos Aires. As Teresa Meade's research has shown, to do this, and to enable the clearance and subsequent reconstruction of the central area, public health campaigns were used to justify the destruction of slum properties and relocation of the inhabitants.[86] By the 1930s and 1940s, while the slums were still seen as ripe for development, there was a broad consensus that they ought to be redeveloped for the existing inhabitants. In 1948, following his visit to Brazil in 1945, Richard Neutra described the Rio hillside slums as 'in a way the most promising ones, because as anybody can well see, they are holding the land quasi free for the best developments to come – a hopeful reserve of the community in spite of currently unsound aspects.'[87] Little was done, however. In 1961 the architect Affonso Eduardo Reidy (1909–64) was still lamenting the fact that Brazil ignored the problem of housing, but he was absolutely clear about the reasons for this. Those at the bottom of the economic scale simply did not earn enough to afford even the most modest of accommodation. As he saw it, this was not a technical problem, nor a sociological or urbanistic problem, but a fundamental economic problem; therefore the only answer lay with the state. Only if the state recognized housing as a public service like the provision of water, sewerage and transport, he argued, could the problem be addressed. The solution would then have to involve urban issues, and any housing programme would have to include other basic necessities – schools of all levels, accessible on foot and in safety, medical and dental centres, a market, sports facilities including a swimming pool, a social club, a library, a film theatre, and so on. All these, for Reidy, were best regarded as an extension of the home. The other crucial factor – as Reidy recognized, but governments often do not – was the issue of transport, and the ideal situation was for people to live as near as possible to their place of work.[88]

Pedregulho

These may seem ambitious preconditions for working-class housing schemes. They are, of course, close to the architects' intentions for those being built in Caracas during the same era, and perhaps Reidy was aware that the health, educational and broader services planned for the Caracas developments were

Affonso Reidy, Pedregulho housing complex, Rio de Janeiro, begun 1947 (photograph c. 1955).

not materializing. But he also speaks from experience, having himself been responsible for the first major housing development in Brazil, in the Pedregulho district of Rio.[89] This scheme, in the industrial district of São Cristóvão, was intended for low-income public employees, and rents were to be subsidized by the government. Reidy had good credentials for a social housing project: in 1930 he had designed and built a Hostel for Homeless Persons in Rio, a thoroughly modern building in structure, design and intentions. In the same year he had been appointed Warchavchik's assistant at the ENBA under Costa's radical directorship, and had taken part in the discussions of modern architecture during the following years as a member of that 'little purist redoubt dedicated to the passionate study not only of the achievements of Gropius and of Mies van der Rohe, but above all of the doctrine and work of Le Corbusier'.[90] In 1936 he was a member of the MES team, and, although during the following years he designed a series of major buildings which were not executed, in 1947 he was appointed architect to Rio's Department of Public Housing, and began planning the Pedregulho development.

The Pedregulho scheme takes into account some of Le Corbusier's ideas and projects, as well as CIAM precepts for high-density urban developments. It announces its modernity in a dramatic way: the dominant architectural feature is the main residential Block A, raised on *pilotis*, snaking 260 metres along the edge of the hillside, following the contours of the terrain in a grand asymmetrical curve. Mindlin suggested Le Corbusier's ambitious, unrealized plans for a similar long, low-curving housing development in Algiers (1931) as a source, but this in turn derives from his scheme for a curving, residential superhighway for Rio two years earlier.[91] Another prototype for the Pedregulho complex is Le Corbusier's Unité d'Habitation in Marseille, on which he began work in 1946 and which was a model for the Caracas superblocks of the 1950s. For Reidy, however, the influence is more from Le Corbusier's ideas than from his practice, as Reidy was already at work on his Pedregulho plans by 1947. More generally, as with other such housing developments in Latin America, Pedregulho is shaped by the ideas of the CIAM's Charter of Athens (1933). Of the mantric 'four functions' it was not designed to include a place of work, but it does emphasize recreation as well as housing, and tackles the transportation problem by consigning it to the perimeter to make the centre a safe pedestrian area, as in the CU in Caracas. There are other functions intrinsic to daily life, especially education and health care, which are not easily susceptible to zoning or urban compartmentalization, and overlap with leisure and living. Reidy recognized these and made them central to his Pedregulho scheme, both geographically and ideologically.

Pedregulho took years to complete. 'The financing of non-speculative building in Brazil is a slow process', as Sigfried Giedion remarked laconically of the still-incomplete project in 1960, but Reidy was well aware of this.[92] Not

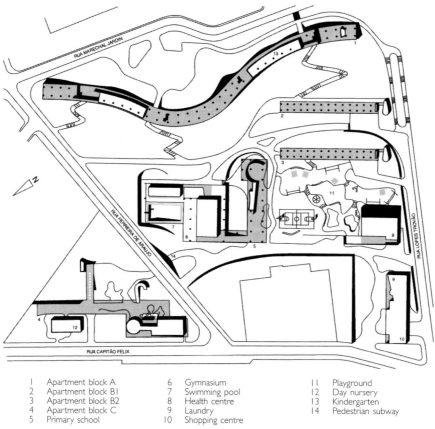

1	Apartment block A	6	Gymnasium	11	Playground
2	Apartment block B1	7	Swimming pool	12	Day nursery
3	Apartment block B2	8	Health centre	13	Kindergarten
4	Apartment block C	9	Laundry	14	Pedestrian subway
5	Primary school	10	Shopping centre		

Affonso Reidy, Pedregulho housing complex, Rio de Janeiro, begun 1947, plan.

trusting the authorities to follow his plans through properly, he ensured that what he regarded as the core shared services – the crèche, nursery and primary schools, pool, gym, commercial centre and dispensary – were completed first, because he recognized that these would not be given priority by the city authorities once the housing blocks were complete.[93] Most of Pedregulho was completed by the late 1950s, including the huge horizontal curve of the main residential block that overlooks the central services. It was the first scheme to include such services in the plans, and it was an adventurous investment on the part of Vargas's populist government – and the prefect of the city, Mendes de Moraes, in particular. It was carefully researched. Reidy and his team interviewed the future tenants; they involved the public services in the discussions, and collected detailed census data.[94] The completed scheme was to house 478 families in flats of between two and four bedrooms, although in the event it took so long to build that most of the individual family requirements had changed by the time they came to move in.

Pedregulho aroused great excitement at the time, and is still visually impressive. In the 1954 'Report on Brazil' in the *Architectural Review* it was the one project singled out by Walter Gropius, Max Bill and Ernesto Rogers for unqualified praise. Bill said of it that it was 'as completely successful from the standpoint of town planning as it is architecturally and socially'.[95] The great curving block extends along the hillside, reaching out over its supporting *pilotis* and the valley below in an optimistic gesture. There are 272 dwelling units, with one-bedroom flats on the first two floors, and two-bedroom duplexes on floors four and five, and six and seven. The third floor is largely open – a great gallery punctuated by supporting pillars – and provides a covered playground area, nursery, kindergarten, and public recreational space,[96] as well as administrative offices (including a social workers' office), and an acoustic shell for children's theatre, a feature which was very popular in Brazil at this time. This block was designed for single tenants and small, young families, and includes all sorts of thoughtful details such as a space on floor three specifically for storing cots. It is hard to think of middle-class male architects identifying this particular issue without some encouragement, so this must surely reflect the care that went into the preliminary consultation process.

The other blocks on the flatter land below are more four-square, but again they are thoughtfully designed, this time for larger families. The four storeys comprise two levels of duplex apartments of three bedrooms each, but the disposition of the upper rooms is flexible so that one can be annexed to the neighbouring apartment to create a two-room and a four-room unit. The living room opens via glass doors on to a balcony partly screened by an openwork concrete grille which acts as an essential sun-breaker while allowing the fresh air to enter. The *pilotis* on the large residential blocks play their part in this system, ensuring that the smaller buildings, such as the lower residential blocks, the schools and the gym, are not cut off from the breeze off the surrounding hills. Throughout the Pedregulho development, as in most early modern architecture in Rio, architects paid close attention to methods of restricting the force of the sun while also encouraging the free circulation of air, and elements which in another context would be of purely aesthetic value are first and foremost functional.

Pedregulho is particularly interesting in that it recognizes and tries to take into account the changing nature of social class in Brazil. The class to which the architects and planners belonged all had domestic servants, and this had a considerable impact on architectural design. Rino Levi's own house in São Paulo, for example, built in 1946, had three bedrooms for himself, his family and guests, and three for the live-in maids. In 1948 Costa began some middle-class apartments in Parque Guinle in Rio, and the three-bedroom flats included two further rooms for maids.[97] The Pedregulho apartments were intended for working-class families, and include no provision for live-in domestics. On the other hand, planning seems to have been designed to encourage upward social mobility, as there was a central laundry where each family was entitled to two kilos of free washing per week, the cost being included in the rent.

Henrique Mindlin explained this in his account of Pedregulho in 1956, when it was very new:

> The machine laundry is mechanical and operated by skilled workers; separate sections deal with the reception, marking, disinfection, washing, drying, ironing, storing and delivery. Despite some initial prejudice motivated by tenants' reluctance to display clothes in bad condition, the central laundry has proved to be one of the most valuable adjuncts to the development.

He goes on to list the advantages this offers: houses have extra space because they do not have individual laundry sinks, the housewife has more time for housework, and 'it makes it easy for every tenant to wear clothes that are washed and ironed'.[98] The other service provided at Pedregulho, which now seems essential for such a scheme, was that the housing blocks were provided with rubbish chutes, and waste was collected and disposed of centrally. The fact that Mindlin, himself one of this generation of innovative Brazilian architects, has to point this out suggests that it was a very novel idea at the time. These types of detail would perhaps not have been considered in a middle-class housing development, where there were always plenty of servants to do such things, and they reinforce Pedregulho's social significance. Women were expected to be house-proud but were released from the drudgery of washing and ironing, and of rubbish disposal. Free laundry would help to ensure that all tenants were tidily dressed in clean, ironed clothes.

Despite the evidence of consultation there is still a strong paternalistic, institutional element to the plans. Perhaps this is inevitable in cases which involve the first such public-financed housing initiatives, and mark a first attempt at moving large groups of people from slums to 'modernity'; this in turn carried expectations that this would – and indeed should – involve a transition from squalor to cleanliness, from sickness to health, from ignorance to education. It was true of the Peabody Trust's rehousing schemes in Victorian England and, as we have seen, of the El Silencio housing scheme in Caracas in the early 1940s. So, for example, in Pedregulho all prospective tenants had to undergo a medical to check for contagious diseases, and the rental agreement allowed for periodic inspections of the property by officials of the Housing Department.

The influence of Richard Neutra's prescriptive utopianism can be detected here. Some of Reidy's features are quite close to the ideas Neutra presented during his visit to Brazil in 1945: the importance of the growth of consumerism for domestic mechanization, for example, and especially his vision of more social and co-operative living arrangements, with shared facilities such as a laundry, social space and the school as the heart of the community.[99] Neutra is passionate, if vague, about the importance of flexible social intercourse, recreation and art:

> The current reconstruction of the world, growing more into a social unit, as staggering a task as ever there was, must be planned. But it must be planned with due regard and *respect for the rationally unplannable....* Only when intuitive architects and planners are accomplishing full scale contemporary housing projects, neighbourhoods, communities – when they have set the stage by manifest examples of recreated human environment – can art regain its fertile prestige, bud and bloom into the consciousness of a broad audience, and of society itself.[100]

Pedregulho was planned as a contribution to such a new world, and represents a modernist and modernizing impulse. It implies a number of fundamental social changes: the move from single family dwellings to apartments probably involved an increased emphasis on the nuclear family; in terms of the basic provision of services like electricity and plumbing it represented a move from underdevelopment to development; these also imply a degree of co-operation on the part of residents. The development encourages a change in the role of the woman of the household, assuming the increasing mechanization of the home and the concomitant bourgeoisification of the lower strata of Brazilian society. The other important feature of Pedregulho is the central importance given to children: as well as schools and nurseries there is a children's theatre, as well as a swimming pool and gym, features from which children had the most to gain. And the environment was intended to be a pleasure to inhabit, with gardens designed by Burle Marx, a tile mural of children's games beside the playground, also by Burle Marx, and another by Portinari – repeated acrobatic figures superimposed by a fluid abstract design that accords well with the forms of the gardens, and other walls with designs in ceramic tiles by Anisio Medeiros, another frequent collaborator on modern architectural projects. The buildings themselves were rendered visually interesting by the different textures of the various concrete screens and *brise-soleils*, by the use of bright colours, and by the juxtaposition of the contrasting serpentine and rectangular blocks; on a smaller scale, the parabolic curve of the gym roof (a much gentler curve than at São Francisco Pampulha) and arches of the changing rooms contrast with the ramps and angles and trapezoidal volumes of the school – all this set against the incomparable landscape of Rio.

Pedregulho, although the first, was not the only major housing development at this time. Reidy himself went on to develop his Pedregulho formula in the Gávea urbanization project begun in 1952, a scheme which involved extensive slum clearances.[101] There were to have been seven large rectangular blocks as well as a dominant serpentine range, striding on *pilotis* across the uneven land, but only the latter was ever completed, and then not until after Reidy's death in 1964. Like Pedregulho, this was a low-rent scheme intended for the displaced slum-dwellers, based on the same idea of a complete neighbourhood unit, 'Unidade de Vizinhança'. It was to have included a church and an open-air amphitheatre as well as a similar range of services to those at Pedregulho. Not only was the scheme incomplete, but in 1982 it was adapted to allow a new motorway to pass right underneath it; so instead of the intended fresh air and good views the inhabitants now enjoy constant fumes and noise, and a view of acres of tarmac.

There were middle-class housing developments aplenty during this time. They explore many of the same ideas: rich surface textures with concrete openwork screens and *brise-soleils*, bright colours, intermediate inside–outside spaces such as screened balconies, covered terraces, and the use of gardens and plants under as well as around the buildings, but they are very traditional in terms of social relations. As I said above, they almost always include provision for live-in domestic help as well as separate servant access, the latter carefully described in Henrique Mindlin's account of his own Tres Leones block of flats in São Paulo (1951).[102] The social niceties of the time are pointed out by Underwood in his account of the Casino at Pampulha, where 'an ingenious backstage access to the dance hall via an elliptical double corridor allowed waiters and gamblers to enter the restaurant without coming into contact with one another'.[103] Reidy's work at Pedregulho and Gávea stands out in this respect, and was informed by different, much more interesting ideas. Reidy used the preliminary sociological research to try to design the new neighbourhood in such a way that, as Bruand says, the architecture 'intervened in the future life of the group, intending to make it progress'.[104] Reidy's intentions were more discreet and less authoritarian than Le Corbusier's or Neutra's, and more practical, but rooted in the same belief that the architect could mould a community into an improved form.

Cidade Universitária

The idea of a Cidade Universitária (CU) for Rio de Janeiro dates back to 1935, when Gustavo Capanema was appointed Minister for Education and Health, so in plan, at least, it predates those of Caracas and Mexico City by about ten years. Capanema later declared this to have been his prime political goal on assuming office: to build a university city, taking the term from the Cité Universitaire in Paris, but unlike Paris, which was primarily residential, he said he had in mind the model of the all-purpose campus universities of the USA and the UK.[105] The MES building was a necessary herald of this larger ambition, but the two projects were always closely linked. Capanema's first move was to invite the Italian Marcello Piacentini to come to Brazil to advise him. Piacentini, who in his work for the University of Rome (1932) had been responsible for establishing the official Fascist architectural style, could spare only a few days – in August 1935 – but he selected a site on the Urca peninsula for which he did a brief sketch. More importantly, he arrived just after the judging of the competition for the MES building. Capanema thought the winning design 'uma coisa horrivel, um pouco "Marajoara"' ('a horrid thing, a bit Marajoara') and wanted external validation for his decision to reject it; Piacentini was apparently happy to oblige.[106] This, as we have seen, led to the setting up of the MES commission of young architects under Costa, and Capanema also established a similar commission, also under Costa, to work on plans for the CU. The architects suggested that Capanema seek Le Corbusier's advice on the MES building, and to make the invitation more attractive they pointed out that he could also help with the CU.[107]

So in July 1936 Le Corbusier came, although he was not alone. Capanema was enthusiastic about inviting foreigners to advise on modernization in Brazil, and in the same year he also invited another French architect, the more conservative Auguste Perret, to come and lecture on city planning and to advise on the MES project. Capanema also tried to arrange a return visit by Piacentini, who, although he could not come himself, sent his assistant Vittorio Morpurgo – 'to help with Le Corbusier's ideas', as Capanema put it.[108] Le Corbusier, however, ignored Piacentini's suggested site – and, presumably, Morpurgo – and got down to business. He divided his time between the CU and the MES building, working on each on alternate days, with the respective (largely overlapping) Brazilian architectural teams in constant attendance. Le Corbusier had come to Rio under the impression that he was to be drawing up plans for the CU, but Brazilian law made the appointment of a non-national architect illegal, so from Capanema's point of view he was coming only to advise.

Le Corbusier saw the CU project as a part of the larger plans for the urbanization of Rio which he had begun to sketch out during his first visit. This was the aspect that really excited him. His sketches began from the idea of a superimposed road network linking the airport, the city centre, the

Le Corbusier, sketch of Rio de Janeiro showing proposed site of University City, labelled *cité universitaire*, Santos Dumont airport and main transport links, 1936.

government ministries, and the beaches with the university, for which at this stage the inland Boa Vista Park was earmarked. Capanema attended Le Corbusier's lectures, and had long discussions with him about the CU and the nature of education.[109] Pietro Maria Bardi (a recent émigré from Italy who, as a modernist and an old rival of Piacentini, had reason to support Le Corbusier) reports that Le Corbusier wanted it to be more than a collection of faculties, more 'a dynamic centre of culture' which, as part of a wider architectural and urbanistic programme, could also lend a new monumentality to the city of Rio.[110] He worked closely with the Brazilian architects – this was where he was most influential – and the results have been described as a sort of collage of earlier ideas:

> The scheme for the *Mundaneum* is taken up again as the *Museum of Knowledge*; the plasticity and structural quality of the [Moscow] *Centrosoyuz* reappears in the *Great Auditorium*; the system of interconnected blocks of the *Ville Radieuse* is used in the majority of the elements of the campus, while the megastructures of the axes of traffic circulation are developments from the *Cité pour trois mille d'habitants*.[111]

After Le Corbusier left for Paris, he and Costa remained in correspondence. Costa angrily reported the sequence of events – how Capanema had appointed two very traditional figures to review the plans, and how, not surprisingly, they had rejected them.[112] Revised plans produced under the two traditionalists by a team which no longer included Costa were then reviewed, this time by Piacentini, and so on. It was altogether a sorry saga; Capanema's later declaration that all he wanted to do was to 'promote the new architecture', and that he did not want to build a CU unless it was going to be 'a great monument of modern art', are disingenuous.[113] On the other hand, there is no doubt that Le Corbusier's ambitious schemes were way beyond the public purse.

The story of the CU was to continue, albeit slowly. The Boa Vista site proved unworkable, and before Capanema left office in 1945 a new location had been identified: the Ilha do Fundão to the north of the city, near Galeão International Airport. This island was to be created by a large landfill scheme that involved linking nine small islands together, a project that took many years to complete: it was still only 'almost concluded' in 1956.[114] The architect in overall charge of the new site was Jorge Moreira, whose first plans date from 1949. Designed for a student population of about 30,000, it included teaching and administration blocks, residential accommodation for 10,000 students, and housing for 300 members of faculty and their families. Moreira, who had been on the commissions for the MES building and the CU in the

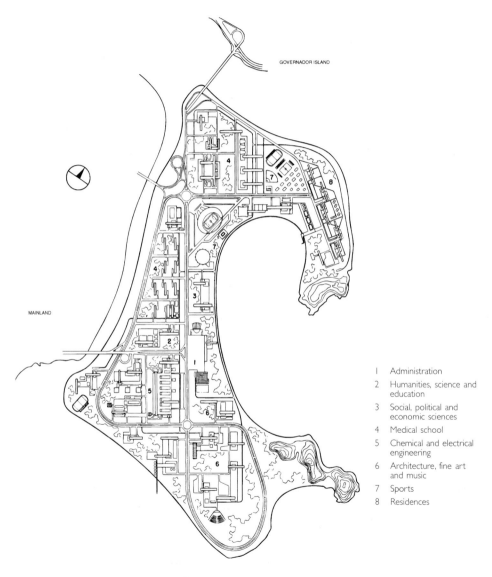

GOVERNADOR ISLAND

MAINLAND

1	Administration
2	Humanities, science and education
3	Social, political and economic sciences
4	Medical school
5	Chemical and electrical engineering
6	Architecture, fine art and music
7	Sports
8	Residences

Jorge Machado Moreira, plan for the CU, Ilha do Fundão, Rio de Janeiro, 1955.

days of Le Corbusier, was well placed to develop some of the original ideas, and to make it an architecturally coherent whole.[115] In practice, however, all he managed to achieve was an outline plan and a few isolated buildings.

What is immediately obvious from the plan is that, unlike the later university cities of Mexico and Caracas, this scheme prioritizes cars over pedestrians.[116] It is organized along the spine of a huge central avenue with curving loops to either side, rather like a race track. Perhaps the imagery of Brazil's growing motor industry was inescapable. The Civic Centre (Le Corbusier's term) was to comprise the central administration building, the main theatre and the university library – this last to be in the spiral form proposed by Le Corbusier.[117] Otherwise there is little evidence of Le Corbusier's ideas, in terms of the organization of the different faculty buildings. For example, in his fifth lecture in Rio in 1936, the one in which he specifically addressed the question of the CU, Le Corbusier had spoken about the importance of locating the art and architectural departments with that of engineering, at the heart of modern production processes, so that they could exchange ideas; but Moreira places engineering in a traditional grouping with chemistry, technology, electronics and nuclear physics. Fine art and architecture are with music.

Moreira's first and most important architectural contribution to the CU was the Institute of Child Welfare. Begun in 1949 and completed in 1953, at the northerly end of the island, it was designed to house a variety of functions concerning child welfare in the widest sense: physical, mental and social. It is approximately E-shaped with long, low ranges partly raised on *pilotis*, clean-cut simple profiles and a thoroughly functional organization of space. It also makes use of what by that time were the more or less standard accoutrements of modern Brazilian architecture: screens and walls of decorative airbricks to provide ventilation and protection from the sun, roof terraces, mosaic murals, cobbled pedestrian areas beneath the buildings, and, of course, gardens by Roberto Burle Marx. It is indicative of the government's priorities that this large, complex design was the first building to be completed, and for some time almost the only building on the site. The Institute of Child Welfare was socially inclusive in its intentions, acknowledging the importance of the future, of the need to understand, nurture and encourage the next generation. Like other state-funded projects – such as Niemeyer's Obra do Berço and the nurseries Reidy included in his housing schemes – the Institute of Child Welfare demonstrates the importance which the Brazilian government accorded to children, even if some of the elements it included (the biometrics department, in particular) were part of a now-discredited ideology about the nature of human development.

The other buildings to be erected under Moreira's directorship were the Faculty of Engineering, begun in 1956, and the Faculty of Architecture and Urbanism, begun in 1957 – both of which were no doubt treated with considerable urgency once Brasília was under construction – and the Clinical Hospital, also of 1957. All slab blocks, raised on *pilotis*, clean and functional, they rework ideas from the Institute of Child Welfare and the MES building. The stylistic arguments had been convincingly won by the mid 1950s, just in time for Brasília to capitalize on it.

Cidade dos Motores

The Cidade de Motores (Motor City) was a rather different project.[118] It was to be a new town based on engineering and the motor industry, and was designed by José Luis Sert and Paul Lester Wiener – the one Catalan, the other German by birth, both resident in New York. Sert and Wiener officially joined forces in 1942 as the Town Planning Associates (TPA), and began developing contacts in Latin America. Wiener, who was well connected with the US State Department, was invited to lecture in Brazil in 1942, and in 1943 the TPA was commissioned by the Chief of the Brazilian Airplane Factory Commission, Brigadier-General Antônio Guedes Muniz, to design a town around the new aeroplane engine factory.[119] As Eric Mumford points out, Brazil reluctantly entered the war in 1942 under pressure from the USA, pressure 'which included the promise of large loan guarantees from the Export–Import Bank for industrial development', and he suggests a link with the patronage of the TPA, given its close relations with the US State Department. This suggestion is reinforced by other factors: in 1936, as we have seen, Brazilian law had prohibited the appointment of Le Corbusier to a similar position, and by 1942 Brazilian architects were well informed on town-planning issues, so they were hardly in need of foreign leadership. And – even more persuasive – the TPA project was the focus of an exhibition in the Museum of Modern Art in New York in 1947, where it was compared with a plan for renovating Chicago's South Side.[120] The MOMA catalogue states that the Brazilian government recognized that unless the development of cities 'can be controlled and di-rected, the result is chaos and near annihilation of the individual', and so for the new Cidade dos Motores, 'wishing to realize the greatest possibilities of the reclaimed land, [it] called in city planners Paul Lester Wiener and José Luis Sert… to design the necessary community for the population attracted by the newly established farms and factories'.[121] We can be sure that the Brazilian government was encouraged to think in this way by representatives of the US government, on behalf of US industry, and, as Mumford points out, to help counter the influence of the Axis powers in Latin America.

The plans for the Cidade dos Motores were drawn up in 1943. It was to be a new town of 25,000 workers and agricultural labourers, to be built on 250 acres of reclaimed marsh to the north of Rio. The TPA's prime responsibility was for planning the residential districts – or, as both Sert and Wiener preferred to term it, the new community – but the broader scheme was for the Cidade dos Motores to develop in three stages beginning with the industrial pro-gramme, then the agricultural, and then, as these grew, so the necessary housing would follow. This sequence is of course illogical because, in order to grow, the 'industrial programme' would have to have workers, and in a pre-planned new town the workers would have to have somewhere to live, but it supports the view that this was a project driven by US industrial interests. In practice the first residential stage of the 'community', the first neighbourhood of six thousand workers and their families, was more or less built by 1946.

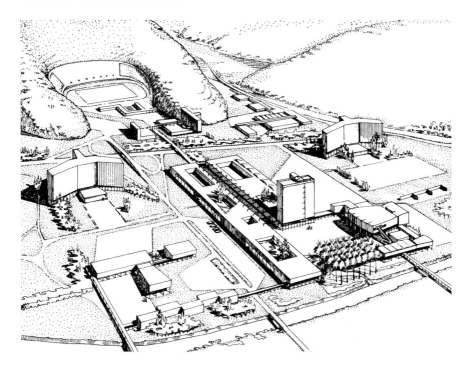

José Luis Sert (Town Planning Associates), perspective view of civic centre,
Cidade dos Motores, c. 1945.

The plans for the Motor City mark an important development from Sert's
theories as published in his study of town planning, *Can Our Cities Survive?*
(1944).[122] This study follows the 1933 CIAM Charter of Athens model of the
four functions of a city – housing, work, recreation and transport – fairly
closely. But even before the book was published, Sert was already having to
face up to the limitations of this scheme. In 1940, Lewis Mumford had refused
an invitation to write an introduction to *Can Our Cities Survive?*[123] He thought
the four functions too narrow, as they did not take into account the political,

educational and cultural functions of a city, and Sert subsequently included a section towards the end on the importance of the 'civic centre'.[124]

For the Cidade dos Motores the TPA designed a multifunctional civic centre with an auditorium, municipal offices, a hotel, a pedestrian arcade with shops and restaurants, a technical high school, a cultural centre, exhibition halls, library and sports stadium.[125] Significantly, these plans for the civic centre – or what Sert later preferred to call the 'community centre' – also included a *praça* and a *passeio*, where people could meet and stroll, see and be seen, in the way traditional in Brazilian – and indeed Mediterranean – town squares. This has both instrumental and responsive origins. Sert believed that 'free thinking did not find its shape in rural regions, neither is it a product of press, radio or television, it owes more to the café table than to the school and … it was mainly spread by the spoken word and born in the meeting places of people.'[126] In other words, a modern equivalent of the traditional town square was important for the nurturing of democracy,[127] but it was also a response to local – and indeed Latin – patterns of social behaviour which Sert and other exiles from Mediterranean Europe missed in democratic New York.

Like Reidy's contemporary housing developments, the TPA combined a sensitivity to local practice with a belief in the many benefits that could follow from good town planning. An example in the TPA's plans for the Cidade dos Motores was that 'all provisions are made for the natural raising of living standards', including nutrition.[128] The MOMA catalogue includes a curious passage that presumably reflects the TPA's views, pointing out the importance of food for town planners. It describes how the Brazilian worker has a varied diet – rice, meat, beans and fruit – but despite this the new development would include communal kitchens to ensure better nutrition and hygiene. The Cidade dos Motores project therefore also included a plan for the industrialization of food production under the aegis of the (better-informed) representatives of the state, so that not only would the right sorts of vegetable be grown, but they would be taken to a centrally located 'kitchen-factory' where the food would be prepared before distribution.[129]

The residential blocks were divided into 'bachelor dormitories' and three- and eight-storey apartment blocks. These were set in 'tropical gardens', separate from the street and from each other, and raised on *pilotis* with corridor access to each flat. They were to be built from standardized parts, and were designed to take the local climate into account. The 1947 MOMA catalogue explains the various measures in some detail:

> An inexpensive sunbaffle is formed by a simple honeycomb of concrete which faces the corridor walls and protects the building from sun and rain. Pivoting wall sections in the living quarters open the rooms to air and view and serve as a sunshade. A special double membrane wall of pre-cast concrete units with a ventilated cavity between them provides insulation against heat for the bedroom walls.[130]

As we have seen, Brazilian architects had been experimenting with methods of screening from the sun while allowing for through-ventilation for some years. It had been an important feature of the Brazilian pavilion at the 1939 World's Fair, and was one of the points Goodwin had consistently stressed in the Brazil Builds catalogue of 1943 as one of Brazil's most innovative and important contributions to modern architecture; but in a telling example of the way in which Latin America's achievements in the field have been forgotten, Maria Rubert de Ventós recently described the Cidade dos Motores details as interesting 'early versions of trellises and blinds and pivoting windows'.[131] These features are not particularly early by Brazilian standards, and indeed are hard to imagine without the Brazilian prototypes.

The TPA's experience in Brazil sensitized them to local and regional factors, which continued to play an important part in their later town-planning projects in Latin America, in Peru, Colombia, Venezuela and Cuba.[132] Sert's ideas on town planning as articulated in his Presidential Address to the 1951 CIAM meeting in Hoddesdon, England, reflect the impact of his projects in Latin America. In emphasizing the need for a community centre where people could gather, he mentions the famous public meeting points of various cities, including 'the Ramblas in Barcelona, the Avenida de Mayo in Buenos Aires, all the "plazas de Armas" in Latin American cities.... [These] are proof that the urge to get together exists in every community, large and small.'[133] In plans for new city centres 'the general trend should be towards the revival of the public squares or "plazas" and the creation of pedestrian districts'. For Sert, as for Burle Marx, nature had an important role to play:

> Trees, plants, water, sun and shade, and all the natural elements friendly to man should be found in such centres. And these elements of nature should harmonize with the buildings and their architectural shapes, sculptural values, and colour. Landscaping must play a very important role.[134]

Although they superficially conform to Le Corbusier's ideas about the importance of greenery in new towns, Sert's gardens differ in that they are above all places where people can meet and talk; Le Corbusier's towns never have crowds, and the landscaped settings are intended for organized sport, or to serve more solitary, meditative purposes, and in particular the contemplation of the architecture.

Prior to Brasília, Brazilian architects had put modern architectural theories into practice in a variety of ways: they had gained experience of modern techniques and materials; they had cleared slums and designed new high-density urban housing schemes; in Santos Dumont they had provided the capital with what must be one of the world's most beautiful airports; they had embarked on a huge university city; they had levelled hills and created beaches to create a more spacious, more orderly city; and they had adapted 'international' modernism to their own climatic and cultural context. They had been visited by numerous foreigners, some of whom had come to advise, some to teach and preach; but there were plenty of others, at home and abroad, who recognized that by the mid 1950s Brazil had earned its architectural spurs and established its own autonomous, alternative, modern voice. To borrow a phrase from James Holston, for the Brazilian government modern architecture had become, 'perhaps more than any other cultural expression in Brazil … the symbol of Brazil's emergence as a modern nation'.[135]

BRASÍLIA

Mention Brasília, and most people – including many Brazilians – sniff dismissively and recite a few clichés about how it bankrupted the country, how it is built on an inhuman scale, how it was designed with no working-class housing, or how dated the architecture looks. All these are superficially true, but Brasília exists – and indeed flourishes – and deserves to be revisited. Brazil's recurrent economic problems can no longer be blamed on Brasília. Tourists may complain that the monumental centre is vast and unwelcoming, but the centre of Washington is on a similar scale, and can hardly be described as friendly. The difference, of course, is that Washington is a world centre and buzzes with self-importance, while Brasília by comparison is quiet, and its monumentality therefore appears vainglorious in the eyes of those predisposed to find Brazil full of picturesque poverty and ramshackle *favelas*. The Brazilian middle class still crack jokes about how the most popular building in Brasília is the airport, and although it is true that there are those who still return to the bright lights of São Paulo and Rio at weekends, such stereotypes are changing, and many who live there would not choose to live anywhere else. Like Canberra, Brasília is valued by middle-class middle-aged civil servants with children, and, like Chandigarh, by the less well-off, for whom it is a source of great pride. Many of the latter were the migrant labourers who came to build the city in the 1950s and 1960s and stayed. They, with their children and grandchildren and the many subsequent immigrants to the region, live in the thriving modern towns surrounding Brasília which have grown up from the much-maligned original satellite shanties. Of course, like any large city in Latin America, Brasília continues to attract rural migrants who establish temporary settlements as and where they can: the original satellites are now centres of business, industry and commerce, with their own high-rise centres and their own shantytowns. As far as the style of the architecture is concerned, Brasília is now old enough to turn the corner into history and leave questions of fashion behind.

Apart from specialists in the work of Oscar Niemeyer, Brasília has received little serious attention from architectural historians, at least outside Brazil.[136] In recent literature on the history of twentieth-century architecture, Brasília attracts little more than a few cursory remarks. In their extensive two-volume *Modern Architecture*, Tafuri and Dal Co devote a single paragraph to Brazil in which, with a passing sneer, they dismiss both Lucio Costa's 'puerile allegorical plan' and Niemeyer's public buildings where, as they put it, 'the gratuitous is tinged with sophistication.… Although they make a fine show, it is one of superficial velleities.'[137] In the section on cities in Jonathan Glancey's recent *Twentieth Century Architecture: The Structures that Shaped the Century* there is no mention of Brasília, although in 1971 it could still be described as 'an epoch-making stride in the evolution of modern architecture … the dream of CIAM, of the Athens Charter, of *Vers une Architecture*, of the Russian Constructivists, the Viennese moderns, the Weimar pioneers, the German diaspora, the English Garden City enthusiasts, the American skyscraper builders'.[138] Can a city that was once described in such terms simply be erased from history? Imagine if Brazil had not built a new capital, if Rio de Janeiro – indisputably one of the most violent cities in the world, and with an international reputation for hedonism and decadence, hopelessly overcrowded and chaotic – was still the capital of Brazil? It is worth remembering that Brasília was built to be the seat of government, and in this respect it is comparable with such *fiat* cities as Byzantium, Canberra, St Petersburg, Chandigarh, and many others.

The most obvious comparison with Brasília, however, has always been Washington. In the 1940s, Brazil, with its vast landmass and a fast-developing economy, was seen by many as on course to become the South American equivalent of the USA. In 1947 the catalogue to the *Two Cities: Planning in North and South America* exhibition at the Museum of Modern Art in New York, which compared the redevelopment of part of Chicago with the new Cidade dos Motores in Rio, made several references to how the latter 'will serve as a model for future Brazilian cities', and drew comparisons between US history and Brazil's future: 'The great undeveloped interior and its rich natural resources are an exciting challenge to pioneers and builders today, as the unopened West of North America stimulated men of vision in the nineteenth century.'[139] The comparison would have been in the mind of President Kubitschek when he began planning the new capital, and it is worth remembering that Washington, too, was met with incredulity in its early years.

> Behind Brasília may be seen an impulse akin to the irrational optimism which once prompted a group of thirteen bankrupt former British colonies to establish a capital so grandiose in its outlines as to provoke derisive comment for at least fifty years after its founding.[140]

Brasília may still provoke derisive comment, but it differs from Washington and from all other *fiat* cities of comparable scale in that it progressed from plan to official inauguration as the working capital in under four years, a breathtaking achievement by any standard.

Brasília is the embodiment of the belief that modern architecture and urbanism could produce a new kind of city that would in turn lead the way towards a new kind of nation. The impulse to design and build a city *ex nihilo*, on mythological virgin land, is a powerful one in Latin America, and one with a long tradition. In the USA, prior to Washington, few cities were laid out before they were inhabited; but in Latin America, from the earliest Spanish settlements in the Caribbean, the conquistadors had staked out the blocks of their grid-plan towns on an optimistic scale, the regularity a deliberate and explicit metaphor for the social order which the Europeans were importing and which they intended to impose on what they saw as the physical and social disorder of the subjugated Indians. First foundations in colonial Brazil were less uniform, but the motivation was the same: cities were founded in orderly fashion with the twin aims of simultaneously demonstrating and instituting 'civilization'.[141] Subsequent regimes continued to embrace the same rhetoric whenever they invested in programmes of urban renovation – as in Rio, where it was behind the arguments in favour of the slum clearances in the early twentieth century.[142] The impulse behind Brasília was similar, although the civilizing force of the new city was directed not at the inhabitants of the interior, whether or not they were Indian, but at the country as a whole, and at its condition of underdevelopment and cultural and economic dependency.

The origins of Brasília

The idea of a new capital in the Brazilian interior had first been suggested as early as 1789, when, as part of the resistance to Portuguese rule, the rebels of Minas Gerais known as the *Inconfidentes* proposed a new capital, free from associations with the colonial regime.[143] The idea surfaced periodically during the nineteenth century, again linked to Republican aspirations, until 1891, when the young Brazilian Republic (the Emperor had finally abdicated in 1889) designated a great tract of land in the central Brazilian plateau as the 'future federal district', within which the new capital was to be sited. Little progress was made for fifty years, however, and then only slowly. President Getúlio Vargas recognized that a new capital would be a way of centralizing control and weakening the individual states, and in particular the rivalrous power of São Paulo and Rio, but it was his successor, Eurico Gaspar Dutra (1946–51), who – during the relatively prosperous postwar years – laid the groundwork with a series of surveys and reports. Article 4 of the 1946 Constitution stipulated the conditions for the transfer of the capital to the central highlands, and in 1948 an investigative team identified an appropriate general area within the federal district. In 1953 Vargas, who had been re-elected in 1951, set a three-year deadline on a research project that would pinpoint the exact location; and in early 1954 the US firm Donald J. Belcher and Associates was commissioned to survey and map the area with regard to its geological, geographical and climatic features.[144] Later that same year Vargas, implicated in a web of corruption and in a failed assassination attempt on a journalist, committed suicide, but despite this the project survived, and in 1955 a Brazilian team – headed by Mareschal José Pessoa, and including architects Affonso Reidy and

Roberto Burle Marx – determined the precise site at the confluence of two rivers, proposing that a dam be built to create a V-shaped lake, and that the centre of the city be located on the peninsula.[145] Nevertheless, this was a moment of considerable political instability, and the possibility of moving from planning to *building* a new capital still seemed a long way off.

Then, during the 1955 presidential election campaign, Juscelino Kubitschek made the realization of Brasília his central election promise.[146] In fact he claimed not to have given it much thought until someone asked him about it at a political rally in Goiás, and on the spur of the moment Kubitschek declared: 'I will implement the Constitution.' This may be part of the subsequent mythologization of Brasília but Kubitschek was as good as his word. To begin with it did not look practicable – he was elected by a slim majority, and the army had to intervene to suppress a coup before he could be inaugurated in 1956 – but Kubitschek was energetic, charismatic and very determined. He saw Brasília as a way of breaking with the politics of the past, of promoting industrialization, stimulating economic growth, and encouraging regional development. He knew that if he did not make enough progress on Brasília during his five-year term of office, the project would be abandoned by his successor. 'Fifty Years' Progress in Five' was his famous slogan, and he succeeded in increasing industrial production by 80 per cent and achieving an economic growth rate of 7 per cent a year. He left Brazil with a self-sufficient motor industry, an international airline, and a brand new modern capital city.[147]

Brasília would not exist were it not for Juscelino Kubitschek, just as the Ciudad Universitaria in Caracas would not have been built without the determination of Pérez Jiménez, nor the Ciudad Universitaria of Mexico City without Miguel Alemán; but as in Mexico and Venezuela, the realization of these ambitious projects also depended on the availability of architects with the experience and the vision to design and build these new worlds. Most accounts of Brasília start with the city plan, the Plano Piloto, but Kubitschek was not prepared to wait for this to be drawn up. He began his own plans even before he was elected, and no sooner had he taken office than he commissioned his old friend Oscar Niemeyer, with whom he had collaborated in Pampulha, to begin by designing a presidential palace to be called the Palace of the Dawn (Palácio da Alvorada). From the start Kubitschek used every opportunity to promote the idea of Brasília in terms of a new dawning in Brazilian history, a new beginning, as the concrete realization of a utopian dream.[148] He visited the site for the first time in October 1956 with Niemeyer, and they decided to position the new palace at the east end of the peninsula that would be formed when the rivers were dammed.[149] In other words, the presidential palace was positioned in such a way that the sun would rise behind it in a dramatic enactment of the way in which the building itself heralded the dawning of the new city and the new Brazil.

Palácio da Alvorada: a prototype for Brasília

The architecture of the presidential palace set the tone for the new capital. In his autobiographical account of the construction of Brasília, Kubitschek describes how he rejected Niemeyer's first proposal for the presidential palace, saying that what he wanted was something that would still be admired in a hundred years' time. Niemeyer went away, and – as is only appropriate for a good origin myth – worked away all night on a new design. The result was just what Kubitschek wanted:

> Here was a building that was a revelation. Lightness, grandeur, lyricism and power – the most antagonistic qualities mingled together, interpenetrating, to achieve the miracle of harmony of the whole… with its columns in the form of inverted fans emerging from the reflections in the water, which constitute, today, the marvellous sculptural symbol of Brasília.[150]

Part of the reason for Brasília's invisibility in recent years is perhaps that just as Burle Marx's gardens now seem elegant rather than controversial, so we no longer recognize these 'antagonistic qualities' in Niemeyer's architecture. Niemeyer's design for the Alvorada Palace is volumetrically simple: a long, low, rectangular glazed box, the flat roof extending out over the length of the back

Oscar Niemeyer, Palácio da Alvorada, Brasília, 1956–58.

and front façades and supported on columns to create a protected arcade. The interior is disposed like a Renaissance palace, with services in the semi-basement, public halls and meeting rooms on the *piano nobile*, and private accommodation above. The most distinctive feature, as Kubitschek recognized, and the point at which the 'antagonistic qualities' arise, is the columniated arcade. Here Niemeyer inverts the traditional arched form so that the roof is apparently supported on a series of points, the inverted arcade like a series of high-peaked waves. Indeed, at the time it was known as 'Oscar's cardiogram'.[151] This inverted arcade is itself supported on shallow arches, this time the right way up, and the meeting of the two arcades articulates the internal division between the semi-basement and the *piano nobile*. The lake in front reinforces the impression that the whole building floats, almost dances on the shallow lower arches, while the open arms of the upper arches reach up in an appropriately expansive and optimistic gesture.

The columniated façade lends itself to multiple readings: as an arcaded colonnade it suggests the colonial past, a link that Niemeyer valued:

> I rejoice in realizing that these forms bestowed individuality and originality upon the Palaces in their modest way and (and this I deem important) established a link with the architecture of colonial Brazil. This was not done through the use of near-at-hand elements dating from that period but by the expression of the same plastic intentions, the same fondness for curves and the rich and gracious lines that gave it its striking personality.[152]

This is not just a formal link – a taste for sweeping curves and striking effects of light and shadow – but also a more ideological link with the rejection of tradition represented by baroque forms. The inversion of the traditional arcade represents a challenge to the rationalist values of classical architecture whereby buildings should be firmly grounded and stable, and columns in particular should look as if they are capable of fulfilling their intended function as supports. Baroque architecture had mounted a similar challenge in Brazil as in Europe with, for example, columns that undulate as if they were made of plasticine, and entablatures that bulge and burst instead of providing a clear horizontal reference point.

But the inverted arcade also involves a technical rupture from that past. At key points of contact – the building with the ground, the roof with the supports – the columns not only refute their traditional role as load-bearers but point literally and metaphorically to the achievements of modern technology, making the irrational rational, the impossible possible. To emphasize the anti-classical-yet-classical contrast – as in Washington and, indeed, grand palaces and seats of government throughout the world – the building is faced up in shining white marble.

The Plano Piloto

In April 1956 Kubitschek founded a development corporation under Israel Pinheiro, the Companhia Urbanizadora da Nova Capital do Brasil, or NOVA-CAP, to oversee the design and construction of the rest of the city. Reidy and Burle Marx, who had worked on the preliminary survey, suggested calling in Le Corbusier to act as adviser, as in 1936, but Brazil's architectural achievements during the intervening twenty years made this hard to justify, and in any case Kubitschek was determined that Brasília should be a Brazilian project through and through.[153] So in September, at Niemeyer's insistence, NOVACAP organized a competition for the design of the city: it was open only to Brazilians, and required of entrants a plan indicating the layout of the key monuments and a written report, to be submitted by the following March. The jury included Niemeyer, and was dominated by his friends and associates, so it is hard to see as surprising the choice of his old mentor and friend Lúcio Costa as winner from the twenty-six entries. As Le Corbusier once remarked of architectural competitions, 'a classic method of choosing your own favourites behind a reassuring "anonymity"',[154] and there was considerable bad feeling among some of the losers. The Milton brothers, who were awarded joint third prize, had invested a great deal of time and money in an extensive, thoroughly researched plan, and were outspoken in their criticism of the system.[155] Reidy and Moreira, who had complained about the composition of the jury, did not take part: they presumably guessed that it would be a stitch-up.

Niemeyer, already at work on the presidential palace, would surely have discussed ideas for the city plan with Kubitschek; Niemeyer knew he could work with Costa and they, too, would have discussed the project together, no doubt at length; and although Costa does not present designs for any of the buildings in his plan, merely some schematic suggestions, the fact that these are in some cases remarkably close to Niemeyer's subsequent architectural forms implies a degree of collaboration. The decision on the winning entry lay, of course, with the international jury, but Niemeyer, as NOVACAP's

Director of Architecture and Urbanism, was himself a member of the jury. The English member of the panel, William Holford of the Royal Institute of British Architects, reported that 'the jury was involved from the start in almost continual discussion with press, public, competitors and officials, even over the period of judging', so the process could not be described as independent. Holford adds, ambiguously, that because of internal tensions it was he and the French jurist who were asked to 'tip the balance in favour of one scheme rather than another'.[156] If the jury were not aware at the outset, Niemeyer would no doubt have reminded them that what Kubitschek was looking for was an idea, a vision of a city and of a future society, rather than a set of measured drawings.

Costa did not submit measured drawings. He submitted what he termed the Plano Piloto, a few deceptively casual-looking sketches together with a carefully crafted report, a piece of highly persuasive poetic rhetoric where, as Holston argues, he presents his plan as a careless trifle. This plan, precisely because it is a careless trifle, appears as a form of inspiration, and thus as the only possible option.[157] Costa begins by denying that he is seriously entering the competition at all but, as he disingenuously puts it, 'merely liberating my mind from a possible solution which sprang to it as a complete picture, but one which I had not sought'.[158] This denial of responsibility for the plan is strikingly similar to Kubitschek's claim not to have thought about Brasília until he was challenged on the subject, at which point his determination to achieve it was suddenly irreversible and unwavering; in other words, Brasília emerges as an almost Platonic Idea which exists regardless of the wishes or plans of either the patron or the designer. Once the non-personal nature of the idea is established, Costa proceeds to present himself as the only person capable of realizing so grand an enterprise as the one he is proposing:

> [Brasília] should be conceived of, I believe, not as a mere organic entity, able to function effortlessly and vitally like any modern town; not as an *urbs*, therefore, but as a *civitas*, having the virtues and attributes appropriate to a true capital city. To achieve this, the town planner must be imbued with a certain dignity and nobility of

purpose – for it is from this basic attitude of his that must spring the sense of order, fitness and proportion which will confer real monumentality on his urban scheme. I use the word not in the sense of ostentation, but as the palpable and conscious expression of true value and significance. He must design a city in which orderly and efficient work may be carried out: but also a city of vitality and charm, conducive to reverie and intellectual speculation, capable of becoming not only the seat of Government, the administrative headquarters of the nation, but also a centre of culture which will attract to it the finest and most perceptive intellects in the country.[159]

The language allies the project for Brasília with the Roman idea of the city, *civitas*, with the justifications of colonizing powers (the imposition of order) and with classical architectural theory from Vitruvius on (to the necessary utility must be added fitness and proportion); it addresses the issue of monumentality, and neatly implies a link between the business of government and 'perceptive intellects'.[160]

Costa then lists twenty-three points, beginning with the origins of this spontaneous idea, via the system of traffic circulation, the monumental heart, the various zones for entertainment, commerce, sport and municipal buildings, to the residential sectors and amenities, including cemeteries which should be 'planted with grass lawns and to be suitably wooded: the gravestones will be the simple, flat slabs used in England, the idea being to avoid any sign of ostentation'.[161] He even proposes a street-numbering system. At the end, after a section on the best ways of making the real estate available to private capital so as to ensure the overall harmony of the original Idea, including the requirement that private developers should submit their plans to NOVACAP for approval, he winds up his Report with an extraordinarily inclusive vision of a city that will be both monumental and 'efficient, welcoming and intimate', 'spread out and compact, rural and urban', whose aims are both 'lyrical and functional'. He ends as he began: by referring to José Bonifácio, 'the Patriarch', who in 1823 had recommended the transfer of the capital from Rio de Janeiro to the inland state of Goiás, and had suggested the name *Brasília*: 'Brasília, capital of the aeroplane and autostrada, city and park. The century-old dream of the Patriach.'[162]

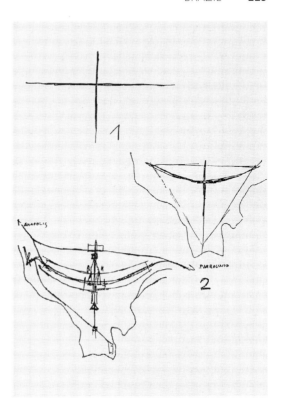

Lúcio Costa, first sketches for the layout of
Brasília from the Plano Piloto, 1957.

The design for Brasília, the realization of the Patriarch's dream, springs ready-formed into Costa's mind: 'It was born of that initial gesture which anyone would make when pointing to a given place, or taking possession of it: the drawing of two axes crossing each other at right angles, in the sign of the Cross.'[163] It is also clear from the second sketch, which included the contour of the planned peninsula, that Costa oriented the arms of his cross to approximate to the points of the compass. Brasília is therefore the primordial sign. It marks the centre, the conceptual (if not the geographical) heart of

Brazil, the crossroads at which the country would come together, from where the new Brazil would grow, the point at which the treasure of the future is buried. Costa's crossroads implies trade and traffic and communication. It provided a neatly symbolic starting point for Kubitschek's goal of 'integration through interiorization', and accorded perfectly with the government's image of Brasília as promoted in a diagrammatic map dating from 1956 which makes it the centre of a sunburst of lines that visually connect the capital to all the other major cities in Brazil, complete with distances. All roads lead to Brasília, even though there were no such roads in 1956. As Holston argues, this image, endlessly repeated in all manner of contexts from school textbooks to government reports, effectively establishes an idea of Brasília as the country's centre of gravity.[164]

Costa then takes this rectilinear 'sign of the Cross' and modifies it by curving the transverse arm, both to adapt it to the local topography and 'to make the sign fit into the equilateral triangle which outlines the area to be urbanized',[165] so again combining elements in a mythicized idea of unity: the four arms of the cross contained within the equilateral triangle. The origins of the plan therefore imply the geometrical purity of Le Corbusier's compelling definition of the right angle as 'the essential and sufficient implement of action because it enables us to determine space with an absolute exactness',[166] but it then evolves into something different: by curving the arms, it breaks out of the 'latent tyranny of the normative orthogonal grid', to borrow a phrase from Kenneth Frampton's discussion of the more organic architects of the 1950s, particularly Alvar Aalto.[167] This allows the Brasília plan to be orthogonal in origin, like a grid-plan colonial town, while simultaneously rejecting such rigidity; it is rooted in the past, but also suggests a development, perhaps a liberation, from the limits of history.

Costa's curved north–south axis animates the design in a remarkable way, opening it up to the most diverse readings. The plan has proved to be – at a symbolic level, at least – phenomenally successful. Some capital cities are rendered distinctive by their ancient origins; others – Buenos Aires or Paris –

by their well-established reputations as centres of culture and sophistication. Closer to home, Rio de Janeiro, the capital Brasília was to replace, is associated with the hedonism of carnival and its singularly dramatic landscape features. Brasília, of course, could lay no claim to history or culture, high or popular; nor were the empty *cerrado* scrubland of the high plateau of the Federal district, or even the vast, beautiful skies, sufficient to give an identity to the city. Costa's Plano Piloto, however, does. It is most commonly described as an aeroplane: the Praça dos Três Poderes the cockpit, the ministries the passenger seats, the curved north–south residential districts, of course, the wings. As a city dominated by its system of highways for cars, and shaped like an aeroplane, it neatly combines two key images of modernity, and points to the improved communications between the various regions of Brazil and with the rest of the world that Brasília was designed to promote.

But Costa's plan has also been described as a bird, a butterfly, or a dragonfly, more poetic metaphors for the city, suggesting natural beauty, grace and liberty. It is also – more subversively but unmistakably (at least in the sketch of the cross with curved arms within the triangle) – a bow and arrow. Even the way in which Costa has traced over the lines again, thickening and coarsening them, suggests a primitive petroglyphic character, as if to remind the ultra-modern city that there is an alternative and much more ancient history of Brazil which can never be completely eradicated.[168] This same multivalent cross-within-triangle sketch also evokes both the crucifix and Leonardo's Vitruvian man, an anthropomorphic form with its extremities touching the corners of the geometrical shape. Originally Brasília's image was that of a very masculine place, built and inhabited by gutsy frontiersmen, but more recently this has given way to a gentler, more domestic idea, reflecting the way the city has been accepted and incorporated into Brazil's sense of itself. As a mark of this domestication of Brasília it is perhaps not surprising, therefore, to find that the plan has been subjected to a new reading: that of a perfectly formed woman, reclining with arms outstretched, and 'sensually bathed in the brilliance of a tropical sun'.[169] Savage, modern, natural, mechanical, male, female: the imagery of Brasília's plan is all-inclusive. Costa's plan and Niemeyer's Palácio da Alvorada establish the formal language of Brasília – what Kubitschek identified as the 'antagonisms' between lyricism and monumentality, but also between tradition and modernity, between continuity and rupture. In fact the distinctive column shape which Niemeyer developed, apparently overnight, is essentially a Latin cross with curved transverse arms, the same idea which Costa claims sprang into his mind unbidden as the root of the city plan.

Geoffrey Broadbent tells a strange story of how, when he was in Brazil in 1969, a taxi driver – whose name was Jeanneret, and who claimed to be a cousin of Le Corbusier – told him that it was Le Corbusier who designed Brasília, and that all Costa had done was to draw it up. On asking Costa if this were true, Broadbent was told: 'Yes, that's right.'[170] In one sense Le Corbusier certainly was responsible for the design of Brasília. In terms of content it is the most thoroughly worked-out example of the sort of city plan proposed by Le Corbusier and the CIAM, according very precisely with their recommendations on zoning, housing and traffic management.[171] In this sense Le Corbusier could be said to have designed it. In its appearance, however, the plan is less Corbusian; in particular, its non-rectilinear nature is more likely to be Costa's. Although Le Corbusier's plan for Rio (1929) was based on a combination of great curving superhighways and high-rise blocks, which in turn inspired his curved 'viaduct building' of the Plan Obus for Algiers (1932), his Ville Radieuse and the CIAM schemes for *ex nihilo* cities are strictly rectilinear. Le Corbusier's Chandigarh (1951) certainly influenced the design of Brasília – the grouping of the ceremonial and government buildings at the apex, for example – but Chandigarh is more of a compact grid-plan city, where the layout of the blocks determines the street pattern. Costa's report emphasizes the CIAM's traditional four functions – housing, work, recreation and traffic – but unlike in Chandigarh, the roads take precedence. Having begun with a crossroads, he proceeds to describe everything in relation to a system of highways, service roads and traffic flow, as illustrated by several of his apparently

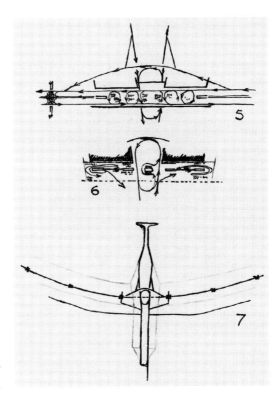

Lúcio Costa, sketches for highway
interchanges, from Plano Piloto, 1957.

hasty sketches. His Brasília is a city on the move, in a country with an
expanding car industry. The junction between the two axes is a gigantic interchange which incorporates the central bus station and a car park.

Costa placed the core functions of Brasília in a triangular plaza at the east
end of the monumental east–west axis: these were the three key government
institutions – the Supreme Court, the Executive Palace and, at the apex, the
Congress. As he explains in his Report: 'These are three, and they are autonomous: therefore the equilateral triangle – associated with the very earliest architecture in the world – is the elementary frame best suited to express them.'[172]

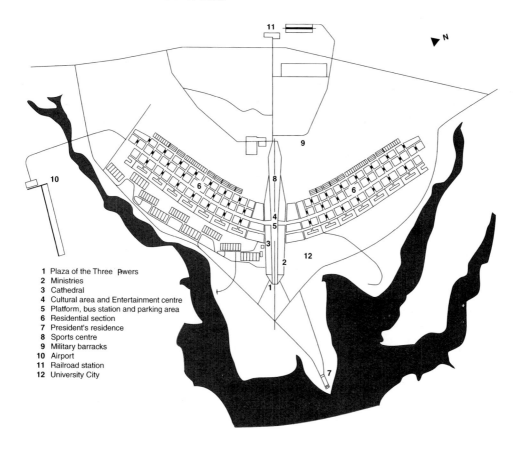

1 Plaza of the Three Powers
2 Ministries
3 Cathedral
4 Cultural area and Entertainment centre
5 Platform, bus station and parking area
6 Residential section
7 President's residence
8 Sports centre
9 Military barracks
10 Airport
11 Railroad station
12 University City

Plan of Brasília.

He does not offer examples of early architecture to authenticate his claim; he is really creating an archetype with an imaginary history.[173] He suggested that this area be called the Praça dos Três Poderes (the Place of the Three Powers), and so it came to pass. To the east of this the monumental axis is flanked by the buildings of the government ministries like a guard of honour protecting the route to the triangular apex. The rest of Brasília is strictly zoned in CIAM fashion. Around the central crossing point of the two arms of the plan are grouped the cultural and entertainment zones, with hotels to the west, and banking and commercial zones to the north and south. The residential districts are contained within the great curving wings of the north–south axis. These were organized into *superquadras*, high-density housing complexes similar to those we have seen elsewhere in Latin America, but of course in Brasília *superquadras* were the rule, instead of being isolated examples of modern high-rise developments in the midst of an otherwise heterogeneous and disorderly urban sprawl.

Costa's submission for the competition was adopted in its entirety, and although as the city has grown there have been some modifications in detail, the overall plan, with its through-routes, its zones and monumental buildings, remains more or less exactly as laid out in the Plano Piloto. Jury member William Holford was in no doubt that Costa's plan, so eloquently justified and explained, was what was needed. Of the submission by the Roberto brothers, he said he had 'never seen, anywhere in the world, a more comprehensive and thorough-going master-plan for a new capital city on a cleared site', but, he continues, damningly, 'everything in it was worthy of admiration except its main objective. It was not an Idea for a capital city.' Costa's Report, however, although at first sight appearing rudimentary, convinced Holford that

> the direction of advance for a government administrative capital had here been indicated in a masterly way, and the fundamental problems of communication, urban residence, metropolitan character and richness of growth within a unity of artistic conception, had all been recognized and anticipated.

He was evidently captivated by Costa's prose: 'Even to me who am no Portuguese scholar, the original version was immediately lyrical and striking.'[174]

The idea, the prose and the easily graspable and attractive graphic shape of the city combined to make Costa's proposal irresistible. Kubitschek's decision to follow Niemeyer's advice and hold a competition must be seen as a compromise between simply appointing Niemeyer as architect-in-charge, which would have infuriated the other Brazilian architects, and going for a fully researched and planned city. He didn't want a plan, he wanted a city. Gilberto Freyre asked angrily: 'Doesn't Brazil also possess economists, ecologists and social scientists?', but a project that would have involved dozens of experts in several different fields would have taken years.[175] Costa, aware of this issue, addressed it in the preamble to his Report when he recognized that the city 'will not be the outcome but the cause of the regional plan'.[176] Costa's view that the creation of Brasília would be instrumental in the future development of the region, and of Brazil, is absolutely in line with the ethos of the European conquerors of the sixteenth century, and Costa himself is conscious of this historical precedent, 'for this is a deliberate act of possession, the gesture of pioneers acting in the spirit of their colonial traditions'.[177] This also attracted Holford, who caught the spirit of the enterprise in his report to the *Architectural Review* (1957):

> [Brasília was needed because] enormous potential wealth, in agriculture, stock, minerals, water-power and other natural resources, remains untapped for lack of centres of communication, marketing and culture, in the partly unexplored hinterland of Brazil.[178]

With the idea of Brasília, the rhetoric of the sixteenth-century conquerors and that of the twentieth-century modernists converge. What was needed next was an architecture to match such aspirations.

Niemeyer's architecture

Niemeyer was architect-in-charge of NOVACAP, and personally responsible for designing almost all the major buildings for the monumental centre, giving Brasília a homogeneity comparable to that of Villanueva's university city in Caracas. For the Praça dos Três Poderes he designed two long low palaces facing each other: the Planalto Palace for the Executive, to the north (Plate

26), and the Palace of the Supreme Court, to the south. The core of both is a glazed International Style box, but as in the Alvorada Palace each is suspended within a form of inverted colonnade. Again the architecture embodies fundamental contradictions, as Niemeyer recognized:

> I did not feel inclined to adopt the usual sections – cylindrical or rectangular columns which would have been far more economical and easier; on the contrary I looked for other forms such as, even if clashing with some requirements of a functional nature, would characterize the buildings, impart greater lightness to them by making them appear almost to float or at least to touch the ground only slightly.[179]

The architecture can been seen as a metaphor for the way in which Brasília would enable Brazil to take flight, to lift off into the future. On several occasions Niemeyer reiterates that he wants architecture to challenge the imagination – that far from being coldly functional and rational it should be inspiring, surprising, astonishing in its beauty and apparent *irrationality*:

> [The architecture] should not seem, as I saw it, cold and technical, ruled by the classical, hard and already obvious purity of straight lines. On the contrary, I visualized it with a richness of forms, dreams and poetry, like the mysterious paintings by Carzou, new forms, startling visitors by their lightness and creative liberty; forms that would seem not to rest heavily on the ground as required by technical reasons but make the Palaces look airy, floating light and white in the endless nights of the Brazilian highland; surprising and breathtaking forms that would lift the visitor, if only for a little while, above the hard and sometimes insuperable problems which life puts in everyone's path.[180]

This is not the modernism of maximum-efficiency-at-minimum-cost functionalism. This is a much more utopian vision of the role of architecture in society, closer to the aims of the Russian Constructivists. It could almost be an adaptation of an early description of Tatlin's *Monument to the Third International* (1920):

> [W]hile the dynamic line of bourgeois society, aiming at possession of the land and the soil, was the horizontal, the spiral, which, rising from the earth, detaches itself from all animal, earthly and oppressing interests, forms the purest expression of humanity set free by the Revolution.[181]

In these palaces Niemeyer creates an architecture which 'rises from the earth', but the Congress buildings at the apex of the triangle provide a strong contrast: twin administrative towers, twenty-eight storeys high, and a broad, low block housing both the Senate and the Chamber of Deputies (Plate 27). These last are represented above the roof line by the twin cupolas of their respective assembly halls: one convex for the Senate, the other concave for the Deputies. The twin towers dominate the vista down the Monumental Axis, and are thus reminiscent of the twin towers at the head of the monumental Avenida Bolívar in Caracas. In Brasília, however, instead of suggesting a gateway, the towers are closely paired, and hold hands, as it were, via a linking bridge between the thirteenth and sixteenth floors. Costa's Report had recommended that the site be landscaped with raised platforms in what he called the 'ancient oriental technique', in order to provide 'an unexpected monumental emphasis'.[182] Here too, however, Niemeyer adds an impression of weightlessness to monumentality – the twin towers float above a pool of water, while the flat roof of the assembly building appears to be suspended between the two lanes of the monumental highway, like a launching pad for the flying-saucer cupolas.

The various Ministry buildings are aligned on either side of the monumental axis in a very similar arrangement to the one sketched in Costa's Plano Piloto. The Ministry of Justice and the Ministry of Foreign Affairs, the Pálacio Itamaraty, are given pride of place at the end of the esplanade nearest the Congress, as stipulated in the text. These two ministries are again 'palaces', like the Planalto and Supreme Court beyond (Plate 28). Each is enclosed within a modern version of a classical peristyle, this time with the colonnades the right way up, but having set up a more traditional type, Niemeyer then backs off again: the structures are not faced in classical marble but left as explicitly modern coarse-textured concrete. Both make use of water to enhance their impact: the Itamaraty colonnades grow out of a still pool, while on the Min-

Oscar Niemeyer, Ministry of Justice, Brasília, 1962–70.

istry of Justice water pours from outsized spouts along the façade, like a version of a motif used by Le Corbusier in Chandigarh. Niemeyer was at pains to make the most of Brasília's greatest natural asset – its vast skies – and the use of water and walls of glass animate the architecture by reflecting the endlessly changing cloud-patterns, another means of incorporating an idea of flight and weightlessness. As if by contrast, however, the other ministries are plain slabs with no columns, water or any form of screening to protect their glass façades from the sun's glare.

Brasília Cathedral is another of Niemeyer's highly original designs. It is set back from the line of the ministries for the reasons listed in Costa's plan: so that it has its own monumentality, so that it does not impinge on the view down to Congress and the Three Powers Plaza from the crossing point of the two axes, and to ensure that the functions of Church and state are visibly distinct.[183] Circular in plan, the structure is essentially sixteen gigantic ribs which curve together and then fan out to form what has been variously described as a crown, praying hands or an opening flower (Plate 29). Niemeyer's ideas, here and elsewhere, were realized by Joachim Cardoso, a brilliant structural engineer whose importance often tends to be overlooked. From the outside it is these structural features which predominate; from inside it is the brilliance of the stained glass, which appears all the more spectacular because the entrance is by means of a dark underground corridor (Plate 30). A further dramatic effect is created by the angels suspended by wires above the nave, which turn in constant slow motion.

The theatricality of the cathedral is akin to that of the baroque churches of Brazil, where the exteriors are relatively plain, with the emphasis on the architectural and the volumetric, while the interiors are a breathtaking riot of carved and gilded woodwork, painted ceilings and gesticulating angels. In another more explicit reference to Brazilian baroque art, along the route leading to the subterranean entrance over-lifesize sculptures of the apostles by Alfredo Ceschiatti form a severe guard of honour in a reworking of Aleijadinho's famous Old Testament prophets on the monumental stairway up to the church of Bom Jesus do Matozinho in Congonhas do Campo, Minas Gerais (Plate 31).

David Underwood sees Niemeyer's 'free-form modernism' as 'rooted in a fundamentally Surrealist project: the attempt to call into question the objects and conventions of the everyday and the commonplace through the deliberate juxtaposition with the extraordinary and the marvelous.'[184] Niemeyer and Cardoso between them certainly achieved visual effects which were deliberately startling in a way that seems to have more to do with either surrealist or baroque art than with much of mainstream modernist architecture. Niemeyer believed that architecture should aspire to the level of a work of art, and in pursuit of this he favoured 'an almost unlimited liberty of forms', regardless of functional constraints:

It is the timid, those who feel safer and more at ease when limited by rules and regulations which leave no room for fantasy, for deviation, for contradiction of the functional principles they adopt and which lead them to accept passively solutions that, repeated again and again, become almost vulgar.[185]

This is a long way from the 'form follows function' formula that was so popular with the earlier generation of modernists – Warchavchik in Brazil and O'Gorman and Legarreta in Mexico. It is a long way from the parsimonious-ness that necessarily underlies the large social projects – schools and housing – in Mexico, Venezuela and Rio; it is far removed from the modernist variant of classical architecture whereby the interior and the exterior of a building should correspond, where honesty in the form of structural and technical clarity (exposed steel frame, supporting members visibly *supporting*, exposed concrete, exposed electric wiring and service elements) is seen as a requirement.

The residential districts

If the monumental centre of the city was designed to lift the spirit above the struggle of daily existence, the living arrangements – equally utopian – were intended to help ease that struggle by moulding the citizens into new patterns of social interaction. Following Costa's plan, the wings of the bird/aeroplane comprise a series of *superquadras*, an enlarged variant of the Neighbourhood Units of Sert and Wiener's Cidade dos Motores. Where the monumental centre demanded distinctive, memorable buildings, the specifications for the residential sectors were more regulated, and the work was undertaken by different archi-tects under Niemeyer's supervision.[186] Each *superquadra* was to include several high-density housing blocks, a primary school, local shops and recreation ar-eas, with a road system that restricted fast traffic to the outside of the block, segregating vehicular traffic from pedestrians everywhere.[187] Four *superquadras*, much like Sert's larger Borough Unit,[188] shared other facilities – a church, a secondary school – while facilities such as the local cinema, garages, work-shops, youth clubs and other retail outlets were located on service roads outside

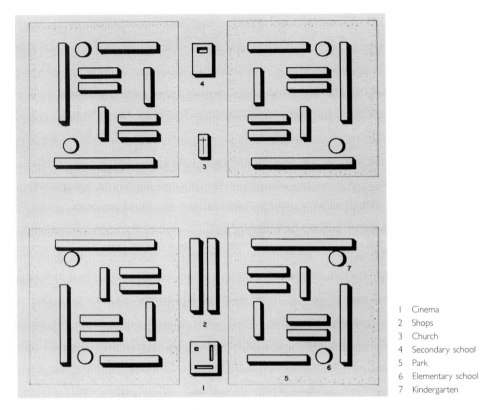

1   Cinema
2   Shops
3   Church
4   Secondary school
5   Park
6   Elementary school
7   Kindergarten

Brasília, diagram of typical neighbourhood unit comprising four *superquadras*.

the strict confines of the *superquadras*, accessible by car. The *superquadras* should be divided from the arterial roads by a band of trees and shrubs.

The social intentions of this housing pattern are also very much in line with CIAM views on the way in which urban planning can be used to improve relations between different classes. Sert claimed that 'Human contacts, now limited by social barriers, would easily expand in a city where everyday life was harmoniously conceived, within a planned frame.'[189] Costa acknowledged that there would be social differences in Brasília, but he believed that the standard-ized *superquadra* system would mitigate the differences in living standards be-tween the different apartment blocks: 'the four-by-four grouping of the super-blocks will, while favouring coexistence of social groups, avoid any undue and undesirable stratification of society'.[190] He also stipulated – famously – that NOVACAP should ensure that no slums be allowed to grow up around the city, and should instead 'make provision for decent and economical ac-commodation for the *entire* population'.[191] Logically, Costa made no provision for slums. On the contrary, he wanted the workers to live in the same *superquadras* as the bureaucrats – perhaps with smaller flats built of lower-quality materials, but sharing the same public facilities. Holston does not find any evidence of a fully socially inclusive intention behind Costa's plan, arguing that Costa was thinking only of housing for the various types of government functionary, but in fact the report does not spell out who will live in Brasília. Niemeyer maintained that the plan was intended to include the construction workers:

> It only saddened us to find out that it would be unfeasible to ensure the workers the standard of living assigned to them by the Master Plan, which situated them, as would have been only just, within the collective housing areas so as to allow their children to grow up in brotherhood with the other children of Brasília, without frustrations, fit for the new station that would be theirs when in time the just claims of humanity were fully granted.[192]

To admit the need for genuinely bottom-of-the-range housing would be to admit that the project as a whole – the economic and social transformation of Brazil which was supposed to radiate out from Brasília like ripples from a stone in a pond – was doomed from the start. The absence of working-class housing was an essential element in the overall theoretical structure. For the architectural plan to work as a 'social condenser' there would have had to have been some real political determination behind it, and there is little evidence that the government was interested.

Housing for the workers

Of course, building a city from scratch meant that at first there was nowhere for *anyone* to live, and temporary accommodation had to be provided for Kubitschek, and for the building workers. Brasília was a honeypot for the under- or unemployed from the rest of Brazil. Most NOVACAP recruits lived on site in camps, but it became clear that those with families needed to be somewhere where they could set up more of a home, with more facilities – a school, a market – than could be made available on a construction site. Holston's account of the building and settlement of Brasília details the way in which NOVACAP tried to prevent informal settlements, and how time and again they were forced to sanction them or to provide alternative, official sites.[193] Where the government was naive (rather than Costa) was in its expectation that once Brasília was complete, the majority of the workers would return to their homes. The parallels between Brasília and the towns and cities founded by the European conquistadors are again striking, and perhaps inevitable: the same idealism, the same hopeless contradictions, obtain. In the sixteenth century the conquerors lived in housing that they considered temporary and rudimentary (which in many cases they had appropriated from the indigenous inhabitants), and arranged for their new city to be built by the Indians. Building a city is generally a slow and messy business. At the end the Indians could be dispensed with and 'sent home', or assimilated into the new city as servants and peons. In practice, they settled in the colonial equivalent of shantytowns around the perimeter of the European settlements. In the case of Brasília the idea – if indeed anyone thought that far ahead – was that those few workers who did not go home after the city was built would be assimilated into the lower echelons of the workforce as servants, cleaners, porters and gardeners.

There was also a structural problem about the question of residency in the city, in that two government bodies were established to transform Brasília from an idea into a reality: NOVACAP – which, as we have seen, was respon-

Brasília Cathedral under construction (photograph c. 1960).

sible for overseeing the construction of the city – and the GTB, the Grupo de Trabalho de Brasília, which was responsible for managing the transfer of governmental functions from Rio de Janeiro to the new capital. Those recruited by NOVACAP, from architects and engineers to labourers, were employed to build the city, but had no rights to live there once it was completed. The GTB, on the other hand, recruited the bureaucrats, their secretaries and servants, or in many cases, of course, were responsible for persuading those already in post in Rio to move, and for facilitating their transfer. All those recruited by or answerable to the GTB had rights of residence in the city.

NOVACAP did not have difficulties in attracting labourers. They were offered good wages and almost unlimited overtime, and encouraged, by skilful propaganda on Kubitschek's part, to feel personally involved in the project. There was a campaign to promote a pioneering spirit among the construction workers, and its success can be summed up in the dramatic change of meaning of the word 'candango' from a term for an illiterate backlands vagrant to a modern hero with a central role in the creation of the new Brazil.[194] But they came not for glory or adventure but for work, and in huge numbers. Most left neither jobs nor even homes behind, and so had absolutely no reason to return once their contract had ended. Satellite settlements were established, officially and unofficially; ironically, in fact, Kubitschek planted the first tree not in the centre of Brasília but in the official NOVACAP camp of Candango-lândia, at the inauguration of the first school, on 21 September 1957.[195]

Failure and success of Brasília

Holston argues that modernism in architecture and urbanism is concerned primarily with social content: it constitutes an attack on the norms of the capitalist city and of capitalist society, and proposes ways of undermining or radically changing these norms.[196] He argues that in this Brasília fails, partly because the only really socially radicalizing element built into the plan was the design of the *superquadras*: no provision was made either in the architectural or the urban context, or in the social or political spheres, for any change in labour relations or working practices;[197] and partly because (although the two are not unrelated) the inhabitants, both official and unofficial, of Brasília re-fused to conform to the patterns of behaviour the city plan implied. The citizens have slowly but surely modified the plan, and thus its intentions, especially in the residential districts. Shopkeepers and public alike rejected the way the plan required shops to open on to quiet pedestrian precincts with entrances facing the roads restricted to deliveries, and have reversed the pattern to re-create something closer to the bustle and confusion of the more traditional type of shopping street. The ambitious plans for mixed-class housing that would act as 'social condensers' have, predictably, ended up as socially homogeneous units with both the richer and the poorer moving, ironically, to more distinctive individualized dwellings outside the Plano Piloto.

A further problem with Brasília, as with much of the theory on which it was modelled, is the low priority given to the wider civic and cultural aspects of city life, which is reflected in the geographical separation between the residential districts and the centrally located entertainment and cultural zones. In Brasília at the local, *superquadra* level, the residents are now well provided for in terms of day-to-day social and commercial needs, partly thanks to the changes they themselves have introduced in the urban fabric, but access to the resources usually associated with a major city – arts, music, theatre, nightlife – is not easy. The Plano Piloto made provision for a 'Cultural Centre' in a park behind the Ministry of Education next to the university city. The culture intended was essentially scholarly, and the centre was to include 'Museums, Library, Planetarium, Academies, Institutes etc.' This was to be connected via 'a lower-level passage' to the entertainment zone with cinemas, cafés, pedestrianized streets and an Opera House, which was to be located on the platform at the crossing point of the two radial arteries, above the bus station.[198] The plan and zoning system imply that everyone in the cultural and entertainment centres is a visitor. Indeed, part of the problem is that in many ways Brasília was conceived as a city to be looked at, visited and driven through. Costa makes frequent reference to the visitor, and the visitor's view of the city and its main architectural monuments from different locations. He saw the city from his own point of view as an outsider looking in; as its creator, he saw it as a work of art. Le Corbusier's Plan Voisin for Paris involved clearing away the old city centre and replacing it with isolated high-rises in parkland, 'the majestic rhythm of vertical surfaces receding into the distance in a noble perspective and outlining pure forms. From one skyscraper to another the relationship of voids and solids is established.'[199] This imaginary Paris, like the Brasília of the Plano Piloto, is not the sort of city where you could visit a gallery, walk up a street calling in at a café or a bar on the way to the theatre, and then afterwards, perhaps, wander on to a restaurant or nightclub.

Related to this is the marked lack of provision for the visual arts. Brasília has no major national art museum, nor was one included in the plan. The logic of the tendency to integrate the arts into architecture – which, as we have seen, was such a significant feature of Brazil and of Latin America as a whole at the time – would perhaps suggest that there would be no need for museums of art in the new modernist world because, as in the CU in Caracas, it belonged on the streets and the walls of buildings, in the public domain. Brasília, however, is a city with very little art, integrated or otherwise. Most strikingly, given the potential for landscaping that the new city offered, Burle Marx was not involved in the planning process at all.[200] His later contributions – to the gardens of the Ministry of Justice, the Itamaraty Palace, and the water gardens of the Ministry of the Army – are not so much integrations as additions to the architecture. The same is true of much of the sculpture that Niemeyer commissioned for the monumental centre: isolated statues which reinforce the sense that the whole area is a sort of sculpture park, dominated by Niemeyer's deliberately sculptural architecture.

William Holford, a key member of the original jury for the Plano Piloto, joined an 'Extraordinary Congress of Art Critics' on a visit to Brasília in 1959. This cannot have been an easy occasion for him, since there was growing hostility to Brasília from foreign critics, but by and large he remained loyal to his original verdict. The question of the synthesis of the arts was much discussed by the delegates, and Holford's comments, published in Niemeyer's mouthpiece, the journal *Módulo*, sound very much like the sort of defence Niemeyer himself would have proffered:

> I am personally against the attempt to create an artificial synthesis of the arts by importing designs for mural paintings and statuary at this stage of the work. As Le Corbusier said ... architecture is itself a synthesis of the arts. And where an architect has already produced a unity of plan and function, such as Brasilia, it would be folly to open a Pandora's box of discordant symbols, to break that unity.... The city is for

Praça dos Três Poderes, Brasília, with Bruno Giorgi's sculpture *Candangos* (also known as *The Pioneers* and *The Warriors*) in front of the Palace of the Supreme Court by Oscar Niemeyer, 1958–60 (photograph 1968).

men, and among them will be artists. At this stage one cannot commission large numbers of works of art; one can only create the conditions in which art can flourish.[201]

This has not happened: the centre of Brasília is itself a sort of museum, and the buildings are its exhibits.

But despite – or perhaps because of – this, what Costa and Niemeyer did achieve was a city with a sort of ready-made identity that has helped people to identify with it, and to feel at home. This they did by establishing from very early on an easily recognizable set of symbols. The plan itself, as we have seen, lends itself readily to a variety of interpretations: aeroplane, bird, butterfly, woman. The plan was prefigured – and, in a sense, legitimized – by the Alvorada Palace columns, whose distinctive, four-pointed star shape, faceted like the head of a lance or a crystal, quickly came to be seen as the symbol of Brasília, and was adopted as the format for the city's coat of arms in

1960.[202] Niemeyer's monumental architecture encourages symbolic or metaphorical readings of a relatively simple kind. I found that the ordinary people of Brasília were very anxious to explain to me that, for example, the twin towers of Congress, with the linking bridge between them to form an H, represents Humanity; or that the military museum was shaped like an M. The arching shape of the military Acoustic Shell was described to me as cleverly designed by Niemeyer so that it could be interpreted as a sword hilt, an image the military would accept, or an all-seeing owl, in which guise it represents the people. Like the owl, the people are always alert, and see everything; the military, on the other hand, can see only what is straight in front of them. Whether or not Niemeyer designed these buildings with such 'popular' readings in mind is not important. What is important is that he created architectural forms which lend themselves to such interpretations. Perhaps it is because they are so 'startling', so new, and therefore carry no ready-made historical interpretations with them. To create monumental architecture which does not speak in an alien, elite language, but is something in which everyone can participate, seems to me an important form of empowerment. It encourages a sense of ownership and pride.

Brasília, for all its problems and contradictions – or perhaps, again, *because of* them – continues to grow and flourish in a way that confounds the critics and confirms the claim Kubitschek made in 1960:

> The founding of Brasília as a way to conquer our 'hinterland', to attract settlers, to extend westward a civilization seemingly rooted to the coastal strip, was in itself a formidable task. It did, of course, materialize an aspiration that is even older than our independence as a nation and expressed anew the pioneer spirit that has always characterized Brazilians; but it is the architectural features of Brasília that reflect the high degree of civilization in my country, just as Greek and Latin architecture and sculpture reflected the magnitude of Greek and Roman civilizations. We imported neither architects nor town planning experts to design Brasília. We planned and built it with our own native talents – Neimeyer and Costa – and the laborers who erected it, from the contractor down to the 'candango' … were all our own people. That is why Brasília depicts, more eloquently than words can convey, our level of civilization and our enterprising spirit.'[203]

FROM REJECTION TO OBLIVION

The decline in interest in Latin American modernist architecture relates to an intertwining of political, economic and cultural factors both internal and external to the region. During the 1960s it became clear that the utopian ideals of the earlier part of the century could not be realized. For a while, modernist high-density social housing developments were new, exciting and fashionable, but as rural migrants poured into the cities in ever greater numbers, residential blocks became mechanistic, any social content largely eliminated or discredited. As the possibility of replacing shantytowns with modern housing faded, so too did the desirability of doing so, and political upheavals affected the way in which the showpieces of government-funded architecture were perceived.

Of the examples considered here, the CU in Caracas was built under the dictatorship of Pérez Jiménez, who wanted it completed in time to welcome the delegates to the tenth Iberoamerican conference in 1954. This was the occasion on which the US Secretary of State, John Foster Dulles, persuaded Venezuela and other military governments in Latin America to support the overthrow of Guatemala's democratically elected left-wing government. After Pérez Jiménez's downfall in 1958, his close identification with the campus provoked a reaction, and in the later 1960s, as part of the much wider student unrest, the architecture and works of art were attacked as the hugely expensive product of a corrupt regime. Brasília more or less bankrupted the country, and after Kubitschek's presidency a backlash was perhaps inevitable. The coup of 1964 effectively converted the monumental Praça dos Três Poderes, symbol of democracy and hope, into a military parade ground, and with a little bit of historical slippage the architecture came to be associated with the dictatorship. The utopian intentions were forgotten in the less-than-utopian reality of a city with no streets or informal social space. It proved to be an urban setting which lent itself perfectly to the new ideology. Similarly, in Mexico during the 1960s, as the regime became more repressive, less tolerant of dissent, the architecture associated with the party machine took on a different significance. The CU campus came to be perceived by the younger generation as 'truly oppressive and at odds with their own socialist ideals'.[1] The key example in Mexico was not the CU, however, but a housing development by Mario Pani, the Tlatelolco–Nonoalco complex (1962–64). This was a gigantic urbanization of over a hundred blocks, several up to twenty-two storeys high, grouped around a sixteenth-century Franciscan church and some of the ruins of what had been the Aztec twin capital of Tlatelolco.[2] To reaffirm Mexico's multi-layered, inclusive society, this site was given the name Plaza de las Tres Culturas. In 1967 Clive Bamford Smith described it as 'Mario Pani's, Mexico's, Latin America's, perhaps this Continent's, most impressive achievement in urban housing'.[3] Its eclipse from the architectural limelight was swift. In 1968, 10,000 people filled the square to protest at the government's failure to live up to the promises of the Revolution, and the government's reaction was to send in the troops. In the ensuing massacre 267 are known to have died, and now a grim monument commemorates them. This event marked the end of innocence – the end of the modernist dream, perhaps – and the style of the architectural context was tainted by the memory.

A further turn of the screw came from a different direction. The Cuban Revolution of 1959 that brought Fidel Castro to power stimulated a brief period of extraordinary architectural creativity, including a series of whimsically inventive schools of art in the grounds of what had been the Country Club

Plaza de las Tres Culturas, Tlatelolco, Mexico City; 'Aztec' dancing, 1996, with 1960s tower blocks by Mario Pani behind.

in Cubanacán on the outskirts of Havana. These schools of art, music, modern dance, ballet and dramatic arts were begun in 1961 by the Cuban Ricardo Porro and two Italians whom Porro had met during a period of self-imposed exile in Venezuela in 1958: Roberto Gottardi and Vittorio Garatti. Influenced by Villanueva's use of intimate, aestheticized spaces at the CU in Caracas, and perhaps also by Niemeyer's playful designs in Pampulha, they produced five village-like compounds where the architecture both suggests and reflects each school's activities. Because the more modern alternatives were expensive and hard to come by, their materials were brick and tile, and the techniques were

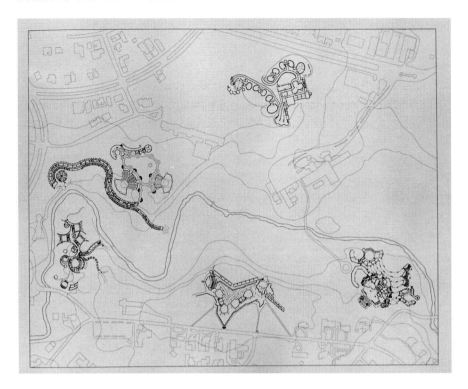

Plan of the Art Schools, Cubanacán, Havana, Cuba; clockwise from the left, Schools of Ballet, Music, Plastic Arts, Drama and Modern Dance.

traditional; the architecture, however, was not. For the modern dance and ballet schools the rehearsal and teaching pavilions are like whirling skirts, and the interlinking paths and corridors undulate like dancers; while in Porro's art school the architecture is as sensual as a woman's body, a sinuous sequence of colonnades and studios leading through to a private patio with a vulva-shaped fountain in the centre (Plate 32). The drama school, on the other hand, is a compact, piled-up design, like a cubist drawing of an Italian hill-top town. The architecture throughout is designed to delight, with the constant interplay of open and closed volumes, light and shade, architecture and vegetation. This is an integrative, anti-hierarchical architecture, an alternative modernism that challenges established ideas of architecture and education at all levels.

The tide was soon to turn, however. John Loomis documents the sad story of the arts schools' fall from grace.[4] Although they were incomplete, they were officially inaugurated in 1965, after which work stopped. As Cuba moved closer to the Soviet Union, the schools came to be repudiated first by architects and critics, especially the influential Roberto Segre, and then by the government: they were extravagant; they made use of outmoded materials and methods of construction; the vaulting system was unsafe; and in their explicitly programmatic architecture they presented a pre-Revolutionary image of Cuba as sensual and indulgent, an amoral tropical paradise. By 1975 non-Cubans were joining the attack: the Mexican architectural critic López Rangel argued, echoing Segre, that 'the works contain a meaning incoherent with the values of the Revolution'.[5]

So Cuba's most original and revolutionary architecture was rejected and forgotten by Cuba, just at the time when the rest of the world lost interest in Latin American architecture in general. It is particularly ironic that Segre, while attacking the architecture of Cubanacán for its exploration of regional characteristics and ideologically unacceptable 'assumptions about cultural roots',[6] was simultaneously criticizing Brasília for its lack of similar qualities:

> [T]he continuity of the spatial and environmental tradition, forged in colonial time and now recovered by the artistic vanguard, which constituted one of the most original aspects of the symbiosis between local traditions and the postulates of the modern movement, is absent from the urban environment of Brasília.[7]

The ideological rejection of Cubanacán contributed to the general muddying of the critical waters, and a loss of confidence: Latin American regionalism was good, but also bad. It was good because it had its roots in the country concerned, bad because such otherness and difference were valued and encouraged by foreigners. It was national when it should have been international, international when it should have been national.

The foreigners, meanwhile, were losing interest. The increasing architectural and geopolitical prominence of the USA and the postwar recovery of Europe both played an important part in the process of occlusion. In the catalogue for the celebratory Latin American Architecture exhibition (1955), Hitchcock compared it with another MOMA exhibition, Built in the USA: Post-war Architecture, of three years previously:

> It will be found, I believe, to exceed that exhibition in variety of interest and at least to equal it in the average level of the work included. In certain fields, notably university cities and public housing, the United States in recent years has little to offer as extensive in scope or as brilliant in design as the best Latin American work.[8]

In the same year – 1955 – there was an exhibition of US architecture at the third Barcelona Bienal which elicited a rapturous review by the Italian Alberto Sartoris: 'Entering the zone reserved for North America one has the clear impression of entering a modern city, new and shining, happy and welcoming, where one immediately feels incorporated into an unexpected magical atmosphere.'[9] Sartoris thought that this was among the most beautiful exhibitions of modern architecture he had ever seen, although he attributes much of this success to the Europeans – Le Corbusier, Gropius, Kahn, Neutra, Mies, Meyer, Lescaze, Sert, Breuer, Saarinen, Aalto – 'who have crossed the ocean in order to enrich the fertile terrain'. This marks a sea-change, because up to that point Sartoris's critical position had been firmly that of the pro-Latin/Mediterranean, anti-Anglo-Saxon camp.

Le Corbusier himself contributed to the exclusion of Latin America from modern architecture. In his lecture in Rio de Janeiro in 1929 he told how Mallet-Stevens had once said to him that they should patent their ideas before younger architects appropriated them. Le Corbusier vigorously disagreed:

> The essence of an idea is to belong to everybody. One must choose between two solutions: give ideas or take ideas. In fact, we do one and the other; we give our

ideas willingly, we use, we recuperate, we exploit.... Ideas are in the public domain. *To give one's idea*, well, it is simple; there is no other solution than that![10]

In one of his lectures in Rio in 1936 he credited his theory of the Ville Radieuse directly to the experience of his earlier trip, and added that the great urbanistic projects of the future would be born in South America, not Europe.[11]

In Paris in 1945 Le Corbusier was shown some photographs of the MES building in Rio, which had been officially opened in 1942. He was startled, and said: 'These young Brazilians have managed to make a building of such significance, on the basis of my principles, the like of which I myself have not yet achieved.'[12] He became more and more angry as he realized that this building was achieving international recognition as a key example of *Brazilian* modern architecture, and indeed that it was the inspiration for other buildings in Rio and elsewhere, which – as he expostulated in a letter to Pietro Maria Bardi in 1949 – were admired 'as the product of Brazil…!!!'[13] He visited Brazil again in 1962, and was guest of honour at a banquet in Reidy's Museum of Modern Art. Capanema delivered a generous eulogy, but Le Corbusier's reply, according to an account by one of the other guests, 'revealed a certain bitterness'. He would not give a direct answer to a question about what he thought of the application of his theories in Brasília, and the commentator suggested that the problem was 'Ce n'est pas beau car ce n'est pas moi qui l'ai fait.'[14] There was too much of himself in Brasília for him to be able to condemn it, but he no doubt felt that he ought to have been invited to advise, if not indeed to design it. In a gesture that smacks of desperation, Le Corbusier did offer to design a cultural centre for the monumental axis of Brasília, for nothing, but the suggestion was not taken up.[15]

History then proceeded to be rewritten according to the perspective of Le Corbusier and his biographers. One example can serve to demonstrate this. In 1956 Le Corbusier designed a youth and cultural centre at Firminy near St Etienne in France, a linear building with walls that incline out towards the roof. Charles Jencks says: 'This balanced formula, two outward canting walls plus a hung ceiling, was then taken up as a unit of architectural meaning around the world, resulting in such buildings as … Alphonse Reidy's Museum of Modern Art, São Paulo [*sic*].'[16] This is impossible. Affonso Reidy's Museum of Modern Art (in Rio, not São Paulo) was designed in 1953–54, and is a development of an idea that Reidy himself had used previously in his Colégio Paraguai–Brasil in Asunción in Paraguay in 1953, and that Niemeyer had used in 1951 in a hotel and a school in Diamantina.[17] Le Corbusier took a keen interest in Brazilian architecture, and was in regular correspondence with a number of Brazilians, including Costa and Niemeyer: he would certainly have known of the Brazilian usage of this form. Perhaps it is time a number of heretical questions were asked – like whether Ronchamps would have been possible without Niemeyer's work at Pampulha, or, more generally, how much *all* of Le Corbusier's work after 1929 owed to Latin America.

Hitchcock was, in fact, to remain an open-minded enthusiast of at least some aspects of Latin American architecture for longer than many others. In the Pelican History of Art volume on nineteenth- and twentieth-century architecture (1958) – the sort of survey which, more recently, would not have devoted more than a few paragraphs to Latin America – there is relatively good coverage, including special praise for the Edificio Polar in Caracas (1953–54). This – built by José Miguel Galia, a Uruguayan who had trained in Montevideo with Julio Vilamajó and Martín Vegas Pacheco, a pupil of Mies van der Rohe – was, for Hitchcock, Latin America's most ingenious and best-designed skyscraper. For him it was better than Lever House in New York by Skidmore, Owings and Merrill (1952), on which it was modelled.[18] It is worth stressing this point: for Hitchcock, Latin American architects could play their part in an even-handed international architectural dialogue, borrowing and then *improving* on the model. This made it possible, as is implied in Hitchcock's earlier work, for Latin America to be a source of inspiration too.

In terms of the dominant critical trend, however, Hitchcock's 1958 Pelican History volume was out of step. Francisco Liernur sums up what he sees as the critical turning point of 1954:

The flirtation with Latin American 'vitalist' architecture lasted the duration of European expiation for having caused the loss of twenty million human lives. With earlier optimism now restored, an unusual court was set up in the prestigious offices in 1954 of *The Architectural Review* to pass 'judgment' (objectively, of course) on Brazilian architecture. The 'force of naturalness' was transformed into 'the anarchy of the jungle', the 'impulse of youth' into 'childish impulses', the 'mystery of the myth' into 'overloaded sensuality.' Ernesto Rogers and Max Bill confidently played their parts as custodians of 'true' modern legality, and from that moment on the accused was expelled from civilized circles.[19]

The 'Report from Brazil' to which Liernur refers was by no means all negative. It had been drawn up, as the editorial introduction explains, because until a group of European architects visited the São Paulo Bienal earlier that year there had been a 'lack of authoritative eye-witnesses' to confirm the extraordinary reports of this 'boom-province of the Modern Movement', where architects were understood to be 'men with Cadillacs, supercharged hydroplanes, collections of modern art to make the galleries blush [and] bikini-clad receptionists'.[20] The British correspondent Peter Craymer was enthusiastic, Gropius cautiously optimistic, and Rogers qualifies his criticism by acknowledging that in the 'orgiastic countryside' of Rio he feels an outsider, unfit to pass final judgement on Niemeyer's work. Max Bill's contribution was a version of a lecture he had delivered at the Bienal. He managed a few words of praise for Reidy's Pedregulho before going on to explain why he felt he had to be so forthright in his criticisms of everything else: 'I want to tell you things which may be useful for the future of your country', because '[p]erhaps, who knows, my plane will crash in the Andes'. He very deliberately establishes an exclusively European genesis for four architectural elements which, he says, are being misused and abused in Brazil. 'Free form' descended via Kandinsky and Arp to Le Corbusier, to whom he gives credit for the 'free form' in garden planning and in architecture. Glass walls were first used by Gropius and then by Le Corbusier, who, in order to protect them from the sun, invented the third element, the *brise-soleil*. Finally he tackles the use of *pilotis*, another Le Corbusian element. He proceeds to denounce the MES building, which, although it represents Le Corbusier's ideas, 'I cannot regard as having been conceived in proper organic relation to the conditions of the country'; but he saves his fire for Niemeyer's half-completed Bienal building in Ibirapuera Park:

> There I saw some shocking things, modern architecture sunk to the depths … the most gigantic disorder I have ever seen.… Here is utter anarchy in building, jungle growth in the worst sense.… Immediately you enter on the building site you are struck by an awesome muddle of constructional systems. Thick pilotis, thin pilotis, pilotis of whimsical shapes lacking any structural rhyme or reason.… One is baffled to account for such barbarism as this in a country where there is a CIAM group, a country in which international congresses on modern architecture are held, where a journal like *Habitat* is published and where there is a biennial exhibition of architecture.[21]

The contradictions are manifold. In following the rules in the MES building, the Brazilians are accused of being academic and not paying sufficient attention to their own context; in failing to follow the rules in other buildings they are accused of barbarism and irresponsibility. But the barbs struck home.[22] The poison spread from Niemeyer's work at Ibirapuera in São Paulo to his buildings in Brasília, and then to that city as a whole. Kenneth Frampton, for example, generally one of the more open-handed of contemporary architectural historians with regard to Latin America, uses Bill's passage to support his negative analysis of Brasília. Frampton is surely correct, however, in identifying Brasília as a turning point, the project which 'brought the progressive development of Brazilian architecture to a point of crisis', and that this crisis eventually provoked 'a global reaction against the precepts of the Modern Movement'.[23]

Brasília certainly contributed to the disappearance of Latin America from the broader stage of twentieth-century architecture. During the 1940s and 1950s the USA was keenly interested in the architectural developments of its southerly neighbours, and was at pains to promote them in books and exhibitions. By the mid 1950s, when Brasília was born, the USA had achieved real political and economic strength, and its attentions were directed elsewhere: to NATO and the USSR. By the later 1960s Brasília was the seat of a vicious military dictatorship ruling over economic crisis – by which time, to para-

Building workers, Brasília, c. 1959.

phrase Serge Guilbaut, the USA had stolen the idea of modern architecture, and had stolen it from Latin America as well as from Europe.[24] Europe, too, had recovered its equilibrium, and between them they could afford to bundle away Latin America into one of those new categories of 'Third World' or 'underdeveloped'. In the process Brasília soon came to be seen not as an outstanding achievement, but as an outrageously ambitious project *for a country like Brazil*. And once the joke had worn off, amnesia set in. Latin American modernist architecture, having been dismissed as puerile, exotic, irrelevant or simply *wrong*, then simply disappeared off the map of architectural history altogether. If we are to restore it to its rightful place, we need to try out some different adjectives. How about, for starters: innovative, shocking, exciting, diverse, challenging, brave, witty, adventurous?

NOTES

INTRODUCTION

1. Leonardo Benevolo's two-volume *History of Modern Architecture* (London 1971) and Charles Jencks's *Modern Movements in Architecture* (New York 1973) scarcely glance in the direction of Latin America. Kenneth Frampton does little better in his *Modern Architecture: A Critical History* (London 1980). Brasília, one of the most ambitious of all modern projects, receives only a brief reference in W.J. Curtis's *Modern Architecture since 1900* (Oxford 1983); while Manfredo Tafuri and Francesco Dal Co, in their two-volume *Modern Architecture* (London 1986), accord it one insultingly dismissive paragraph. Other great architects and major projects are either ignored or reduced to little more than footnotes.

2. Le Corbusier's only executed town plan was that of Chandigarh, capital of the Punjab, which was designed for an initial population of 150,000; Brasília was designed for 500,000.

3. Philip Goodwin, *Brazil Builds: Architecture Old and New, 1652–1942 / Construção brasileira: arquitetura moderna e antiga 1642–1942*, photographs by G.E. Kidder Smith, Museum of Modern Art, New York 1943.

4. Henry-Russell Hitchcock, *Modern Architecture in Latin America since 1945*, New York 1955, p. 13. The text is a cautious balance of generosity and criticism: almost every positive remark is offset by a disparaging one.

5. Introduction by Authur Drexler, to Hitchcock, *Modern Architecture in Latin America since 1945*, p. 9.

6. See Stamos Papadaki, *Oscar Niemeyer: Work in Progress*, New York 1956; Klaus Frank, *Affonso Eduardo Reidy: Works and Projects*, New York 1960; Colin Faber, *Candela the Shell Builder*, New York 1963; Olivia Zuñiga, *Mathias Goeritz* [English text], Mexico City 1963; Gianni Rigoli, *The Work of Amancio Williams*, Buenos Aires 1966. Other important architects who missed this early boom, including the Mexican Juan O'Gorman and the designer of Brasília Lúcio Costa, have never been the subject of a study in English.

7. See Irving E. Myers, *Mexico's Modern Architecture*, New York 1952; Max Cetto, *Modern Architecture in Mexico*, New York 1961; Clive Bamford Smith, *Builders in the Sun: Five*

Mexican Architects, New York 1967; Hans Beacham, *The Architecture of Mexico: Yesterday and Today*, New York 1969. Francisco Bullrich, *New Directions in Latin American Architecture*, London 1969, provides an excellent overview. Leopoldo Castedo, *A History of Latin American Art and Architecture,* London 1969; and Gilbert Chase, *Contemporary Art in Latin America*, New York 1970, are more general books, both with useful chapters on modern architecture.

8. Paul Damaz synthesized this view in his *Art in Latin American Architecture* (New York 1963), which deals with the incorporation of non-architectural elements – sculpture, murals, tiles, mosaics and vegetation – into and on to the buildings.

9. See Aloisio Magalhães and Eugene Feldman, *Doorway to Brasília*, New York 1959, a poetic evocation of the half-built city with out-of-focus art photos and a visionary introduction by John Dos Passos; or, at the other end of the spectrum, the thoroughly documented account of Willy Stäubli, *Brasília*, New York 1965.

10. Klaus Frank, *The Works of Affonso Eduardo Reidy*, London 1960, introduction by Sigfried Giedion, pp. 10–11.

11. Interestingly, Latin American architectural historians, unlike art historians, have always tended to take a lively interest in the work of the region as a whole, and publications are often the result of collaboration between practitioners from several different countries. A good example is Roberto Segre (ed.) *Latin America in its Architecture*, New York 1981. Italy has always maintained its interest in modern Latin American architecture. The very useful *Arquitectura latinoamericana en el siglo XX*, co-ordinated by Ramón Gutiérrez (Madrid 1998), was first published in Milan in 1996, for example; and the architectural journal

Zodiac, also published in Milan, had a special issue on modern Latin American architecture in 1992, with contributions by several Latin American scholars. Jorge Francisco Liernur's 'Un nuovo mondo per lo spirito nuovo: le scoperte dell'america Latina da parte della cultura architettonica del XX secolo/A new world for the new spirit: twentieth-century architecture's discovery of Latin America') is particularly relevant to my argument in that it traces the rise and fall of interest in Latin American architecture in fascinating detail: *Zodiac* 8, 1992, pp. 84–121.

12. See Erich Mendelsohn, 'The Problem of a New Architecture', 1919 (excerpt published in Ulrich Conrads (ed.), *Programmes and Manifestoes on 20th-century Architecture*, London 1970, pp. 54–5); Le Corbusier's *Towards a New Architecture* (New York 1986) was first published in French as simply *Vers une Architecture* (Paris 1923), but the book was a compilation of articles from the review *L'Esprit Nouveau*, and in 1926 he published his 'Five Points towards a New Architecture' (reprinted in Conrads, *Programmes and Manifestoes on 20th-century Architecture*, pp. 99–101); Walter Gropius, *The New Architecture and the Bauhaus*, London n.d. [*c.* 1937]. Similarly the Brazilian Lúcio Costa wrote an essay in 1930 entitled 'Razões da nova arquitetura' (Arguments for a New Architecture), reprinted in Alberto Xavier (ed.), *Arquitetura moderna brasileira: depoimento de uma geração*, São Paulo 1987, pp. 26–43 (discussed in Chapter 3 below).

13. Quoted in Frampton, *Modern Architecture: A Critical History*, p. 248.

14. Ibid., p. 269. See also James Holston, *The Modernist City: An Anthropological Critique of Brasília*, Chicago 1989, ch. 2, pp. 31–58.

15. The Charter of Athens was closely related to ideas developed by Le Corbusier from

258 BUILDING THE NEW WORLD

about 1930 and published in 1935 as *La Ville Radieuse*. The tenets of the Charter of Athens were expanded and developed by José Luis Sert in *Can Our Cities Survive? An ABC of Urban Problems, Their Analysis, Their Solutions*, Cambridge, MA 1944.

16. Future research may prove me wrong, but for the period under consideration the sources I have been drawing on suggest that while there were many high-profile talented women painters and sculptors, architecture was almost exclusively a male profession, presumably because it was precisely that, a profession.

17. The term 'unidad habitacional' seems to be a relatively recent introduction in Mexico, however. At the time of their construction the earliest housing blocks were referred to as 'multifamiliares', and a group of them was a 'centro urbano', but they are now referred to, retrospectively, as 'unidad habitacional'.

18. See Jeffrey Needell, *A Tropical Belle-Époque: Elite Culture and Society in Turn of the Century Rio de Janeiro*, Cambridge 1987; Arturo Almandoz Marte, *Urbanismo europeo en Caracas (1870–1940)*, Caracas 1998.

19. 'The Anthropophagite Manifesto', May 1928, translated in Dawn Ades, *Art in Latin America*, London 1989, p. 313.

20. Liernur documents many examples of architectural exchange and influence in 'Un nuovo mondo per lo spirito nuovo'.

21. Again, this was an area in which Latin America was very modern: it had moved, as Hitchcock later noted, directly from the horse to the aeroplane: Hitchcock, *Modern Architecture in Latin America since 1945*, p. 12. Avianca of Colombia and Varig of Brazil are among the oldest-established airlines in the world.

22. Le Corbusier, *Precisions on the Present State of Architecture and City Planning*, Cambridge, MA 1991, figs 202, 223, 224.

23. Ibid., p. 242, figs 225, 226.

24. Charles Jencks, *Le Corbusier and the Tragic View of Architecture*, Harmondsworth 1987, p. 103, credits the appearance of curves to Le Corbusier's drawings of Josephine Baker, with whom he travelled back to Europe from Rio.

25. See Aracy Amaral (comp.), *Arte y arquitectura del modernismo brasileño (1917–1930)*, Caracas 1978, p. 159.

26. I develop this idea in 'Cannibalizing Le Corbusier: The MES Gardens of Roberto Burle Marx', *Journal of the Society of Architectural Historians*, June 2000, pp. 180–93.

27. Le Corbusier, *Precisions*, pp. 203–5.

28. Jean Franco, *The Modern Culture of Latin America*, Harmondsworth 1967, p. 65; Gerald Martin, *Journeys through the Labyrinth*, London 1989, p. 21.

29. Alfred Bossom, *An Architectural Pilgrimage to Old Mexico*, New York 1924, p. x.

30. Helen Delpar, *The Enormous Vogue of Things Mexican: Cultural Relations between the United States and Mexico 1920–1935*, Tuscaloosa 1992.

31. Susana Torre, 'En busca de una identidad regional: evolución de los estilos misionero y neocolonial hispano en California entre 1880 y 1930', in Aracy Amaral (ed.), *Arquitectura neocolonial: América Latina, Caribe, Estados Unidos*, São Paulo 1994, pp. 47–60.

32. Marjorie Ingle, *Mayan Revival Style*, Salt Lake City 1984.

33. Francisco Mujica, *The History of the Skyscraper*, Paris and New York, 1929.

34. Francis Violich, *Cities of Latin America: Housing and Planning to the South*, New York 1944, pp. 34–5.

35. Hitchcock, *Modern Architecture in Latin America since 1945*, p. 29.

36. Sibyl Moholy-Nagy, *Carlos Raúl Villanueva and the Architecture of Venezuela*, New York 1964, p. 69.

37. Goodwin, *Brazil Builds*, p. 7.

38. Alison McClean-Cameron, 'El Taller de Gráfica Popular: Printmaking and Politics in Mexico and Beyond, from the Popular Front to the Cuban Revolution', PhD thesis, University of Essex, 2000, p. 254; Serge Guilbaut, *How New York Stole the Idea of Modern Art*, Chicago 1983, p. 3.

39. Hitchcock and Johnson's term 'International Style' has proved accurate in that although the European theorists and their Latin American followers argued that the new architecture was style-less, and constituted a new generic category of architecture, removed from the constraints of time and place to which a 'style' belongs, with hindsight we can see that it was indeed a style.

40. Le Corbusier claimed to have discovered the aesthetic qualities of exposed concrete, terming it *béton brut*, but in Latin America it was an inevitable by-product of technical constraints, a necessity which architects made into a virtue.

41. Oriana Baddeley and I used the term in our *Drawing the Line: Art and Cultural Identity in Contemporary Latin America*, London 1989; it was taken up and developed by David Craven in 'The Latin American Origins of "Alternative Modernism"', *Third Text* 36, Autumn 1996, pp. 29–44.

42. Quoted in Bullrich, *New Directions In Latin American Architecture*, p. 83.

43. Simon Collier, Harold Blakemore and Thomas Skidmore (eds), *The Cambridge Encyclopedia of Latin America and the Caribbean*, Cambridge 1985, pp. 285–6.

44. Holston, *The Modernist City*, p. 18.

45. As used, for example, in the title of Richard Neutra's *Architecture of Social Concern in Regions of Mild Climate*, São Paulo 1948.

46. Franco, *The Modern Culture of Latin America*, p. 222.

47. Raúl Flores Guerrero, quoted in Smith, *Builders in the Sun*.

48. Currently the name most people associate with twentieth-century Mexican architecture is that of Luis Barragán, but he features only briefly in these pages because he played no part in the major state-funded projects of the period. Also, given that my emphasis throughout this book is historical rather than critical, Barragán's lack of special status here is no more than an accurate reflection of his position at the time; indeed, as Eggener has recently demonstrated, his work was regarded as problematic by the leading members of the architectural confraternity and, in a phrase attributed to O'Gorman, 'what Mexican architecture shouldn't be': Keith L. Eggener, 'Contrasting Images of Identity in the Post-war Mexican Architecture of Luis Barragán and Juan O'Gorman', *Journal of Latin American Cultural Studies*, vol. 9, no. 1, 2000, pp. 27–45.

49. Holston, *The Modernist City*, p. 84.

MEXICO

1. This lack of an avant-garde voice among architects is identified by Antonio Toca Fernández, *Arquitectura contemporánea en México*, Mexico 1989, p. 118; and Rafael López Rangel, *La modernidad arquitectónica mexicana: antecedentes y vanguardias 1900–1940* (Cuadernos Temporales 15), Mexico 1989, p. 41.

2. J.H. Haddox, *Vasconcelos of Mexico: Philosopher and Poet*, Austin 1967, p. 59.

3. José Vasconcelos, Barcelona 1921.

4. Luis Cardoza y Aragón, *Diego Rivera: Los Murales en la Secretaría de Educación Pública*, Mexico 1986, p. 21.

5. José Vasconcelos, *A Mexican Ulysses*, trans. Rex Crawford, Bloomington 1963, p. 196.

6. Cardoza, *Diego Rivera*, pp. 19–22.

7. Quoted in López Rangel, *La modernidad arquitectónica mexicana*, p. 44.

8. Jorge Alberto Manrique, 'México quiere ser otra vez barroco', in Aracy Amaral (ed.), *Arquitectura neocolonial: América Latina, Caribe, Estados Unidos*, São Paulo 1994, pp. 35–46.

9. Antonio E. Méndez-Vigatá, 'Politics and Architectural Language: Post-Revolutionary Regimes in Mexico and their Influence on Mexican Public Architecture, 1920–1952', in Edward R. Burian (ed.), *Modernity and the Architecture of Mexico*, Austin 1997, p. 67.

10. Vasconcelos, *A Mexican Ulysses*, pp. 187–8.

11. Louise Noelle and Carlos Tejeda, *Catálogo guía de architectura contemporánea: ciudad de México*, Mexico 1993, p. 25.

12. Vasconcelos, *A Mexican Ulysses*, p. 191.

13. Carlos G. Mijares Bracho, 'The Architecture of Carlos Obregón Santacilia', in Burian (ed.), *Modernity and the Architecture of Mexico*, pp. 151–61.

14. On the popularity of Deco in Mexico, see the exhibition catalogue *Art Déco: un país nacionalista, un México cosmopolita*, Mexico 1997.

15. Published in the magazine *Cemento*, December 1927, quoted in López Rangel, *La modernidad arquitectónica mexicana*, p. 113. López Rangel, however, sees the building as more transitional, retaining strong Deco accents.

16. Fernando González Gortázar (co-ord.), *La arquitectura mexicana del siglo XX*, Mexico 1994, p. 104.

17. Antonio Luna Arroyo, *Juan O'Gorman: autobiografía, antología, juicios críticos y documentación exhuastiva sobre su obra*, Mexico 1973, p. 89.

18. Ibid., p. 97.

19. Lilia Gómez O, 'Entrevista con el arquitecto José Villagrán García, el dia 28 de octubre 1979', in *Testimonios vivos: veinte arquitectos* (Cuadernos de Arquitectura y Conservación del Patrimonio Artístico, 15–16), 1981, p. 63.

20. Ibid., p. 63; Luna Arroyo, *Juan O'Gorman*, p. 129.

21. Luna Arroyo, *Juan O'Gorman*, p. 129.

22. 'A stridentist prescription penned by Manuel Maples Arce', 1921, in Dawn Ades, *Art in Latin America*, London 1989, p. 308.

23. In ibid., pp. 322–3.

24. Ibid., p. 323; original emphasis.

25. Luna Arroyo, *Juan O'Gorman*, p. 89.

26. Ibid., p. 93.

27. Ibid., p. 92.

28. Le Corbusier, *Towards a New Architecture*, New York 1986, p. 91.

29. Ibid., p. 117.

30. Ibid., p. 25.

31. Ibid., p. 107.

32. Ibid., p. 288.

33. Luna Arroyo, *Juan O'Gorman*, p. 100.

34. Ibid.

35. This was a very popular maxim among early modernists, but it was easily distorted. The CIAM warned in its 1928 La Sarraz Declaration that 'the idea of "economic efficiency" does not imply production furnishing maximum commercial profit, but production demanding a minimum working effort': Ulrich Conrads (ed.), *Programmes and Manifestoes on 20th-Century Architecture*, London 1970, p. 109. In Mexico it was sometimes interpreted precisely in this way: the explicit policy of the Mier and Pesado Foundation, an investment company involved in urban development, was to get the maximum profit for the minimum investment. This Foundation constructed the first private multifunctional buildings in Mexico,

beginning with Juan Segura's Ermita Building (1930–31), which incorporated apartments, offices and commercial outlets. Burian (ed.), *Modernity and the Architecture of Mexico*, p. 166.

36. Luna Arroyo, *Juan O'Gorman*, p. 102.

37. The Rivera–Kahlo house has recently been admirably restored by Victor Jiménez: Victor Jiménez, 'Las casas de Juan O'Gorman para Diego y Frida, crónica de su restauración', *México en el Tiempo, Revista de Historia y Conservación*, vol. 3, no. 20, 1997, pp. 35–41.

38. Ibid., p. 53.

39. Le Corbusier, *Towards a New Architecture,* p. 81, exterior and p. 262, interior of the Ozenfant studio.

40. Reproduced in Jiménez, 'Las casas de Juan O'Gorman', p. 38.

41. López Rangel, *La modernidad arquitectónica mexicana*, p. 84.

42. Lilia Gómez O, 'Entrevista con el arquitecto Juan O'Gorman, el dia 10 de octubre 1979', in *Testimonios vivos*, p. 132.

43. Le Corbusier, *Towards a New Architecture*, pp. 14–15, original emphasis.

44. Luna Arroyo, *Juan O'Gorman*, p. 118.

45. Conrads (ed.), *Programmes and Manifestoes*, p. 112.

46. Luna Arroyo, *Juan O'Gorman*, p. 110.

47. Bassols and O'Gorman published a joint statement explaining the current situation and spelling out the criteria for the new schools. Reprinted in Marisol Aja, 'Juan O'Gorman', *Apuntes para la historia y la crítica de la arquitectura mexicana del siglo XX, 1900–1980*, vol. 2 (Cuadernos de Arquitectura y Conservación del Patrimonio Artístico, 22–3), Mexico 1982, pp. 25–7.

48. Luna Arroyo, *Juan O'Gorman*, p. 117.

49. Ramón Vargas Salguero and Rafael López Rangel describe early Mexican functionalism as leading to 'an almost devastating poverty' in architectural terms: 'The Current Crisis in Latin American Architecture', in Roberto Segre (ed.), *Latin America in its Architecture*, New York 1981, p. 132; see also López Rangel, *La modernidad arquitectónica mexicana*, p. 127.

50. López Rangel, *La modernidad arquitectónica mexicana*, pp. 198–9.

51. Luna Arroyo, *Juan O'Gorman*, pp. 118–19.

52. Aja, 'Juan O'Gorman', p. 32.

53. In 1922 O'Gorman's first job was with the Eureka factory, which produced sheets, tanks and tubes of cement and asbestos, and his familiarity with these new products led him to make good, and sometimes quirky, use of them in his designs: ibid., p. 17.

54. O'Gorman defended his schools in a vigorous debate between the socialist and conservative architects organized by the Sociedad de Arquitectos Mexicanos in 1933. O'Gorman's speech is reprinted in López Rangel, *La modernidad arquitectónica mexicana*, p. 199.

55. Luna Arroyo, *Juan O'Gorman*, p. 119.

56. MacKinley Helm, *Modern Mexican Painters* [1941], New York 1968, p. 102, records seeing a panel in a Polytechnic Institute which read 'Let us dynamite the schools and cut off the ears of the teachers'.

57. Bernard Myers, *Mexican Painting in our Time*, New York 1956, p. 60.

58. Manuel Ortiz Monasterio, quoted in Aja, 'Juan O'Gorman', p. 27.

59. Luna Arroyo, *Juan O'Gorman*, p. 120; López Rangel, *La modernidad arquitectónica mexicana*, pp. 119–25.

60. Gómez O, 'Entrevista con el arquitecto Juan O'Gorman', p. 132.

61. López Rangel, *La modernidad arquitectónica mexicana*, p. 201.

62. González Gortázar, *La arquitectura mexicana*, p. 110. The choice of the cast of the Victory of Samothrace was not arbitrary. In the 'Stridentist' manifesto of 1921, the

poet Manuel Maples Arce had quoted Marinetti's dictum from the Futurist Manifesto, 'A racing car is more beautiful than the Victory of Samothrace'; see Ades, *Art in Latin America*, p. 131.

63. Quoted in Toca Fernández, *Arquitectura contemporánea en Mexico*, p. 122.

64. López Rangel, *La modernidad arquitectónica mexicana*, p. 116.

65. González Gortázar, *La arquitectura mexicana*, p. 111.

66. Quoted in López Rangel, *La modernidad arquitectónica mexicana*, p. 114.

67. Le Corbusier, *Towards a New Architecture*, p. 264.

68. *Arquitectura en México: Porfiriato y movimiento moderno* (Cuadernos de arquitectura y conservación del patrimonio artístico, 28–9), catalogue of an exhibition in the Instituto Nacional de Bellas Artes, Mexico, 1983, p. 76, no. 230.

69. Le Corbusier, *Towards a New Architecture*, has many examples. His slightly later combined high-rise block and viaduct designs for Rio (1929) and Algiers (1930) are curved, but it seems unlikely that O'Gorman would have known of these examples by 1932.

70. He uses the flag and the cacti again on his design for the building for the Union of Cinematographers in 1934.

71. González Gortázar, *La arquitectura mexicana*, p. 202.

72. Toca Fernández, *Arquitectura contemporánea en México*, pp. 124–5.

73. Ibid., pp. 123–4.

74. Louise Noelle Merles, 'The Architecture and Urbanism of Mario Pani', in Burian (ed.), *Modernity and the Architecture of Mexico*, pp. 177–89.

75. Frampton suggests that Le Corbusier's crossover duplex units of 1932 are a development of the ideas of the Russian Association of Contemporary Architects

(OSA) of 1927: Kenneth Frampton, *Modern Architecture: A Critical History*, London 1985, p. 179. The source for Pani's duplex flats was probably Le Corbusier, but there was considerable interest in and knowledge of Russian architecture in Mexico, especially via Hannes Meyer.

76. Photograph in González Gortázar, *La arquitectura mexicana*, p. 207.

77. Henry-Russell Hitchcock, *Modern Architecture in Latin America since 1945*, New York 1955, p. 123.

78. Villagrán García, introduction to Clive Bamford Smith, *Builders in the Sun: Five Mexican Architects,* New York 1967, p. 10.

79. Cardoza, *Diego Rivera*, p. 22.

80. Celia Ester Arredondo Zambrano, 'Modernity in Mexico: The Case of the Ciudad Universitaria', in Burian (ed.), *Modernity and the Architecture of Mexico*, p. 92.

81. Smith, *Builders in the Sun*, pp. 66–7.

82. Luna Arroyo, *Juan O'Gorman*, p. 142.

83. From his speech on receiving the Pritzker Prize in 1980: *Barragán: The Complete Works*, London 1996, p. 97.

84. Jorge Alberto Manrique provides a useful history of the CU in 'El Futuro Radiante: La Ciudad Universitaria', in González Gortázar, *La arquitectura mexicana*, pp. 125–48.

85. Armando Franco, Enrique Molinar and Teodoro González de León; the latter went on to become one of the most successful Mexican architects of recent decades, often in collaboration with Abraham Zabludovsky.

86. Conrads (ed.), *Programmes and Manifestoes*, p. 142, Charter paragraph 86.

87. Here I am using 'campus' in its English sense; in the context of the CU in Mexico the term is used to refer to the huge main square only, not the complex as a whole.

88. Manrique makes the comparison with cathedrals, 'El futuro radiante', pp. 138–9; the image of the cathedral as the product

of an ideal communal – indeed proto-communist – effort was very popular among architectural theorists in the early twentieth century.

89. Villagrán García, introduction to Smith, *Builders in the Sun*, p. 10.

90. Alberto Kalach, 'Architecture and Place: The Stadium of the University City', in Burian (ed.), *Modernity and the Architecture of Mexico*, p. 110. As we have seen, Villagrán García built the previous national stadium of concrete on the grounds that although it was expensive nothing else would have been strong enough; the economic arguments in both cases were no doubt only one factor among many.

91. There were precedents for this in Mexico. The Plaza de Toros of Mexico City, for example, made use of the hole excavated for clay for brickworks to create the arena: González Gortázar, *La arquitectura mexicana*, p. 140.

92. Bruno Taut's Glass Pavilion (1914) and Mies van der Rohe's project for a glass skyscraper (1922) being early examples, foreshadowed by Paxton's Crystal Palace (1857).

93. In 1947 the railway reached Palenque, and President Miguel Alemán visited it in 1950: Augusto Molina Montes, 'Palenque, the Archaeological City Today', in Merle Greene Robertson, (ed.), *Sixth Palenque Round Table*, Norman 1991.

94. For a full list of the architects involved on the different buildings, see Noelle, *Catálogo Guía de arquitectura contemporánea, Ciudad de México*, p. 49.

95. Zambrano, 'Modernity in Mexico', pp. 102–3.

96. Ibid., p. 105, n. 9.

97. Conrads (ed.), *Programmes and Manifestoes*, p. 46.

98. Philip Stein, *Siqueiros, His Life and Works*, New York 1994, pp. 215–28.

99. Ibid., p. 219.

100. Quoted in ibid., p. 225.

101. Ibid., pp. 216–17.

102. Luna Arroyo, *Juan O'Gorman*, p. 143.

103. Raúl Flores Guerrero, *Cinco pintores mexicanos*, Mexico 1957, p. 77.

104. Colin Faber, *Candela the Shell Builder*, New York 1963.

105. *Barragán: The Complete Works.*

106. For an apposite recent review of Barragán's work at this time, see Keith L. Eggener, 'Contrasting Images of Identity in the Post-war Mexican Architecture of Luis Barragán and Juan O'Gorman', *Journal of Latin American Cultural Studies*, vol. 9, no. 1, 2000, pp. 27–45. For Legorreta, see John V. Mutlow, *The Architecture of Legorreta*, London 1997.

107. Olivia Zúñiga, *Mathias Goeritz*, Mexico City 1963.

VENEZUELA

1. Arturo Almandoz Marte, 'European Urbanism in Caracas, 1870s-1930s', PhD thesis, Architectural Association, London University 1996, p. 26.

2. Gordon Brotherston, *Book of the Fourth World*, Cambridge 1992, pp. 10, 37.

3. Ciro Caraballo Perichi, 'Venezuela: la arquitectura tras la quimera de la historia', in Aracy Amaral (ed.), *Arquitectura neocolonial: América Latina, Caribe, Estados Unidos*, São Paulo 1994, p. 131; Beatriz Gil Scheuren, 'El Goticismo en la arquitectura religiosa venezolana', in *De Arquitectura*, Revista de la Facultad de Arquitectura y Arte de la Universidad de los Andes, vol. 2, no. 2, July 1994; Mérida, *Venezuela*, pp. 22–31.

4. William Curtis, *Venezuela: The Land Where It's Always Summer*, London 1896, p. 51.

5. Graziano Gasparini and Juan Pedro Posani, *Caracas a través de su arquitectura*, Caracas 1998, pp. 241–2.

6. Ibid., pp. 185–6.

7. Caraballo Perichi, 'Venezuela: la arquitectura tras la quimera de la historia', pp. 133–4.

8. 'Manuel Mujica Millán: La Catedral de Mérida', in *De Arquitectura*, pp. 5–21.

9. *Wallis, Domínguez, Guinand: arquitectos pioneros de una época*, Caracas, Galería de Arte Nacional 1998.

10. Iris Peruga in collaboration with José María Salvador, *Museo Nacional de Bellas Artes de Caracas, Cincuentenario*, Caracas 1988.

11. Gerald Martin, *Journeys through the Labyrinth: Latin American Fiction in the Twentieth Century*, London 1989, p. 46.

12. Curtis, *Venezuela: The Land Where It's Always Summer*, p. 55.

13. *Wallis, Domínguez, Guinand*, pp. 10–12.

14. Caraballo Perichi, 'Venezuela: la arquitectura tras la quimera de la historia', p. 138.

15. *Exposition Internationale: Art and Crafts in Modern Life*, Official Guide (English edition), Paris 1937, p. 71.

16. Caraballo Perichi, 'Venezuela: la arquitectura tras la quimera de la historia', p. 139.

17. *Wallis, Domínguez, Guinand*, p. 52.

18. In this Mujica is similar to the Argentine Alejandro Bustillo, also a consummate and flexible craftsman, best remembered for his own grand version of Beaux-Arts classicism; in 1927, however, he agreed to collaborate with Victoria Ocampo, avant-garde author and patron of letters, to build her the perfect, radically modern house. The difference is that she designed it herself. On visiting her house in Buenos Aires in 1929, Le Corbusier commented on her impeccable good (Le Corbusian) architec-

tural taste: Pablo Grementieri, 'El legado estético de una pionera', *La Prensa* (Buenos Aires), 17 August 1997.

19. Gasparini and Posani, *Caracas a través de su arquitectura*, p. 319.

20. *Wallis, Domínguez, Guinand*, p. 152.

21. Ibid., p. 56.

22. Ricardo de Sola Ricardo, *La reurbanización 'El Silencio', crónica 1942–1945*, Caracas 1987, p. 76.

23. Gasparini and Posani, *Caracas a través de su arquitectura*, p. 344.

24. Jorge Francisco Liernur, 'Un nuovo mondo per lo spirito nuovo: le scoperte dell'America Latina da parte della cultura architettonica del XX secolo/ A new world for the new spirit: twentieth-century architecture's discovery of Latin America', *Zodiac* 8, 1992, p. 94.

25. Francis Violich, 'Caracas: Focus of the New Venezuela', in H. Wentworth Eldridge (ed.), *World Capitals: Towards Guided Urbanization*, New York 1975, p. 265.

26. Quoted in Sibyl Moholy-Nagy, *Carlos Raúl Villanueva and the Architecture of Venezuela*, New York 1964, p. 141. These rehousing schemes were intended only for those with sufficient income to pay the rent. In 1968, for example, they were only for those with incomes of between 500 and 1,500 bolívares a month: *Banco Obrero, Plan Nacional de vivienda 1965–1968*, Caracas n.d. [*c.* 1968], p. 11.

27. Gasparini and Posani, *Caracas a través de su arquitectura*, pp. 366–7.

28. Sola Ricardo, *La reurbanización 'El Silencio'*, p. 78.

29. Ibid., p. 80.

30. Especially the flats in the rue Mallet-Stevens (1926–27).

31. Tim Benton, 'Rome Reclaims its Empire', in *Art and Power: Europe under the Dictators 1930–1945*, Hayward Gallery, London 1995, p. 121; Sola Ricardo, *La reurbanización 'El*

Silencio', pp. 66–7.

32. Ibid., p. 142.

33. *Banco Obrero, Plan nacional de vivienda 1965–1968*, p. 17.

34. An earlier proposal for Caracas drawn up by Mujica in 1928 included a subterranean railway station underneath a refurbished Plaza Bolívar: Gasparini and Posani, *Caracas a través de su arquitectura*, p. 493.

35. The road system has been much altered since the Centro Bolívar was built, with most of the traffic now below ground.

36. An exception is the experimental housing scheme Nuevo Prado de María, designed by Leopoldo Martínez Olavarría (1946–49), begun during Rómulo Betancourt's presidency: Ramón Gutiérrez (co-ord.), *Arquitectura latinoamericana en el siglo XX*, Madrid 1998, p. 365.

37. Moholy-Nagy, *Carlos Raúl Villanueva*, p. 141.

38. Le Corbusier, *The City of Tomorrow and its Planning* [1929], New York 1987, p. 280.

39. Ulrich Conrads (ed.), *Programmes and Manifestoes on 20th-Century Architecture*, London 1970, p. 141.

40. Walter Gropius, *The New Architecture and the Bauhaus*, New York n.d. [*c.* 1937], pp. 72–3.

41. José Luis Sert, *Can Our Cities Survive? An ABC of Urban Problems, Their Analysis, Their Solutions*, Cambridge MA 1944, p. 230. Sert was working on the Cidade dos Motores in Brazil from at least 1946; see Chapter 3 below.

42. Gasparini and Posani, *Caracas a través de su arquitectura*, p. 374.

43. Gutiérrez, *Arquitectura latinoamericana en el siglo XX*, p. 98.

44. Henry-Russell Hitchcock, *Latin American Architecture since 1945*, New York 1955, p. 137.

45. Hitchcock also suggests Powell and Moya's De Quincey House in London as

a source: ibid., p. 135.

46. Moholy-Nagy, *Carlos Raúl Villanueva*, pp. 158–9.

47. Hitchcock, *Latin American Architecture since 1945*, p. 137.

48. *Sert: Arquitecto en Nueva York*, Museu d'Art Contemporani, Barcelona 1997, p. 58.

49. Walter Bor, 'Venezuela', *Architectural Design*, August 1969, p. 425.

50. Violich, 'Caracas: Focus of the New Venezuela', p. 256.

51. William Mangin, 'Urbanization: Case History in Peru', *Architectural Design*, August 1963, pp. 366–70.

52. Gasparini and Posani, *Caracas a través de su arquitectura*, p. 374.

53. Moholy-Nagy, *Carlos Raúl Villanueva*, p. 142.

54. Ibid., p. 173.

55. Ibid., p. 172.

56. Marina Gasparini, 'La Ciudad Universitaria de Villanueva: Las obras de un obra', in *Obras de Arte de la Ciudad Universitaria de Caracas*, Caracas 1991, p. 19.

57. Moholy-Nagy, *Carlos Raúl Villanueva*, p. 34, fig. 40, shows a model of this first project.

58. Ibid., p. 40.

59. Ibid., p. 72.

60. Enrique Larrañaga, 'La ciudad universitaria y el pensamiento arquitectónico en Venezuela', in *Obras de Arte de la Ciudad Universitaria de Caracas*, p. 56.

61. William Hogarth, *Analysis of Beauty*, London 1753, p. 24.

62. Quoted in Larrañaga, 'La ciudad universitaria', p. 79; translation modified.

63. Ibid., p. 74; translation modified.

64. *Los Disidentes* 2, Paris, April 1950, p. 2.

65. Ibid., p. 5.

66. *Los Disidentes*, 5, Paris, September 1950, pp. 10–12.

67. Bernardo Moncada Cárdenas, personal communication.

68. Le Corbusier, *Towards a New Architecture*

[1923], New York 1986, p. 19.

69. Ibid., p. 20.

70. Conrads (ed.), *Programmes and Manifestoes*, p. 80.

71. Ibid., p. 66.

72. Ibid., pp. 46–7.

73. Ibid., p. 49.

74. Moholy-Nagy, *Carlos Raúl Villanueva*, p. 171; my translation.

75. Gasparini, 'Las obras de un obra', p. 23.

76. Ibid., p. 18.

77. Le Corbusier, *Towards a New Architecture*, p. 29.

78. Gasparini, 'Las obras de un obra', p. 21.

79. Ibid., p. 19.

80. Miguel Arroyo, 'La Ciudad Universitaria de Caracas y el Proyecto de Integración de las Artes', in *Obras de Arte de la Ciudad Universitaria de Caracas*, p. 77.

81. *Historia de un Boleto: El Metro de Caracas*, Caracas 1989, p. 10.

82. It was discussed, for example, by Anthony Penfold, 'Metro', *Architectural Design*, August 1969, pp. 431–3.

83. *Historia de un Boleto*, p. 123.

84. Ibid., p. 142.

85. Ibid., p. 147.

86. Alejo Carpentier, *Consagración de la Primavera*, Mexico 1978, p. 407.

87. Ibid., pp. 411, 515.

BRAZIL

1. Philip L. Goodwin, *Brazil Builds: Architecture New and Old 1652–1942*, Museum of Modern Art, New York 1943, p. 42.

2. Henry-Russell Hitchcock, *Architecture: Nineteenth and Twentieth Centuries*, Harmondsworth 1958, p. 385.

3. Sigfried Giedion, introduction to Klaus Frank, *The Works of Affonso Eduardo Reidy*, London 1960, p. 8.

4. Rachel Sisson, *Rio de Janeiro as Capital: A Study on Historic Landmarks and Spatial Structures*, ICOMOS, [Rio de Janeiro?] 1987; Rachel Sisson, 'Rio de Janeiro, 1875–1945: The Shaping of a New Urban Order', *The Journal of Decorative and Propaganda Arts*, Brazil theme issue, 21, 1995, pp. 138–55; David Underwood, '"Civilizing" Rio de Janeiro: Four Centuries of Conquest through Architecture', *Art Journal*, vol. 51, no. 4, 1992, pp. 48–56.

5. It still faces out to sea except that landfill of part of the bay means that it is now further inland.

6. Teresa Meade, *'Civilizing' Rio: Reform and Resistance in a Brazilian City 1889–1930*, Penn-sylvania 1997, documents how the poor, mainly black communities were swept out of the city centre under the guise of health and urban redevelopment schemes.

7. Sisson, 'Rio de Janeiro, 1875–1945', fig. 14.

8. Henrique Mindlin, *Modern Architecture in Brazil*, London 1956, p. 5.

9. David Underwood, *Oscar Niemeyer and the Architecture of Brazil*, New York 1994, p. 218 n. 3.

10. Yves Bruand, *Arquitetura contemporânea no Brasil*, São Paulo 1981, p. 83.

11. I discuss this issue in 'Cannibalizing Le Corbusier: The MES Gardens of Roberto Burle Marx', *Journal of the Society of Architectural Historians*, June 2000, pp. 180–93.

12. Sigfried Giedion, introduction to Mindlin, *Modern Architecture in Brazil*, p. ix.

13. Pietro Maria Bardi, *Lembrança de Le Corbusier*, São Paulo 1984, p. 155.

14. Le Corbusier, *Precisions on the Present State of Architecture and City Planning*, Cambridge, MA 1991, p. 245.

15. Le Corbusier and Pierre Jeanneret, *The Complete Architectural Works, Vol. III, 1934–*

1938, ed. Max Bill, London 1964, pp. 78–80.

16. Liernur notes the similarity between Le Corbusier's project and Agache's in Jorge Francisco Liernur, 'Un nuovo mondo per lo spirito nuovo: le scoperte dell'America Latina da parte della cultura architettonica del XX secolo/ A new world for the new spirit: twentieth-century architecture's discovery of Latin America', *Zodiac* 8, 1992, p. 94.

17. Le Corbusier and Jeanneret, *The Complete Architectural Works, Vol. III*, p. 78.

18. Mindlin, *Modern Architecture in Brazil*, p. 9.

19. Bruand, *Arquitetura contemporânea no Brasil*, p. 85 n. 22; these are the drawings reproduced in Le Corbusier and Jeanneret, *The Complete Architectural Works, Vol. III*, pp. 78–80.

20. Underwood, *Oscar Niemeyer and the Architecture of Brazil*, p. 24.

21. Le Corbusier, *Precisions*, pp. 44, 48, 56.

22. Ibid., p. 49.

23. Ibid., p. 235.

24. Goodwin, *Brazil Builds*, pp. 84–5.

25. Bruand, *Arquitetura contemporânea no Brasil*, p. 87.

26. Mindlin, *Modern Architecture in Brazil*, p. 12.

27. In Rio a good example of the use of *azulejos* is the eighteenth-century church of Nossa Senhora da Glória do Outeiro: it includes hunting scenes in the sacristy and Old Testament figures in the choir; the nave has scenes of pastoral love loosely based on the Song of Songs: T.C. Tribe, 'The Heroic and the Gallant: Tile Painting in Portugal and Brazil, 1670–1780', PhD thesis, University of Essex, 1994.

28. Goodwin, *Brazil Builds*, pp. 90, 110.

29. I am grateful to Oswaldo Aurelio da Silva for showing this tile to me during my visit in 1995.

30. Le Corbusier and Pierre Jeanneret, *The Complete Architectural Works, Vol. IV, 1938–*

1946, ed. W. Boesiger, London 1964, p. 82.

31. Bardi, *Lembrança*, p. 94. Biddle was a friend and former classmate of Roosevelt who encouraged his interest in the Mexican muralists: Laurance P. Hurlburt, *The Mexican Muralists in the United States*, Albuquerque 1989, p. 8.

32. Bruand, *Arquitetura contemporânea no Brasil*, p. 93 n. 46.

33. Le Corbusier, *Precisions*, p. 44.

34. Ibid.

35. Ibid., p. 40.

36. Claude Vincent, 'The Modern Garden in Brazil', *Architectural Review*, May 1947, pp. 165–72.

37. Reproduced in Dawn Ades, *Art in Latin America: The Modern Era, 1820–1980*, London 1989, pp. 310–11.

38. Maria Marta Camissasa, 'Modern Architecture and the Modernist Movement in Brazil during the 1920s and 1930s', PhD dissertation, University of Essex, 1994.

39. Gregori Warchavchik, 'Acerca da arquitetura moderna', reproduced in Alberto Xavier (ed.), *Arquitetura moderna brasileira: depoimento de uma geração*, São Paulo 1987, pp. 23–6.

40. In fact the Italian version of Warchavchik's article was published under the title 'Futurismo?' Futurist ideas were introduced into Brazil in 1912 by Oswald de Andrade: Amaral (ed.), *Arte y arquitectura del modernismo brasileño*, p. 157. In 1928 Warchavchik, while acknowledging that Le Corbusier was important, emphatically denied that he was a proselyte of his: Ricardo Christiano de Souza, 'Do modernismo oficial à realidade brasileira', *AU: Arquitetura Urbanismo* 44, October–November 1992, pp. 78–91, p. 79.

41. Amaral (ed.), *Arte y arquitectura del modernismo brasileño*, p. 80.

42. Ibid., p. 84.

43. Maria Marta Camisassa, 'Problemas em

perspectivas históricas: Le Corbusier e a arquitetura moderna no Brasil', *O Estudo de História na Formação do Arquiteto* (Revista Pós, Número Especial 2), FAUUSP, São Paulo 1996, pp. 43–9.

44. Warchavchik, 'São Paulo y la nueva arquitetura' (1929), reproduced (in Spanish translation) in Amaral (ed.), *Arte y arquitectura del modernismo brasileño*, p. 99.

45. Bruand, *Arquitetura contemporánea no Brasil*, pp. 65–7.

46. Maria Marta Camissasa points out the importance of gardens in relation to modern Brazilian architecture, 'Modern Architecture and the Modernist Movement in Brazil during the 1920s and 1930s', p. 168. Mina Klabin's influence was probably much greater than has been suggested: she would certainly repay further study.

47. Rino Levi, 'A arquitetura e a estética das cidades' (1925), reproduced in Xavier (ed.), *Arquitetura moderna brasileira*, pp. 22–3.

48. Amaral (ed.), *Arte y arquitectura del modernismo brasileño*, p. 78.

49. Ibid., pp. 101–2.

50. Ibid., p. 104.

51. Bardi, *Lembrança*, p. 52.

52. The book's production was evidently a family affair: Warchavchik wrote the preface, the text was translated by Mina Klabin and the paper was produced by Klabin Irmãos & Co. of São Paulo.

53. Richard Neutra, *Architecture of Social Concern in Regions of Mild Climate*, São Paulo 1948, p. 34.

54. Ibid., p. 38.

55. Ibid., p. 39.

56. Ibid., p. 69.

57. Ibid., pp. 199–200.

58. Lúcio Costa, quoted in Marcos Sá Corrêa, *Oscar Niemeyer*, Rio de Janeiro 1996, p. 94.

59. Amaral (ed.), *Arte y arquitectura del modernismo brasileño*, p. xxv.

60. Lúcio Costa, 'Razões da nova arquitetura',

reproduced in Xavier (ed.), *Arquitetura moderna brasileira*, pp. 26–43. Costa's terminology is fluid: he uses the terms 'modern', 'new' and 'contemporary' to refer to the architecture he is promoting, and distinguishes this from what he calls 'false modernism' which he sees as dishonest and equivocal, and from grotesque 'modernistic' fictions.

61. Xavier (ed.), *Arquitetura moderna brasileira*, p. 33.

62. Ibid., p. 34.

63. Ibid., p. 43.

64. Bruand, *Arquitetura contemporánea no Brasil*, p. 70.

65. Xavier (ed.), *Arquitetura moderna brasileira*, p. 88.

66. For example, Fernando Cocchiarale and Anna Bella Geiger (eds), *Abstracionismo geométrico e informal*, Funarte, Temas e Debates 5, Rio de Janeiro 1987, makes no mention of his work.

67. Fraser, 'Cannibalizing Le Corbusier', pp. 180–93.

68. Lúcio Costa, 'Depoimento de um arquiteto carioca' (1951), in Xavier (ed.), *Arquitetura moderna brasileira*, p. 92.

69. Peter Craymer, in 'Report on Brazil', *Architectural Review*, October 1954, p. 236.

70. In Xavier (ed.), *Arquitetura moderna brasileira*, p. 303.

71. William Howard Adams, *Roberto Burle Marx: The Unnatural Art of the Garden*, Museum of Modern Art, New York 1991; Emilio Ambatz, *The Architecture of Luis Barragán*, Museum of Modern Art, New York 1976.

72. Interview with Damián Bayón, in Xavier (ed.), *Arquitetura Moderna Brasileira*, p. 312.

73. José Lins do Rego, 'O homen e a paisagem' (1952), in ibid., pp. 303–4.

74. Bardi, *Lembrança*, p. 153.

75. Santos Dumont Airport was very badly damaged by fire in 1998. It was fully re-

stored and reopened in August 1999.

76. Stamis Papadaki, *Oscar Niemeyer*, New York 1960, p. 17.

77. Bruand, *Arquitetura contemporânea no Brasil*, p. 105.

78. Given the bridge-building intentions of the exhibition, it is perhaps no accident that in Goodwin's illustration the flag that appears to be flying above the building is that of the USA; in Mindlin's illustration of the same façade but from a different angle the brand-new flag of the United States of Brazil is prominently displayed in the foreground; Goodwin, *Brazil Builds*, p. 195; Mindlin, *Modern Architecture in Brazil*, p. 181.

79. Josefina Alix Trueba, *Pabellón Español, Exposición Internacional de París 1937*, catalogue of an exhibition at the Centro de Arte Reina Sofía, Madrid 1987, pp. 31–47. Underwood also points to the German pavilion in Barcelona in 1929 by Mies van der Rohe: Underwood, *Oscar Niemeyer and the Architecture of Brazil*, p. 46.

80. Underwood, *Oscar Niemeyer and the Architecture of Brazil*, p. 54.

81. Ibid., p. 69.

82. Papadaki, *Oscar Niemeyer*; Rupert Spade, *Oscar Niemeyer*, London 1971; Underwood, *Oscar Niemeyer and the Architecture of Brazil*; David Underwood, *Oscar Niemeyer and Brazilian Free-form Modernism*, New York 1994.

83. Oscar Niemeyer, 'De Pampulha ao Memorial da América Latina', *Módulo* 100, March 1989, p. 23, quoted in Underwood, *Oscar Niemeyer*, 1994, pp. 206–7.

84. Goodwin, *Brazil Builds*, p. 96.

85. Le Corbusier, *Precisions*, p. 9.

86. Meade, *'Civilizing' Rio*.

87. Neutra, *Architecture of Social Concern*, p. 190.

88. Affonso Reidy, 'Inquérito nacional de arquitetura' (1961), in Xavier (ed.), *Arquitetura moderna brasileira*, pp. 183–4.

89. The official title of the development is the *Conjunto Residencial Prefeito Mendes de Moraes*. See Alberto Xavier, Alfredo Brito and Ana Luiza Nobre, *Arquitetura moderna no Rio de Janeiro*, São Paulo 1991, p. 26.

90. Costa, 'Depoimento de um arquiteto carioca', p. 88.

91. Mindlin, *Modern Architecture in Brazil*, p. 122.

92. Giedion, in the introduction to Frank, *The Works of Affonso Eduardo Reidy*, p. 10. The one remaining housing block was never built.

93. Bruand, *Arquitetura contemporânea no Brasil*, p. 225 n. 10.

94. Mindlin, *Modern Architecture in Brazil*, p. 120.

95. Max Bill in 'Report on Brazil', *Architectural Review*, 1954, p. 238.

96. Labelled 'lounge' in the English edition of Mindlin, *Modern Architecture in Brazil*, p. 123.

97. The Nova Cintra (1948), Bristol (1950) and Caledônia (1954) Buildings: ibid., pp. 90–93.

98. Ibid., p. 128.

99. Reidy, 'Inquérito nacional de arquitetura', p. 186; Neutra, *Architecture of Social Concern*, p. 191.

100. Neutra, *Architecture of Social Concern*, pp. 217–18; original emphasis.

101. The official title of the development is the *Conjunto Residencial Marquês de São Vicente*. See Xavier, Brito and Nobre, *Arquitetura moderna no Rio de Janeiro*, p. 79. Frank, *Reidy*, has interesting period photographs showing the serpentine block towering above the wooden shacks below.

102. Mindlin, *Modern Architecture in Brazil*, p. 98.

103. Underwood, *Oscar Niemeyer and the Architecture of Brazil*, p. 60.

104. Bruand, *Arquitetura contemporânea no Brasil*, p. 225.

105. Gustavo Capanema, 'Depoimento sobre o edifício do Ministério da Educação' (1985), in Xavier (ed.), *Arquitetura moderna brasileira*, p. 116. Stamford would be an

obvious example, but the lack of pre-1930s campus-style universities in the UK suggests that this was a later justification on Capanema's part. The idea for a CU in Mexico was first mooted in 1928, but was not seriously discussed until 1943.

106. Capanema, 'Depoimento sobre o edifício do Ministério da Educação', p. 117; even though the design by Archimedes Memoria was in the plain classical style favoured by Piacentini himself. Marajoara was the term given to a popular form of decoration derived from the Amazonian Indians of the island of Marajó. Underwood, *Oscar Niemeyer and the Architecture of Brazil,* p. 218 n. 2.

107. Capanema, 'Depoimento sobre o edifício do Ministério da Educação', p. 119.

108. Ibid., p. 122.

109. Bardi, *Lembrança*, p. 154.

110. Ibid., p. 71.

111. Fernando Pérez Oyarzún, *Le Corbusier y Sudamérica: viajes y proyectos*, Santiago de Chile 1991, p. 46.

112. Ibid., p. 48.

113. Capanema, 'Depoimento sobre o edifício do Ministério da Educação', p. 122.

114. Mindlin, *Modern Architecture in Brazil*, p. 236.

115. Pérez Oyarzún lists all the members of both teams: *Le Corbusier y Sudamérica*, p. 45 n. 14

116. Mindlin, *Modern Architecture in Brazil*, p. 237.

117. Le Corbusier, 5th Rio lecture (1936), reprinted in Bardi, *Lembrança*, p. 156. This was a scheme Le Corbusier suggested on several different occasions, including in 1962 during his last visit to Brazil, where he proposed it as a cultural centre for the central axis of Brasília: ibid., p. 114.

118. Jaume Freixa, *Josep Ll. Sert: obras y proyectos*, Barcelona 1989, pp. 58–9; *Sert: arquitecto en Nueva York*; *Progressive Architecture*, September 1946.

119. Eric Mumford, 'CIAM and Latin America', in *Sert: Arquitecto en Nueva York*, Museu d'Art Contemporani, Barcelona 1997, pp. 48–75.

120. MOMA, *Two Cities: Planning in North and South America*, Museum of Modern Art, New York 1947.

121. Ibid., p. 4.

122. José Luis Sert, *Can Our Cities Survive? An ABC of Urban Problems, their Analysis, their Solutions*, Cambridge, MA 1944.

123. Mumford, 'CIAM and Latin America', p. 52.

124. *Can Our Cities Survive?*, pp. 230–34.

125. MOMA, *Two Cities*, p. 10.

126. 'Centres of Community Life', reprinted in *Sert*, p. 134.

127. Mumford, 'CIAM and Latin America', p. 48.

128. MOMA, *Two Cities*, p. 6.

129. Ibid., p. 6.

130. Ibid., p. 8. The pivoting wall sections were designed a bit like up-and-over garage doors; Richard Neutra used a similar system in some of his schools in Puerto Rico, and illustrates them in his *Architecture of Social Concern*, diagram p. 43, photograph p. 51.

131. Maria Rubert de Ventós, 'Cities in Latin America: The Work of the Town Planning Associates 1943–1956', in *Sert*, p. 82.

132. Lima (Peru) 1947; Chimbote (Peru) 1948; Medellín (Colombia) 1949; Cali (Colombia) 1950; Bogotá (Colombia) 1951–53; new towns in Maracaibo, Venezuela (1950–53); Havana (Cuba) 1955–58: *Sert*, 1997, pp. 48–101; Freixa, *Josep Ll. Sert*, pp. 53–79. The TPA's plans for Chimbote in Peru (1947) included renovating ancient Inca canal systems, 'an attempt to bring the old and good tradition of the colonial "Plaza de Armas" into a modern application'; the low-rise brick housing was designed in the local patio-style tradition and included room for animals, because the

new residents would be rural migrants from the Andes: *Sert,* p. 58.

133. 'Centres of Community Life', reprinted in *Sert,* p. 134.

134. Ibid., p. 138.

135. James Holston, *The Modernist City: An Anthropological Critique of Brasília,* Chicago 1989, p. 95.

136. Holston considers the urban plan and the architecture in his fascinating anthropological study of Brasília: Holston, *The Modernist City.*

137. Manfredo Tafuri and Francesco Dal Co, *Modern Architecture,* 2 vols, London 1986, vol. II, p. 354.

138. Jonathan Glancey, *Twentieth Century Architecture: The Structures that Shaped the Century,* London 1999. Glancey includes only two examples of Latin American architecture: the MES building and Niemeyer's Yacht Club at Pampulha. Rupert Spade, *Oscar Niemeyer,* London 1971, p. 17.

139. MOMA, *Two Cities,* p. 4.

140. Norma Evenson, 'Brasília: "Yesterday's City of Tomorrow"', in H. Wentworth Eldridge (ed.), *World Capitals: Toward Guided Urbanization,* New York 1975, p. 503.

141. Valerie Fraser, *The Architecture of Conquest: Building in the Viceroyalty of Peru 1535–1635,* Cambridge 1990, pp. 49–50; Holston, *The Modernist City,* pp. 201–2.

142. Meade, *'Civilizing' Rio.*

143. Evenson, 'Brasília: "Yesterday's City of Tomorrow"', pp. 472–3.

144. Willy Stäubli, *Brasília,* London 1966, p. 10.

145. Bruand, *Arquitetura contemporânea no Brasil,* p. 354.

146. Evenson, 'Brasília: "Yesterday's City of Tomorrow"', pp. 474–5.

147. Simon Collier, Harold Blackmore and Thomas Skidmore (eds), *The Cambridge Encyclopedia of Latin America and the Caribbean,* Cambridge 1985, p. 272.

148. The dawn image is ubiquitous. For example, the official hymn to Brasília, sanctioned by decree in 1961, and the popular song 'Brasília, Capital da Esperança/ Brazil, Capital of Hope', both refer to the city as marking the dawn of a new era: *Brasília Tourist Guide,* Brasília 1995, p. 12.

149. Stäubli, *Brasília,* p. 131.

150. Juscelino Kubitschek, *Por que construí Brasília,* Rio de Janeiro 1975, p. 60.

151. William Holford, 'Brasília: A New Capital for Brazil', *Architectural Review* 122, December 1957, p. 396.

152. Stäubli, *Brasília,* pp. 22–3.

153. Bruand, *Arquitetura contemporânea no Brasil,* p. 354.

154. Le Corbusier, *When the Cathedrals Were White,* London 1947, p. 21.

155. Bruand, *Arquitetura contemporânea no Brasil,* p. 355, n. 24.

156. Holford, 'Brasília', p. 397.

157. Holston, *The Modernist City,* p. 64; the competition rules and Costa's Report are reprinted in *Relatório do Plano Piloto de Brasília,* Brasília 1991. Costa's Report is included in the official English translation in William Holford's account of the competition for Brasília in the *Architectural Review* 122, pp. 394–402.

158. Le Corbusier also liked to boast of the spontaneous generation of some of his architectural ideas – as, for example, in one of his lectures in Rio (1936), when he claimed that the term *Ville Radieuse* 'was born accidentally', inspired by his earlier trip to South America and his speedily evolved solutions to the urban problems of Buenos Aires, Montevideo, São Paulo and Rio: Bardi, *Lembrança,* p. 138.

159. Plano Piloto in Holford, 'Brasília', p. 399.

160. I develop some of these ideas in Valerie Fraser, 'Brasília, A National Capital without a National Museum', in Michaela Giebelhousen (ed.), *The Architecture of Museums,* Manchester (forthcoming).

161. Plano Piloto in Holford, 'Brasília', p. 401.
162. Holford, 'Brasília', p. 402.
163. Plano Piloto in ibid., p. 399.
164. Holston, *The Modernist City*, p. 19.
165. Plano Piloto in Holford, 'Brasília', p. 399.
166. Le Corbusier, *The City of Tomorrow and its Planning*, London [1924] 1987, p. 13, a text with which Costa was very familiar.
167. Kenneth Frampton, *Modern Architecture: A Critical History*, London 1985, p. 202.
168. In the popular imagination of the 1950s there were those who viewed Brasília as fit only for Indians. Holston quotes from a samba of 1958: 'I'm not going to Brasília … I'm not an Indian or anything; I don't have a pierced ear': Holston, *The Modernist City*, p. 321 n. 12.
169. *Brasília Tourist Guide*, p. 4.
170. *Independent*, 22 June 1998, Letters to the Editor.
171. Holston details the relationship between Brasília and the CIAM ideals in his chapter 'Blueprint Utopia', in *The Modernist City*.
172. Plano Piloto in Holford, 'Brasília', p. 400.
173. No one seems to have commented on one of the accompanying sketches: a triangular plaza with buildings that correspond closely to those later designed by Niemeyer. The sketch is labelled 'Forum de palmeiras imperiaes proposto em 1936 por Le Corbusier/Forum of imperial palms proposed in 1936 by Le Corbusier'. The Praça dos Três Poderes would therefore seem to be lifted directly from something Le Corbusier suggested while he was in Rio in 1936, which would support the story told to Geoffrey Broadbent.
174. Holford, 'Brasília', pp. 397–8.
175. Freyre quoted in Evenson, 'Brasília: "Yes-

176. Plano Piloto in Holford, 'Brasília', p. 399.
177. Ibid.
178. Holford, 'Brasília', p. 396.
179. Stäubli, *Brasília*, p. 22.
180. Ibid., p. 23.
181. Quoted in *Art in Revolution: Soviet Art and Design since 1917*, Hayward Gallery, London 1971, p. 22.
182. *Relatório*, 1991, p. 22.
183. Plano Piloto in Holford, 'Brasília', p. 400.
184. Underwood, *Oscar Niemeyer and Brazilian Free-Form Modernism*, p. 79.
185. Stäubli, *Brasília*, p. 21.
186. Underwood, *Oscar Niemeyer and the Architecture of Brazil*, p. 41.
187. Plano Piloto in Holford, 'Brasília', pp. 400–401.
188. Sert, *Can our Cities Survive?* p. 72.
189. Ibid., p. 230.
190. Plano Piloto in Holford, 'Brasília', p. 401.
191. Ibid.
192. As quoted in Holston, *The Modernist City*, pp. 334–5, n. 6.
193. Ibid., ch. 6, 'Rights to the City'.
194. Ibid., p. 209.
195. *Brasília Tourist Guide*, p. 11.
196. Holston, *The Modernist City*, pp. 9–10.
197. Ibid., p. 80.
198. Plano Piloto in Holford, 'Brasília', p. 400.
199. Le Corbusier, *The City of Tomorrow*, p. 282.
200. Adams, *Roberto Burle Marx*, p. 13, gives various reasons for this.
201. William Holford, 'Problems and Perspectives of Brasilia', *Módulo: Revista de arquitetura e artes visuais no Brazil* 17, 1960, unpaginated English supplement.
202. *Brasília Tourist Guide*, p. 11.
203. Foreword to Stäubli, *Brasília*, p. 7.

AFTERMATH

1. Alberto Pérez Gómez in interview with Edward Burian, in R. Burian (ed.), *Moder-

nity and the Architecture of Mexico*, Austin 1997, p. 41.

terday's City of Tomorrow"', p. 476.

2. The urbanization which was, in effect, a small town. The statistics themselves are impressive: Pani laid out the 200-acre site with 101 buildings ranging in height between four and twenty-two storeys. These provided nearly 12,000 apartments of between one and three bedrooms, to house a population of 70,000. The buildings, roads and paths took up just under half of the total acreage, leaving the rest as open space, a density of over 400 people per acre. As well as open parkland, the urbanization also included thirteen schools, twelve crèches, three clinics, three sports and social clubs, a cinema, shopping areas and round-level and subterranean parking. Clive Bamford Smith, *Builders in the Sun: Five Mexican Architects,* New York 1967, p. 185.

3. Ibid., p. 184.

4. John A. Loomis, *Revolution of Forms: Cuba's Forgotten Art Schools,* New York 1999.

5. Quoted in ibid., p. 161.

6. Roberto Segre, Eliana Cárdenas and Lohania Aruca, *Historia de la arquitectura y del urbanismo: América Latina y Cuba,* La Habana 1988, p. 314. This is a revised edition of a 1981 text.

7. Roberto Segre, 'The Territorial and Urban Conditioning of Latin American Architecture', in Roberto Segre (ed.), *Latin America in its Architecture,* New York 1981, p. 68.

8. Henry-Russell Hitchcock, *Latin American Architecture since 1945,* New York 1955, p. 13.

9. Alberto Sartoris, 'La arquitectura en la III Bienal Hispanoamericano', *Goya* 8, September–October 1955, p. 110.

10. Le Corbusier, *Precisions on the Present State of Architecture and City Planning,* Cambridge, MA 1991, p. 237.

11. Pietro Maria Bardi, *Lembrança de Le Corbusier,* São Paulo 1984, p. 141.

12. Ibid., p. 89.

13. Ibid., p. 107.

14. 'It isn't beautiful because it is not I who did it': ibid., p. 113; French in the original.

15. Ibid., p. 114. This would probably have been for a spiral 'musée de la connaissance', an idea he had worked on since the 1920s, and which had a part in the early plans for the CU in Rio.

16. Charles Jencks, *Le Corbusier and the Tragic View of Architecture,* Harmondsworth 1987, p. 161.

17. See Yves Bruand, *Arquitetura contemporânea no Brasil,* São Paulo 1981, p. 168, for Niemeyer's work in Diamantina, p. 237 for Reidy's work in Asunción and pp. 237–40 for his Museum of Modern Art in Rio.

18. Henry-Russell Hitchcock, *Architecture: Nineteenth and Twentieth Centuries,* Harmondsworth 1958, pp. 416–17. Sartoris thought the plan of Lever House was 'not particularly ingenious', 'La arquitectura en la III Bienal Hispanoamericano', p. 113.

19. Francisco Liernur, 'Un nuovo mundo per lo spirito nuovo: le scoperte dell' America Latina da parte della cultura architettonica del XX secolo/A new world for the new spirit: twentieth-century architecture's discovery of Latin America', *Zodiac* 8, 1993, pp. 107–9.

20. 'Report on Brazil', *Architectural Review,* October 1954, pp. 235–40.

21. Max Bill in 'Report on Brazil', *Architectural Review,* October 1954, pp. 238–9.

22. Bill's criticisms of the MES building, and of Brazilian modernist architecture in general, have been echoed ever since, as in Rafael Cardoso, 'Brazilian Blend', *Architectural Review,* November 1990, pp. 40–42.

23. Kenneth Frampton, *Modern Architecture: A Critical History,* London 1985, pp. 256–7.

24. Serge Guilbaut, *How New York Stole the Idea of Modern Art; Abstract Expressionism, Freedom, and the Cold War,* Chicago 1983.

SELECT BIBLIOGRAPHY

This is a guide to the main sources on Latin American architecture used in this study. More specialist material is included in the Notes. In the following bibliographical references I make a small stand against the prevailing tendency to include more detail than is necessary in order to track down a book; it just makes extra work for scholars and publishers alike.

Adams, William Howard, *Roberto Burle Marx: The Unnatural Art of the Garden*, Museum of Modern Art, New York 1991.

Ades, Dawn, *Art in Latin America: The Modern Era*, South Bank Centre, London 1989.

Almandoz Marte, Arturo, *Urbanismo europeo en Caracas (1870–1940)*, Caracas 1998.

Amaral, Aracy (comp.), *Arte y arquitectura del modernismo brasileño (1917–1930)*, Caracas 1978.

Amaral, Aracy (ed.), *Arquitectura neocolonial: América Latina, Caribe, Estados Unidos*, São Paulo 1994.

Ambatz, Emilio, *The Architecture of Luis Barragán*, Museum of Modern Art, New York 1976.

Bardi, Pietro Maria, *Lembrança de Le Corbusier*, São Paulo 1984.

Beacham, Hans, *The Architecture of Mexico: Yesterday and Today*, New York 1969.

Born, Esther, *The New Architecture in Mexico*, New York 1937.

Browne, Enrique, *Otra arquitectura en América Latina*, Mexico 1988.

Bruand, Yves, *Arquitetura contemporânea no Brasil*, São Paulo 1981.

Bullrich, Francisco, *Arquitectura latinoamericana 1930–1970*, Buenos Aires 1969.

Bullrich, Francisco, *New Directions in Latin American Architecture*, London 1969.

Burian, Edward R. (ed.), *Modernity and the Architecture of Mexico*, Austin 1997.

Cardoza y Aragón, Luis, *Diego Rivera: Los Murales en la Secretaría de Educación Pública*, Mexico 1986.

Castedo, Leopoldo, *A History of Latin American Art and Architecture*, London 1969.

Cetto, Max, *Modern Architecture in Mexico*, New York 1961.

Chase, Gilbert, *Contemporary Art in Latin America*, New York 1970.

Conrads, Ulrich (ed.), *Programmes and Manifestoes on 20th-Century Architecture*, London 1970.

Costa, Lúcio, *Registro de uma vivência*, São Paulo 1997.

Damaz, Paul, *Art in Latin American Architecture*, New York 1963.

Eldridge, H. Wentworth (ed.), *World Capitals: Towards Guided Urbanization*, New York 1975.

Evenson, Norma, *Two Brazilian Capitals: Architecture and Urbanism in Rio de Janeiro and Brasilia*, New Haven 1973.

Faber, Colin, *Candela the Shell Builder*, New York 1963.

Fernandes Cardoso, Luiz Antonio and Olívia Fernandes de Oliveira, *(Re)Discutindo o modernismo: universalidade e diversidade do movimento moderno em arquitetura e urbanismo no Brasil*, Salvador 1997.

Ferraz, Geraldo, *Warchavchik e a introdução da nova arquitetura no Brasil: 1925 a 1940*, São Paulo 1965.

Flores Guerrero, Raúl, *Cinco pintores mexicanos*, Mexico 1957.

Franco, Jean, *The Modern Culture of Latin America,* Harmondsworth 1967.

Frank, Klaus (introduction by Sigfried Giedion), *The Works of Affonso Eduardo Reidy*, London 1960.

Gasparini, Graziano and Juan Pedro Posani, *Caracas a través de su arquitectura*, Caracas 1998.

González Gortázar, Fernando (co-ord.), *La arquitectura mexicana del siglo XX*, Mexico 1994.

Goodwin, Philip, *Brazil Builds: Architecture Old and New, 1652–1942/Construção brasileira: arquitetura moderna e antiga 1642–1942*, photographs by G.E. Kidder Smith, Museum of Modern Art, New York 1943.

Gutiérrez, Ramón, *Arquitectura y urbanismo en Iberoamérica*, Madrid 1983.

Gutiérrez, Ramón (co-ord.), *Arquitectura Latinoamericana en el Siglo XX*, Madrid 1998.

Hardoy, Jorge (ed.), *Urbanization in Latin America: Approaches and Issues*, Museum of Modern Art, New York 1975.

Hitchcock, Henry-Russell, *Modern Architecture in Latin America since 1945*, New York 1955.

Holford, William, 'Brasilia: A New Capital for Brazil', *Architectural Review* 122, December 1957, pp. 394–402.

Holston, James, *The Modernist City: An Anthropological Critique of Brasília*, Chicago 1989.

Kubitschek, Juscelino, *Por que construí Brasília*, Rio de Janeiro 1975.

Larrosa, Manuel, *Mario Pani: Arquitecto de su época*, Mexico 1985.

Liernur, Jorge Francisco, 'Un nuovo mondo per lo spirito nuovo: le scoperte dell'america Latina da parte della cultura architettonica del XX secolo/A new world for the new spirit: twentieth century architecture's discovery of Latin America'. *Zodiac* 8, 1992, pp. 84–121.

Loomis, John A., *Revolution of Forms: Cuba's Forgotten Art Schools*, New York 1999.

López Rangel, Rafael, *La modernidad arquitectónica mexicana: antecedentes y vanguardias 1900–1940*, (Cuadernos Temporales 15), Mexico 1989.

Luna Arroyo, Antonio, *Juan O'Gorman: autobiografía, antología, juicios críticos y documentación exhuastiva sobre su obra*, Mexico 1973.

Meade, Teresa, *'Civilizing' Rio: Reform and Resistance in a Brazilian City 1889–1930*, Pennsylvania 1997.

Mindlin, Henrique (introduction by Sigfried Giedion), *Modern Architecture in Brazil*, London 1956.

Moholy-Nagy, Sibyl, *Carlos Raúl Villanueva and the Architecture of Venezuela*, New York 1964.

Mujica, Francisco, *The History of the Skyscraper,* Paris and New York 1929.

Myers, Irving E., *Mexico's Modern Architecture*, New York 1952.

Neutra, Richard, *Architecture of Social Concern in Regions of Mild Climate*, São Paulo 1948.

Noelle, Louise and Carlos Tejeda, *Catálogo guía de architectura contemporánea: Ciudad de México*, Mexico 1993.

Obras de Arte de la Ciudad Universitaria de Caracas, Caracas 1991.

Papadaki, Stamos, *The Work of Oscar Niemeyer*, New York 1950.

Papadaki, Stamos, *Oscar Niemeyer: Work in Progress*, New York 1956.

Papadaki, Stamos, *Oscar Niemeyer*, New York 1960.

Pérez Oyarzún, Fernando, *Le Corbusier y Sudamérica: viajes y proyectos*, Santiago de Chile 1991.

Posani, Juan Pedro, *The Architectural Works of Villanueva*, Caracas 1985.

Posani, Juan Pedro, and Alberto Sato, 'Riflessioni dai Tropici/Reflections from the Tropics', *Zodiac* 8, 1992, pp. 48–83.

Sola Ricardo, Ricardo de, *La reurbanización 'El Silencio', Crónica 1942–1945*, Caracas 1987.

Rigoli, Gianni, *The Work of Amancio Williams*, Buenos Aires 1966.

Sá Corrêa, Marcos, *Oscar Niemeyer*, Rio de Janeiro 1996.

Segre, Roberto (ed.), *Latin America in its Architecture*, New York 1981.

Segre, Roberto, Eliana Cárdenas and Lohania Aruca, *Historia de la arquitectura y del urbanismo: América Latina y Cuba*, La Habana 1988.

Smith, Clive Bamford, *Builders in the Sun: Five Mexican Architects,* New York 1967.

Spade, Rupert, *Oscar Niemeyer*, London 1971.

Stäubli, Willy, *Brasília*, New York 1965.

Stein, Philip, *Siqueiros, His Life and Works*, New York 1994.

Toca Fernández, Antonio, *Arquitectura contemporánea en México*, Mexico 1989.

Toca Fernández, Antonio (ed.), *Nueva arquitectura en América Latina: presente y futuro*, Mexico 1990.

Underwood, David, *Oscar Niemeyer and the Architecture of Brazil*, New York 1994.

Underwood, David, *Oscar Niemeyer and Brazilian Free-Form Modernism*, New York 1994.

Vallmitjana, Marta (co-ord.), *El Plan Rotival: La Caracas que no fue*, Caracas 1991.

Villanueva, Carlos Raúl, *Caracas en tres tiempos*, Caracas 1966.

Violich, Francis, *Cities of Latin America: Housing and Planning to the South*, New York 1944.

Wallis, Domínguez, Guinand: Arquitectos pioneros de una época, Galería de Arte Nacional, Caracas 1998.

Xavier, Alberto (ed.), *Arquitetura moderna brasileira: depoimento de uma geração*, São Paulo 1987.

Xavier, Alberto, Alfredo Brito and Ana Luiza Nobre, *Arquitetura moderna no Rio de Janeiro*, São Paulo 1991.

Zuñiga, Olivia, *Mathias Goeritz*, Mexico 1963.

INDEX

Figures in **bold** refer to illustrations.